THE U.S. ARMY GHQ MANEUVERS OF 1941

by

Christopher R. Gabel

MILITARY INSTRVCTION

CENTER OF MILITARY HISTORY
UNITED STATES ARMY
WASHINGTON, D.C., 1992

Library of Congress Cataloging-in-Publication Data

Gabel, Christopher R. (Christopher Richard), 1954–
    The U.S. Army GHQ maneuvers of 1941 / by Christopher R. Gabel.
       p.   cm. — (CMH pub ; 70–41)
    Includes bibliographical references and index.
    1. United States.   Army—Maneuvers.   I. Title.   II. Series.
U253.G33   1991
355.5'2'0973—dc20   91–17502
                                                   CIP

First Printed 1991—CMH Pub 70–41–1

For sale by the Superintendent of Documents, U.S. Government Printing Office
Washington, D.C. 20402

Foreword

The 1941 maneuvers, the largest ever conducted by the U.S. Army, exercised an incalculable influence on the development of the American force structure in World War II. They served to test emerging assumptions about doctrine, organization, and equipment. Equally important, they allowed the service's leaders to take the measure of the rising crop of field grade officers who would soon direct the fortunes of the largest military force the nation ever raised. The training tests in Louisiana and North Carolina also helped develop the combined-arms doctrine, with infantry-artillery teams supported by independent tank battalions as its centerpiece, that prevailed during the war. The reactions of Army Ground Forces headquarters to the maneuvers and Lt. Gen. Lesley J. McNair's consequent decisions about training cast important light on the process by which the Army created its doctrine for battle before and during World War II.

The U.S. Army GHQ Maneuvers of 1941 forms part of the Center of Military History's ongoing effort to commemorate the fiftieth anniversary of World War II. It also provides an important and useful addition to the emerging body of historical literature on military training. The evolution of training in the U.S. Army, particularly the linkage between maneuvers and changes in doctrine and organization, is an extremely worthy field for study by military students. I especially urge our young officers and noncommissioned officers to read and reflect on this important milestone in our Army's victory in World War II.

Washington, D.C.   HAROLD W. NELSON
25 February 1991   Brigadier General, USA
                                                   Chief of Military History

The Author

Christopher R. Gabel received the Ph.D. degree in history from Ohio State University in 1981. Since 1983 he has served on the faculty of the Combat Studies Institute, the military history department of the U.S. Army Command and General Staff College, where he specializes in the U.S. Army of the interwar and World War II periods. His publications include *Seek, Strike, and Destroy: U.S. Army Tank Destroyer Doctrine in World War II.*

Preface

I first discovered the 1941 maneuvers while researching the Army's antitank doctrine of World War II. According to a number of prominent soldiers and authors, the great prewar maneuvers played an important role in shaping the wartime Army. Surprisingly, I could find no secondary account that analyzed these maneuvers in detail or substantiated claims of their efficacy in preparing the military for war. I attempted to fill this void with a doctoral dissertation which, in revised form, has become this book. In the process of preparing this study I came to appreciate that the maneuvers themselves were but the final act of an even more intriguing drama—the prewar mobilization of 1939–41. I hope further to explore this broader subject in research and writing.

Foremost among the many individuals who helped make this book possible is Harry L. Coles, my doctoral adviser and mentor. During the research phase Gibson B. Smith of the National Archives, John Jacob of the George C. Marshall Research Library, Richard J. Sommers and John J. Slonaker of the U.S. Army Military History Institute, and James C. Dorsey of the U.S. Army Command and General Staff College Research Library guided me to the essential primary documents. Martin Blumenson kindly answered my queries, giving freely of his own enormous expertise.

The U.S. Army Center of Military History intervened decisively on two separate occasions. In 1980 Brig. Gen. James L. Collins, Jr., Maurice Matloff, and the staff of the Center provided a generous fellowship and made available the resources of their organization. In 1989 John Greenwood urged me to revise the original dissertation and offer it for publication. My thanks to all those who made this manuscript presentable, especially Jeffrey Clarke, Theodore Wilson, John B. Wilson, Joyce Hardyman, Sherry Dowdy, Diane Sedore Arms, Joycelyn Canery, and Catherine Heerin. Thanks also to Lu Welch, my typist in Leavenworth.

Moral support came from Lou Gabel, who told me his war stories on summer nights in Pennsylvania; from Charlie O'Connell during the years at Ohio State; and especially from Ann, who will never forget the day we went looking for Good Hope Church. To Matthew and Eric I offer the good hope that this nation has seen its last world war.

25 February 1991   CHRISTOPHER R. GABEL

Contents

Appendixes

Charts

Maps

Illustrations

THE U.S. ARMY
GHQ MANEUVERS OF 1941

Introduction

> They do not wait for war to begin before handling arms, nor do they sit idle in peacetime and take action only when the emergency comes. . . . It would not be far from the truth to call their drills bloodless battles, their battles bloody drills.
>
> Josephus, *The Jewish War* [1]

The sun rising over the Silesian village of Leuthen on the misty morning of 5 December 1757 presented a daunting spectacle to Frederick II of Prussia. His opponent, Prince Charles of Lorraine, had posted 65,000 Austrians on well-chosen terrain athwart Frederick's intended route toward Breslau. Although he brought only 35,000 troops onto the frozen battlefield, Frederick moved immediately to attack his enemy. In broad daylight the superbly trained Prussians marched across the front of the Austrians, shattered their line with a flank attack, and sent them reeling from the battlefield in disorder. [2]

In spite of his numerical inferiority, Frederick enjoyed an enormous advantage at the battle of Leuthen. In time of peace, it was Frederick's habit to conduct autumn maneuvers at the close of each summer's training season. These maneuvers were full-sized simulated battles in which Frederick perfected his tactics and tested the skills of his generals. Autumn maneuvers helped make the Prussian Army, man for man, the finest in Europe. Leuthen was, in fact, one of the "battlegrounds" on which those exercises took place, meaning that Frederick was intimately familiar with every fold of the ground. Little wonder that Frederick sought battle there so readily. [3]

Maneuvers such as those conducted by the Prussian Army departed significantly from the eighteenth century norm. In that era, most training took the form of drill, in which the individual soldier acquired an automatic, mechanical obedience to orders. The objective of this training was to weld the regiment into a single responsive weapon. Maneuvers, on the other hand, involved large units locked in simulated battle replete with the fog and friction of real war. The objective here was to test for weakness and to accustom all ranks to the sights and sounds of battle. The free maneuver, in which two forces competed for victory free from the restrictions of script or scenario, represented the ultimate such exercise.

Although Frederick apparently originated the practice of ending each training season with autumn maneuvers, the use of simulated battle in military training is probably as old as organized warfare itself. Certainly the legions of Rome were noted for the warlike character of their training, as Josephus suggested.[4] In more recent times, Peter the Great of Russia, who as a boy enjoyed playing war with living toy soldiers, modernized his army through the use of professionally run maneuvers involving tens of thousands of troops.[5] Napoleon's *Grande Armee* of 1805, one of history's most celebrated fighting forces, prepared itself for Ulm and Austerlitz through a comprehensive unit training program that included corps-level maneuvers.[6]

In the last half of the nineteenth century, annual autumn maneuvers became a fixture on the European military scene. Armies composed of conscripts and reservists, headed by general staffs, capped off summer training with simulated battles that tested doctrine, training, and leadership. In some instances, the routine of maneuvers hardened into ritual. Under Wilhelm II, the German autumn maneuvers always concluded with the utter annihilation of one army by the other. Predictably, the Kaiser was always to be found in command of the winning side.[7]

There were no autumn maneuvers in the U.S. Army of the late nineteenth century and, in fact, little unit training of any sort. Scattered across a continent in constabulary garrisons and seacoast fortifications, the Army languished in obscurity until the Spanish-American War of 1898 dramatized the inadequacies and anachronisms of the military establishment. Subsequent reforms implemented by Secretary of War Elihu Root included provisions for bringing together Regular and National Guard units in summer encampments which usually included maneuvers. The emphasis at these exercises was on instruction rather than the realistic simulation of large-scale engagements.[8]

Reforms such as these set important precedents for the future, but for the present their impact was limited. World War I revealed that the U.S. military was still quite unprepared for modern war. Doctrine was out of date, experience in the command of large forces was nonexistent, and the coordination of arms and services was largely a matter of theoretical conjecture. Once war was declared, it took a year and a half to create an American field army capable of mounting an offensive on the Western Front. Even in the very last major operation of the war, the Meuse-Argonne offensive, American amateurism remained painfully obvious. Overoptimistic planners set unrealistic objectives. Some division commanders proved inadequate and had to be replaced. Logistics and communications foundered. Tactical commanders, who had never mastered the employment of supporting weapons, resorted instead to ruinous frontal attacks by their brave but artless infantry. Col. George C. Marshall, of the American Expeditionary Forces (AEF) staff, noted with dismay the "stumbling, blunderings, failures, appeals for help, and hopeless confusion" that characterized the initial phases of the Meuse-Argonne campaign.[9]

Two decades later, Marshall was the Army chief of staff. Before him lay the task of readying the United States Army for another world war. Although Marshall endeavored to avoid the heartbreaking amateurism he had witnessed in 1918, the Army's state of unreadiness held scant prospect of improvement. Twenty years of inadequate funding and skeletonized units had made the U.S. Army little more than a token establishment. The periodic Regular Army–National Guard maneuvers conducted in those years were little more than playacting between notional forces.

The circumstances of America's entry into World War II did, however, afford Marshall one enormous advantage that no other Army chief had ever enjoyed—a period of partial mobilization that actually preceded the formal declaration of war. In the two years between the German invasion of Poland and the Japanese attack on Pearl Harbor, reservists and conscripts expanded the Army eightfold. With these men the War Department was able to field thirty-three divisions, some of which were nearly combat ready by the time Congress declared war.

Maneuvers were a central feature of this prewar mobilization period. Lt. Gen. Lesley J. McNair, placed in charge of the Army's training, used maneuvers to give small units experience in teamwork and combined arms. Marshall, who referred to maneuvers as the "combat college for troop leading," wanted mistakes made and corrected during maneuvers, not battle.[10] Equally important was the utilization of maneuvers as field laboratories for the armored, antitank, and air forces that had come of age since 1918.

Culminating the period of prewar mobilization were the great GHQ (General Headquarters) maneuvers that pitted entire field armies against each other in the summer and fall of 1941. Nearly half of the Army's total manpower participated in these enormous field exercises. All of the arms and services played their parts under conditions of simulated warfare. Scores of news correspondents made the maneuvers a focal point of national attention.

Whether viewed as the final episode of peacetime mobilization or the first demonstration of wartime military might, the GHQ maneuvers mark a turning point in the history of the U.S. military and of the American nation.

Notes

1. Josephus, *The Jewish War*, trans. G. A. Williamson (Middlesex, UK: Penguin, 1959, 1969), pp. 194–95.

2. Christopher Duffy, *The Military Life of Frederick the Great* (New York: Atheneum, 1986), pp. 146–53.

3. Ibid., pp. 50, 80–81.

4. For a description of Roman training, see the classic account by Vegetius in Thomas R. Phillips, ed., *Roots of Strategy: The 5 Greatest Military Classics of All Time* (Harrisburg: Stackpole, 1985), pp. 81–96.

5. Vasili Klyuchevsky, *Peter the Great* (New York: Vintage, 1958), pp. 22–23.

6. James R. Arnold, "Bold Gamble's Unexpected Crises," *Military History*, Oct 86, pp. 26–33.

7. Walter Goerlitz, *History of the German General Staff, 1657–1945* (New York: Praeger, 1967), p. 139.

8. See Charles Douglas McKenna, "The Forgotten Reform: Field Maneuvers in the Development of the United States Army, 1902–1920," Ph.D. dissertation, Duke University, 1981.

9. George C. Marshall, *The Papers of George Catlett Marshall*, vol. 1, *"The Soldierly Spirit," December 1880–June 1939* (Baltimore: Johns Hopkins, 1981), pp. 334–38 (Lecture, "Development in Tactics").

10. George C. Marshall, *The Papers of George Catlett Marshall*, vol. 2, *"We Cannot Delay," July 1, 1939–December 6, 1941* (Baltimore: Johns Hopkins, 1986), pp. 94–99 (Speech to the National Guard Association of the United States, 27 Oct 39).

CHAPTER 1

Protective Mobilization

We didn't know how soon war would come, but we knew it was coming. We didn't know when we'd have to fight, but we knew it might come at any time, and we had to get together *something* of an Army pretty darn fast. We didn't dare stop for the progressive and logical building of a war machine. As a result, the machine was a little wobbly when it first got going. The men knew it. The officers knew it. Everyone knew it.[1]

Lt. Gen. Lesley J. McNair

On 1 September 1939, the day that Germany's attack on Poland signaled the beginning of World War II, the U.S. Army ranked approximately seventeenth in effectiveness among the armies of the world, just behind that of Rumania.[2] The Regular Army totaled less than 190,000 personnel, including the Philippine Scouts and the Army Nurse Corps. Of 174,000 enlisted men, 45,300 were stationed overseas.[3]

Aside from paper organizations, the Army possessed few tactical units larger than battalion. Within the United States, there were only three functioning infantry divisions, each at half strength, and six others listed as partially organized that consisted of skeleton cadres. Two cavalry divisions, one organized and one partially organized, and one understrength experimental mechanized cavalry brigade completed the Army's roster of Regular field units. The air arm comprised less than 20,000 men organized into sixty-two tactical squadrons equipped with obsolete aircraft. There were no corps or field army headquarters functioning full time.[4]

The National Guard was in a comparable state of emaciation. Its 200,000 part-time soldiers were just sufficient to keep its eighteen divisions alive as maintenance-strength cadre units.[5]

Six years later, the Army numbered more than eight million, with eighty-nine divisions and over two hundred combat air groups engaged in a massive war effort that girdled the globe.[6] Most of the Army's remarkable growth took place after the bombing of Pearl

Harbor and the formal declaration of war. This wartime mobilization, however, built upon the foundation of an earlier expansion program, effective 1939–41, known as the Protective Mobilization Plan (PMP).

The Protective Mobilization Plan was itself a product of the Army's lean interwar years. During the 1930s, Chief of Staff Douglas MacArthur and his successor, Malin C. Craig, recognized that the skeletal Army they commanded was incapable of affording even the most basic protection to the United States. Under Craig's direction, the War Department drafted the first Protective Mobilization Plan in 1937–38.

The objective of this plan was the raising of a small but combat-effective Army as quickly as possible in time of emergency. This was to be accomplished by fleshing out existing Regular and National Guard units, concentrating first on the most nearly combat-ready units. Only after a battle-worthy PMP Army of 1,224,357 officers and men was trained and equipped (within eight months of mobilization day) would new units be activated. This ambitious plan was predicated on the assumption that all of the equipment for the PMP Army would be produced and stockpiled in advance, something that Congress did not consider feasible.[7]

Even though stockpiles of modern equipment did not exist, and the sequence of events was not exactly as planned (there was, for example, no unambiguous "mobilization day" to trigger the plan), Army mobilization from 1939 to 1942 followed the general outlines of the Protective Mobilization Plan. This meant that few new ground combat units were activated in that period, manpower and resources being dedicated instead to the existing Regular and National Guard forces.

A reasonable starting date to posit for the onset of protective mobilization is 8 September 1939, when President Franklin D. Roosevelt proclaimed a "limited national emergency . . . for the purpose of strengthening our national defense within the limits of peacetime authorizations."[8] General Marshall, who had formally ascended to the position of Army chief of staff just one week earlier, moved immediately to resuscitate the moribund Regular Army, utilizing the modest increases in manpower and money voted by an increasingly alarmed Congress.

One of Marshall's first acts as chief of staff was to force through a long-deferred restructuring of the Army's principal fighting formation, the infantry division. The structure that he ordered replaced, known as the square division, dated from 1917 and reflected a pre-occupation with trench warfare as practiced on the Western Front in

CHART 1—SQUARE INFANTRY DIVISION, 1941

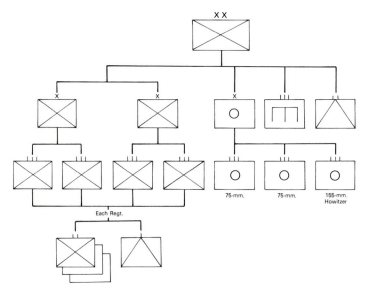

World War I. *(Chart 1)* The square division was a huge force of 28,000 men (trimmed to 22,000 by 1939) tailor-made for attrition warfare. Typical World War I tactics involved placing the division's four regiments (hence *square*) on line, with battalions in column within each regiment. Following a rolling barrage, successive waves of infantry, supported by massed machine gun fire, hurled themselves against the enemy defenses. Such tactics, obsolescent by 1918, were wholly anachronistic by 1939, as was the square division itself.

To replace the old doctrine, the Army of the late 1930s borrowed from the Germans. Maj. Gen. George A. Lynch, chief of the Infantry from 1937, discarded the old scheme, dominated as it was by rigid planning, centralized control, and self-sacrifice on the part of the rifleman. He provided each company and battalion with the weapons (mortars and machine guns) to establish its own base of fire and directed the riflemen to secure successive objectives by maneuver and by enfilading of enemy strongpoints.[9]

The division organization that Marshall adopted in 1939 to facilitate this doctrine was also borrowed from the Germans. It was called the triangular division because nearly every echelon within the division possessed three maneuver elements, plus a means of fire support. *(Chart 2)* Be it the division itself or the rifle company, each echelon could establish a base of fire using both direct and indirect fire support, fix the enemy with one maneuver element,

CHART 2—TRIANGULAR INFANTRY DIVISION, 1941

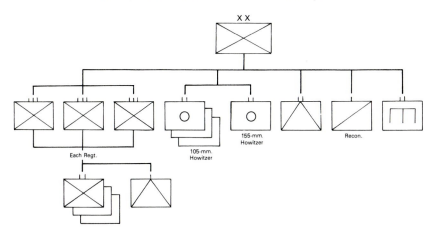

find his flank with a second, and maintain a third in reserve. Thus doctrine and organization meshed elegantly.

Artillery doctrine had also evolved since 1918, and the triangular division incorporated this development, too. Accuracy, responsiveness, and flexibility supplanted sheer volume as measures of effectiveness. Accordingly, the triangular division's artillery consisted of three battalions of light artillery, each of which could be attached to an infantry regiment to create a regimental combat team, and a battalion of medium artillery for general support. Improved communications and advances in the techniques of observation and fire direction enabled the field artillery to decentralize its batteries for maximum responsiveness, yet retain the ability to mass fires when needed.

Another innovation within the triangular division was the replacement of all animals by motor transport (though the infantry still traveled on foot). Finally, to keep the triangular division lean (around 15,000 men) the War Department streamlined all support and service elements not essential to the division and pooled them in reserve at higher echelons until needed.[10] The smaller size enabled Marshall to create five embryonic triangular divisions out of three skeletonized square divisions when he converted the Regular Army to the new formation in September 1939.[11]

These new doctrines and force structures called for a broad array of new equipment. Like the square division, much of the Army's existing stocks dated from another war and another era. The principal infantry weapon in 1939 was still the venerable 1903 Springfield rifle, although the M1 Garand semiautomatic rifle had been in limited production for three years.[12] The Field Artillery relied on 75-mm. guns and 155-mm. howitzers of World War I vintage until 1941, when the first of a superb new breed of 105-mm. howitzers arrived. The Army stepped up the development and procurement of these and other less glamorous but equally necessary items such as water purifiers, cooking ranges, and food containers.[13]

By the spring of 1940, the process of modernizing the still minuscule Regular Army had progressed sufficiently to permit field tests of the new organizations, equipment, and tactics. In March and April the Army assembled and tested IV Corps, its first corps to take the field since 1918. This force, comprising the newly triangular 1st, 5th, and 6th Divisions, conducted field exercises at Fort Benning, Georgia, and in May traveled to Louisiana to face the provisional IX Corps (2d Division and 1st Cavalry Division) in the first corps-versus-corps maneuvers in Army history.[14]

As of June 1940, the Army had made a good start towards modernizing its Regular forces after twenty years of neglect. The triangular division had been adopted and tested, and commanders had gained valuable experience in employing it under field conditions. Although modern equipment was still critically scarce, Maj. Gen. Walter C. Short, IV Corps commander, commented at the conclusion of the spring exercises that ". . . the [Regular Army's] equipment problem is on its way to being solved in another year if Congress continues its liberal appropriations."[15]

The Army that had once had the time to modernize but not the money now had the money but not the time. In accordance with the Protective Mobilization Plan, General Marshall intended to continue the modernization and reequipping process while pursuing only a limited expansion program. Both he and his naval counterpart, Admiral Harold R. Stark, the chief of naval operations, believed a drastic increase in munitions production should precede any large-scale augmentation of military manpower.[16]

However, Germany's stunning conquest of France and subsequent aerial assault on Britain in the summer of 1940 induced preparedness-minded legislators, specifically Senator Edward Burke and Congressman James Wadsworth, to propose expanding the Army at once, not by inducting the reserve components, as called for in the Protective Mobilization Plan, but through the first peacetime conscription in the nation's history. They introduced the selective service bill on 20 June, and, although a protracted debate ensued, as the summer progressed passage seemed increasingly likely.

Meanwhile, General Marshall pressed for the induction of the National Guard and Reserve. Not only were these components vital elements of the PMP Army, but the eighteen undermanned Guard divisions could absorb thousands of selectees who would otherwise swamp the nine regular infantry divisions and undo the modernization process entirely.

The reports that emanated from National Guard training camps in August reconfirmed Marshall's determination to bring the Guard under federal control. Operating under the optimistic assumption that sixty evenings a year spent in armory drills had provided the 200,000 Guardsmen with adequate basic, technical, and theoretical training, the War Department ordered the commanders of the four (paper) field armies to bring together all of the Guard units in their geographic areas for massed unit training.[17] Each encampment was to conclude with a corps-versus-corps maneuver between supposedly field-worthy Guard divisions.[18]

When the earnest but ill-prepared Guardsmen reported to camp in early August 1940, they embarked upon three-week training programs, written by their army commanders and approved by the War Department, which allowed them about five days for platoon, company, and battalion training; two days of regimental and brigade training; and two days of division training. Ready or not, the divisions then gathered into provisional corps for the climactic maneuvers. Although the corps-versus-corps maneuvers in each of the encampments varied in detail, they all revealed that the National Guard's state of training was wholly inadequate. Individual soldiers, physically unprepared for marching and living in the field, collapsed from exhaustion with alarming frequency. Observers noted that enlisted men were poorly trained in basic discipline as well. Platoons, companies, and battalions wandered aimlessly through the exercises, demonstrating clearly that the few days devoted to small-unit training had been grossly insufficient. At the higher levels, officers frequently failed to issue coherent orders and often disobeyed the orders they received. Brigade and division commanders proved generally inept at coordinating the weapons and units under their control. Communications were usually in a state of collapse, and in some cases even the administration of supply broke down, leaving the Guardsmen without food.[19]

Few of the deficiencies exhibited in the August maneuvers were truly the fault of the National Guard. The War Department had neglected to form triangular divisions in the National Guard, and, in fact, would not do so until 1942. Virtually every type of equipment was obsolete, or scarce, or both. Guardsmen reported to their encampments with World War I tents, webbing, shoes, and blankets in various stages of decay. Their khaki clothing looked old and worn even before field maneuvers began. News correspondents (147 at First Army's encampment alone) who covered the August maneuvers paid particular attention to the numerous items of equipment that the National Guard did not have at all. A shocked public read about trucks with "TANK" painted on the sides, Springfield rifles labeled ".50 CALIBRE," and simulated antitank guns constructed of drainpipe.[20]

Americans who had opposed conscription, in the belief that the National Guard represented a combat-ready force, were rudely shaken. The 1940 summer encampments demonstrated beyond dispute that, in terms of ground forces, the nation was virtually defenseless. On 27 August, just as the maneuvers were winding down, a joint resolution of Congress authorized the War Department to call up the nearly 300,000 Guardsmen and Reservists for twelve months of federal service. Only three weeks later, the Selective Service Act cleared Congress, empowering the Army to draft up to 900,000 men, also for a year's service. The National Guard's make-believe guns spoke louder in Congress than they did on the maneuver field.[21]

Faced with the imminent prospect of attaining Protective Mobilization Plan manpower objectives, the Army had already begun activating higher tactical headquarters on a permanent basis. On 26 July 1940, the War Department activated the nucleus of General Headquarters (GHQ) in accordance with mobilization plans dating from the 1920s. GHQ was to be the analogue of General Pershing's AEF headquarters in France during World War I. Its initial duty would be to train all of the Army's tactical units and prepare them for commitment to the theater of operations. At that point, GHQ would become the combat command post for the general of the Army, who would be either the Army chief of staff or another officer designated by the president.[22]

General Marshall, who was both Army chief of staff and commanding general of General Headquarters, chose to delegate the responsibility for training the Army to the newly designated GHQ chief of staff, then Brig. Gen. Lesley J. McNair. General McNair came to General Headquarters following a tour as commandant of the Army's Command and General Staff School at Fort Leavenworth, Kansas. He held the reputation of being "the brains of the Army" and would in time win acclaim as the chief architect of the Army's ground forces in World War II.

One of General McNair's first acts as de facto head of General Headquarters was to recommend the fleshing out of the four field army and nine tactical corps headquarters that had existed on paper since the 1920s. McNair wanted these headquarters to supervise the training of the divisions that they might someday take into battle. General Headquarters was the capstone, overseeing the training of the entire Army.[23]

General Headquarters dedicated the remainder of 1940 to the task of absorbing National Guard units, Reservists, and selectees and incorporating them into divisions, corps, and field armies. By the end of the year, the Army had grown to a total of 620,000 soldiers, and in February 1941 the General Staff produced concrete plans for raising the Army to the new Protective Mobilization Plan establishment of 1.4 million by July and maintaining it at that level for one year.[24]

From the outset, GHQ's efforts to create a combat-ready PMP Army encountered numerous difficulties, not the least of which was simply the problem of imposing a uniform, Army-wide training program where none had existed before. Training had previously been the province of the field army commanders (even when the field armies had been paper organizations). McNair, as a staff officer, had only indirect authority over the lieutenant generals who commanded the field armies.

At the lower levels, unit commanders found it increasingly difficult to provide meaningful instruction for their troops. The admixture of raw selectees, half-trained Guardsmen, and seasoned Regulars made it necessary for many units to conduct basic and advanced training at the same time. Furthermore, training facilities were swamped and equipment was more scarce than ever. In one typical case, a National Guard division received only one-quarter of the M1 rifles it needed, forcing the division's four regiments to take turns training with them. Other Guard units were stripped of whatever equipment they possessed in order that the government might fulfill lend-lease obligations.[25]

Undoubtedly, the major obstacle to training in the winter of 1940–41 was the serious shortage of officers who were qualified to train troops and command field units. Two decades of peace left many Regular officers mentally and physically unprepared for the demands of mobilization. Promotions in the Army officer corps operated on the seniority system, as represented on a single promotion list. This list was hopelessly clogged by a logjam of some 4,200 World War I era officers, virtually all of whom were still captains and majors. Inept officers had little trouble retaining their rank, and talented young men had no means of advancing.

In June 1940, Congress approved a War Department plan to automatically promote Regular officers according to a schedule based on time in service. This measure shoved the Army's majors forward in rank, virtually en masse, while they were still young enough to be useful as lieutenant colonels. In October, Congress authorized the granting of temporary promotions to and within the general officer ranks in order to fill the command positions of the expanding Army, a policy normally reserved for wartime. Finally, in 1941, the War Department inaugurated a removal procedure under which officers who had served honorably but who had outlived their usefulness could be retired quickly irrespective of age.[26]

National Guard officers, although partially trained in peacetime, as a group fell short of the Army's expectations. At the conclusion of the 1940 summer encampment, the National Guard Bureau estimated that 20 percent of staff and division officers were unqualified for their positions, in part because less than one-third of the National Guard officers inducted during 1940 and 1941 had ever completed an Army course in leadership.[27] However, Guard officers who failed to meet the demands of active duty could be, and were, removed by the National Guard's own review system. This necessitated the appointment of Regular officers to some of the vacancies in National Guard units, causing friction and further reducing the Regular Army's officer pool.

That the officer shortage did not lead to the complete collapse of mobilization and training was because 106,000 Reserve officers were eligible for call-up. By the end of 1940, these graduates of Reserve Officers Training Corps (ROTC) courses and summer training camps constituted 90 percent of the Army's lieutenants and 60 percent of all officers on duty with field units.[28] The chief of the Field Artillery reported that these reservists "have in most cases taken hold with an enthusiasm and competence which more than justifies the time and money spent in developing and building up the Officers' Reserve Corps."[29]

Inevitably, the attempt to merge officers from three sources into the same Army (and often into the same unit) led to instances of friction and discontent. Regular officers who had labored for years to attain their ranks resented the ease with which Guardsmen and Reservists stepped from the comforts of civilian life into positions of authority. For their part, Guard officers suspected the Army of trying to supplant them completely with Regulars. Stories circulated about Regular officers who, being assigned to National Guard units, deliberately undercut their Guard associates so as to further their own careers. There is a grain of truth in the accusation that General McNair and his staff at General Headquarters failed fully to appreciate the National Guard's distinct character, and that GHQ observers were sometimes quicker to recommend the relief of a Guard officer than to offer him constructive aid.[30]

Although there was no shortage of enlisted men, troop morale declined as the crisis atmosphere of 1940 subsided. Shortages of equipment and training facilities resulted in makeshift work and poorly utilized training time, which the troops were quick to point out to their families and legislators. The officer shortage contributed to a generally low quality of instruction, which in turn aggravated the morale problem. Undeniably, some "old Army" officers and noncoms were decidedly unsympathetic toward their citizen-soldier subordinates. There were also too many cases of "business as usual" staff officers whose insistence on proper procedure resulted in inadequate provisioning of the troops. General Marshall personally investigated some of the soldiers' complaints and issued pointed directives for their redress. He maintained, however, that overprotective families and scandal-hunting newsmen were themselves partly responsible for depressing the morale of the troops.[31]

But of all the problems that General Headquarters encountered in trying to train the PMP Army, the one over which it had the least control, and the one that magnified every other difficulty, was the shortage of time. Although Guardsmen and selectees entered federal service for one-year terms, a shortage of training facilities forced the Army to stagger the induction of National Guard divisions over a six-month period. The last Guard division reported for duty in April 1941, at which time the first divisions to report had only six months of federal duty remaining. September 15—the day that the National Guard would begin to demobilize—was General Headquarters' target date for attaining the Protective Mobilization Plan training objectives.[32]

In spite of difficulties that defied enumeration, General McNair was determined to produce the best-trained Army in American history. He formulated a training program that was carefully integrated and progressively structured, in spite of the need for haste. The policy that McNair prescribed, and that General Headquarters sought to implement in 1940 and 1941, started with training the individual soldier, progressed to integrating individuals into small units, and then turned to training successively larger units uniformly, step by step. McNair believed that ". . . these steps are the foundation of military efficiency. They can be hurried or slighted only at a price." [33] Even though altogether too many steps would be hurried, slighted, or omitted because of the dictates of time and the scarcity of equipment, the McNair training program was, in theory, the best that the Army had ever pursued.

The soldier who entered the Army in 1940–41 began his training with a mobilization training program (MTP) that lasted about thirteen weeks. Prior to March 1941, soldiers took such training in their permanent tactical units. After that time most recruits went to one of twelve replacement training centers established for that express purpose, thus freeing the tactical units for more advanced training.

Mobilization training began with several weeks of basic training, which involved physical conditioning, instruction in fundamental military knowledge, and an introduction to the rudiments of discipline and Army life. The recruit spent little time on such formalities as close-order drill. Instead, basic training provided him with practical knowledge in such matters as map reading, sanitation, and first aid. The second phase introduced the recruit to his service specialty and taught him to function as part of a small unit. If he was slated to become a rifleman, the recruit learned to fire his weapon and to fulfill his role in squad, platoon, and company tactics. Other troops learned to cook, to drive or maintain trucks, and to serve artillery pieces.[34]

While the recruit engaged in mobilization training, some of his officers attended the service schools operated by the different combat arms. The Army encouraged National Guard and Reserve officers in particular to attend their branch service school. Courses of study included both general instruction in the art of command and technical branch training. Division commanders and staffs could attend one of the special two-month courses offered at the Command and General Staff School.[35]

When officers and enlisted men had mastered their individual skills and the small units had become proficient in minor tactics, the MTP phase ended and the combined training phase began. The purpose of this phase was the development of combined arms teamwork leading eventually to the forging of a field-worthy infantry division. Under combined training, infantry units learned to request, and artillery units to deliver, timely and accurate artillery fire. Engineers performed repairs and demolitions for the other arms, and supply echelons gained experience in sustaining the combat units.

Combined training focused most closely on the development of the regimental combat team (RCT), an infantry regiment reinforced by a battalion of field artillery. (Square divisions received training in the analogous brigade combat team.) The regimental combat team being the basic subdivisional task force, two-thirds of the combined training period, thirteen to sixteen weeks, were devoted to it. Much of this training took place in the field, where regimental combat teams conducted a series of controlled (scripted) maneuvers of increasing complexity that introduced various types of operations one by one. The first exercise simply involved moving the team from place to place. In later maneuvers, the team learned deployment, attack, defense, and withdrawal under pressure. The regimental combat team field exercises culminated with a free maneuver between regiments that assayed the RCT's ability to function as a well-orchestrated combination of elements.[36]

Once the regimental and brigade combat teams had demonstrated their proficiency, they progressed to four weeks of division training. There the combined training process was repeated at the division level until the division was able to maneuver in the field and fight a simulated battle against another division.[37]

The completion of division training marked the conclusion of the combined training phase. In World War I there had been no training beyond that stage, but the GHQ schedule for the summer of 1941 entailed combining divisions into corps and corps into field armies, with free maneuvers punctuating each phase. If war came, this PMP Army would escape the "stumbling and blunderings" of 1918. As of 30 June 1941, Army manpower stood at 1,460,998, surpassing the Protective Mobilization Plan establishment.[38]

Notes

1. Eli J. Kahn, *McNair, Educator of an Army* (Washington, D.C.: Infantry Journal Press, 1945), p. 24.

2. "Gaps in U.S. Preparedness," *Newsweek*, 28 Aug 39, p. 11.

3. Mark S. Watson, *Chief of Staff: Prewar Plans and Preparations*, U.S. Army in World War II (Washington, D.C.: U.S. Army Center of Military History, Government Printing Office, 1950), p. 16; *The War Reports of General George C. Marshall, General H. H. Arnold, and Admiral Ernest J. King* (New York: Lippincott, 1947), p. 17.

4. *War Reports*, pp. 16–17.

5. Watson, *Chief of Staff*, pp. 149, 193.

6. *War Reports*, pp. 264–67.

7. Marvin A. Kreidberg and Merton G. Henry, *History of Military Mobilization in the United States Army, 1775–1945* (Washington, D.C.: Department of the Army, Government Printing Office, 1955), pp. 475–92.

8. Franklin D. Roosevelt, *The Public Papers and Addresses of Franklin D. Roosevelt*, vol. 10, *The Call to Battle Stations, 1941* (New York: Russell and Russell, 1950), p. 194.

9. "From the Chief's Office," *Infantry Journal*, Mar–Apr 40, pp. 185–93.

10. Kent Roberts Greenfield, Robert R. Palmer, and Bell I. Wiley, *The Organization of Ground Combat Troops*, U.S. Army in World War II (Washington, D.C.: U.S. Army Center of Military History, Government Printing Office, 1947), pp. 274–75, 300–318.

11. George C. Marshall, *Papers 2*, pp. 59–60 (Marshall to Gen Malin C. Craig, 19 Sep 39).

12. Constance M. Green, Harry C. Thomson, and Peter C. Roots, *The Ordnance Department: Planning Munitions for War*, U.S. Army in World War II (Washington, D.C.: U.S. Army Center of Military History, Government Printing Office, 1955), p. 177.

13. "Final Annexa of IV Corps Maneuvers, March 1940," Record Group 337 57D, HQ AGF, GHQ GS G–3, Subject File 1940–March 1942, National Archives (NA), Washington, D.C.

14. Ibid.; *War Reports*, p. 18.

15. Annex 20, "Final Annexa of IV Corps Maneuvers, March 1940," RG 337 57D, NA.

16. Stetson Conn and Byron Fairchild, *The Framework of Hemisphere Defense*, U.S. Army in World War II (Washington, D.C.: U.S. Army Center of Military History, Government Printing Office, 1960), pp. 38–39.

17. Chief, National Guard Bureau, to CG, Corps Area, 25 Apr 40, General Files AG 353 (12–28–39), RG 94, Office AG Central Files 1926–39, NA.

18. "First Army Maneuvers, 1940, Final Report," p. l, RG 337 57D, NA.

19. "First Army Maneuvers, 1940, Final Report"; "Report, Second Army Maneuvers August 1940"; "Report, Third Army Maneuvers, August 1940, Sabine Area." All in RG 337 57D. Memo for Gen McNair, 31 Aug 40, Maneuvers Memoranda, General Corresp, RG 337 57, HQ AGF, GHQ, NA.

20. For public reaction, see magazine articles such as Herbert B. Nichols, "Prepare for Action," *Christian Science Monitor Magazine*, 28 Sep 40, pp. 8–14, and "Rehearsal," *Time*, 2 Sep 40, pp. 18–19.

21. See Garry J. Clifford and Samuel R. Spencer, Jr., *The First Peacetime Draft* (Lawrence: University Press of Kansas, 1986) for a comprehensive analysis of the 1940 selective service legislation.

22. Greenfield, Palmer, and Wiley, *Organization*, p. 5; Russell F. Weigley, *History of the United States Army* (New York: Macmillan, 1967), pp. 405–07.

23. Greenfield, Palmer, and Wiley, *Organization*, pp. 10–12; Ray S. Cline, *Washington Command Post: The Operations Division*, U.S. Army in World War II (Washington, D.C.: U.S. Army Center of Military History, Government Printing Office, 1951), pp. 61–63.

24. Watson, *Chief of Staff*, pp. 202, 319.

25. Edmund G. Love, *The 27th Infantry Division in World War II* (Washington, D.C.: Infantry Journal Press, 1949), p. 13; Jim Dan Hill, *The Minute Man in Peace and War* (Harrisburg: Stackpole, 1964), p. 427.

26. Watson, *Chief of Staff*, pp. 241–42, 247–48. See also *Army and Navy Journal*, especially the issue of 5 Oct 40.

27. Greenfield, Palmer, and Wiley, *Organization*, pp. 11, 34.

28. Weigley, *History of the U.S. Army*, p. 428; Watson, *Chief of Staff*, pp. 263–64.

29. "Annual Report of the Chief of Field Artillery, Fiscal Year 1941," File 319.1/C., Command and General Staff College Library, Fort Leavenworth, Kan.

30. Hill, *Minute Man*, pp. 392–95, 411, 424–25.

31. Forrest C. Pogue, *George C. Marshall: Ordeal and Hope* (New York: Viking, 1966), pp. 110–19, 156.

32. Hill, *Minute Man*, p. 373.

33. Kahn, *McNair*, p. 22.

34. Robert R. Palmer, Bell I. Wiley, and William R. Keast, *Procurement and Training of Ground Combat Troops*, U.S. Army in World War II (Washington, D.C.: U.S. Army Center of Military History, Government Printing Office, 1948), pp. 377, 414, 444; WD Press Release, 23 May 41, Training (5–23–41) (5–31–41), RG 407, Army AG Decimal File 1940–45, NA.

35. Palmer, Wiley, and Keast, *Procurement*, p. 261; Greenfield, Palmer, and Wiley, *Organization*, p. 36.

36. CofS GHQ to All Army Commanders, 4 Jan 41, sub: Combined Training, 353 Training Directives, GHQ Binder 2, RG 337, Records of AGF, NA.

37. Ibid.

38. Watson, *Chief of Staff*, p. 202.

CHAPTER 2

Preparing for Mechanized War

The period of American protective mobilization (1939–41) coincided with Nazi Germany's great tide of conquest in Europe. Spearheading Germany's seemingly invincible military machine were her panzer (tank) divisions. These were powerful, mobile formations that exemplified the principles of speed, surprise, and shock. Henceforth, any nation with pretensions of military greatness must come to terms with mechanization—the large-scale employment of armored fighting vehicles.

Armored vehicles as such were not new to the U.S. Army. In 1918 General John J. Pershing had authorized the establishment of a 30-battalion, 15,000-man tank corps for the American Expeditionary Forces. Only four battalions actually saw action in World War I, but the fulfillment of contracts after the war left the Army with over 1,000 tanks, of British and French design. For a few months there even existed an autonomous Tank Corps, U.S. Army.[1]

The National Defense Act of 1920 assigned all tanks to the Infantry, where the tank's role was "to facilitate the uninterrupted advance of the riflemen in the attack."[2] Doctrine called for medium tanks to advance immediately behind a rolling barrage, their objective being the enemy antitank positions. Light tanks, accompanying the infantry, would help subdue machine gun positions and other enemy strongpoints.[3] This doctrine, while logical, did little to explore the potential of the tank as a weapons system. Obsolete equipment and chronically short funding prevented infantry from doing more. By 1940 the Infantry's tank establishment totaled eight battalions.[4]

Beginning in 1930, the Cavalry branch created its own experimental mechanized force. (To circumvent the National Defense Act, which assigned all tanks to the Infantry, the Cavalry called its tanks combat cars.) The Cavalry's attitude toward mechanization was somewhat more innovative than the Infantry's even though hardcore horse troopers deeply resented the intrusion of motor vehicles. The 7th Cavalry Brigade (Mechanized), organized at Fort

Knox in the 1930s, eventually grew into a prototype combined-arms mechanized force that included two cavalry regiments, an artillery battalion, observation aircraft, and, in 1940, even an attached regiment of infantry. Under the leadership of Col. Adna R. Chaffee, this brigade compiled an enviable record of accomplishments during field tests and maneuvers, leading Chaffee to conclude that a properly organized mechanized unit could strike the decisive blow in battle.[5]

Three of the four field armies vied to obtain Chaffee's brigade for their spring 1940 maneuvers. Lt. Gen. Stanley B. Embick not only won the 7th for Third Army's Louisiana maneuvers, he also obtained the Provisional Tank Brigade, Brig. Gen. Bruce Magruder commanding, that the Infantry branch created by pooling seven of its eight tank battalions. The Louisiana maneuvers climaxed with an exercise in which the two brigades joined to form the Army's first provisional mechanized division.[6]

Up to this time, American officers remained sharply divided on the issue of mechanization. Germany's blitzkrieg in Poland, many believed, could not be duplicated against a first-rate opponent. But while the 1940 Louisiana maneuvers were in progress, Germany launched its mechanized forces against the Western Allies. By 25 May, the day the Louisiana maneuvers ended, the once-proud French Army was a shattered and discredited force, many of its finest elements either destroyed or penned up ignominiously along the Channel coast. In the space of ten days, a German army group spearheaded by nine panzer divisions had punched a clean hole through the French defenses along the Meuse River and raced to the English Channel. This time there could be no claim that special circumstances alone made the mechanized triumph possible. France had been well armed, alerted, and mobilized and had opened the battle on ground of her own choosing. This campaign made clear to all that mechanization had established a new era in warfare.

On the last day of the Louisiana maneuvers, a little-noticed but important meeting took place in the basement of the Alexandria, Louisiana, high school. Generals Chaffee and Magruder, the mechanized brigade commanders, and other interested officers such as Col. George S. Patton, once the Army's leading expert in tank warfare, and Brig. Gen. Frank Andrews, assistant chief of staff, met to discuss the creation of an American mechanized branch.[7] They agreed that independent status was necessary because the Cavalry and Infantry branches had procrastinated too long already. (Significantly, the chiefs of Cavalry and Infantry were in Louisiana to observe the maneuvers but were not invited to the meeting.) [8]

The basement conspirators sent their recommendations to Washington with General Andrews, who laid them before the Army chief of staff. On 6 June General Marshall informed the branch chiefs of his decision to create the autonomous force that the Louisiana group had recommended. The Cavalry and the Infantry, long the reluctant custodians of mechanization, were ordered to turn their tanks over to the new branch. The War Department officially activated the experimental Armored Force on 10 July 1940 and named General Chaffee as chief. Five days later the 7th Cavalry Brigade became the 1st Armored Brigade and the Provisional Tank Brigade was redesignated the 2d Armored Brigade. (*Armored* was chosen for the new force because it avoided the Cavalry's *mechanized* as well as the Infantry's *tank*.)

At its inception the Armored Force comprised the I Armored Corps and two armored divisions, the 1st and 2d, which were built around the existing brigades. The corps was strictly a headquarters organization, having no organic troops of its own, and as such it remained contiguous with Armored Force headquarters until May 1941, when Maj. Gen. Charles L. Scott assumed the corps command. The most crucial of General Chaffee's early duties was the design and establishment of the two armored divisions, the real fighting force of the armored command.

It would have been natural enough for Chaffee to copy the organization and doctrine of the German panzer division. The fundamental characteristics, and many of the details, of panzer warfare could be discerned from open sources, such as the American service journals, although a good deal of fright literature had to be discounted. In 1940, a typical panzer division consisted of one tank regiment of two or three battalions, one motorized infantry brigade totaling four battalions, a regiment of motorized artillery, plus antitank, antiaircraft, engineer, reconnaissance, signal, and supply elements, all motorized. Panzer divisions, like other German forces, often divided up into all-arms *Kampfgruppen*—battle groups or task forces generally of regimental strength—each one tailored to its specific tactical mission. The actions of tanks, infantry, and artillery were integrated at the company or battalion level.[9]

The 1940 armored division devised by Chaffee contained the same basic elements as the panzer division. It consisted of an armored brigade (three armored regiments and an artillery regiment); an infantry regiment of two battalions; an additional artillery battalion; a battalion of engineers; and reconnaissance, supply, and command echelons.[10] As with the panzer division, the entire command was fully motorized. (*Chart 3*)

CHART 3—1940 ARMORED DIVISION

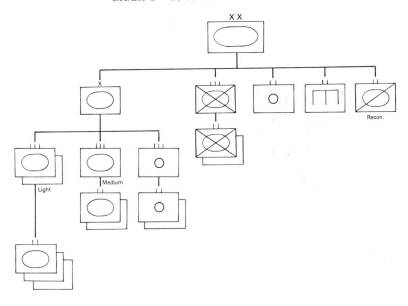

The 1940 armored division differed markedly from the panzer division, however, in that it could not subdivide into battle groups. Under Chaffee's scheme, the armored division's principal fighting element was the strike echelon consisting solely of the armored brigade. It was his intent that the brigade's two regiments of light tanks would conduct rapid, deep envelopments of the enemy while the medium regiment (two battalions as compared to the light regiment's three) provided support and tackled major centers of resistance.[11] Infantry and engineers were found in the support echelon, which existed primarily to protect the lines of communication, secure captured objectives, and prepare the way for the strike echelon's decisive attacks.[12] There is no indication that Chaffee expected infantry, artillery, and armor to fight side by side in the *Kampfgruppe* manner. Overall, the 1940 armored division reveals that Chaffee valued the speed and mobility of his light armored regiments over the firepower, staying power, and protective armor of the other elements, an attitude that was consistent with his Cavalry background. Stated simply, the principle of combined arms was not effectively observed.

In another respect, however, Chaffee was in fundamental agreement with the tactical philosophy of Heinz Guderian, the father of the German panzer force. Both men believed that armored units were all-purpose forces, not merely arms of exploitation, that

An M3 light tank of the 2d Armored Division on maneuvers. *(Armor magazine.)*

when grouped together in suitable mass were capable of striking the decisive blow of a battle. Chaffee expressed his views to Congress in 1941: "The role of an armored division is the conduct of highly mobile ground warfare, particularly offensive in character, by a self-sustained unit of great power and mobility, composed of specially equipped troops . . . on missions either strategical or tactical, whose accomplishment will effect to the maximum the total destruction of the enemy."[13] Chaffee was unswerving in his advocacy of massed armored units, even to the level of armored armies. With the exception of five independent tank battalions that the Army kept in general reserve to reinforce infantry divisions, the Armored Force he forged embodied that principle.

With a tentative table of organization and a tactical doctrine in hand, the Armored Force activated the 1st and 2d Armored Divisions in July 1940. To dilute old branch ties, General Chaffee assigned General Magruder (Infantry) to command the 1st Armored Division, which was built around the 1st Armored Brigade (the renamed 7th Cavalry Brigade). General Scott (Cavalry) assumed command of the 2d Armored Division, which included the 2d Armored Brigade (the Infantry's old Provisional Tank Brigade). Patton, now a brigadier general, also from the Cavalry, succeeded Scott in December 1940. This shrewd tactic succeeded in loosening old affiliations, as evidenced by the esprit that quickly suffused the new force. This development was fortunate indeed considering the multitude of difficulties that remained to be overcome and overcome quickly, for General Chaffee set 1 October 1940 as the date on which the armored divisions were to be ready for field training.

The most serious initial obstacle confronting the two division commanders was a shortage of trained personnel. Whereas each armored division was to have a peacetime establishment of 9,500 and a wartime strength of 11,200, at its inception the entire Armored Force consisted of only 9,500 men.[14] The passage of the Selective Service Act in September assured an adequate supply of manpower, but mere numbers would not solve the problem.

The intricacies of mechanized warfare demanded highly trained and motivated soldiers, officers and enlisted men alike. General Chaffee estimated that 50 percent of an armored division's enlisted men ranked as occupational specialists.[15] At the outset, the Armored Force lacked essential specialized training programs and had to adapt existing Infantry and Cavalry materials. Even after satisfactory training manuals were published, the need to expand and train at the same time meant that individual and unit training proceeded simultaneously. What is more, the two divisions had barely filled their ranks when, in October, they surrendered some of their best personnel as cadre for the 3d and 4th Armored Divisions.[16]

Equipment shortages also plagued the early days of the Armored Force. In place of the 3,243 vehicles that each division needed to attain full combat strength, the Armored Force inherited less than 1,000.[17] Of the 287 light and 120 medium tanks required for each division, a total of 400 light and only 18 medium tanks were on hand.[18] Many of the existing vehicles fell below the mark in quality, particularly the M2 medium tank, which was abandoned altogether in favor of the makeshift M3. General Chaffee thought that the M3 possessed "barely satisfactory performance characteristics," although it did have the advantage of carrying a 75-mm. gun mounted into the right side of the hull.[19] The M3 did not appear in production until April 1941, and even then many went to lend-lease instead of to the Armored Force. Light tanks with "M" painted on their hulls helped fill the medium regiments throughout 1941.

The Armored Force did acquire from both the Cavalry and the Infantry a variety of serviceable light tanks which were designated, respectively, the M1 and M2 series. The Armored Force adopted a standardized M3 (not to be confused with the M3 medium) in July 1940. All of these models were roughly similar in appearance and characteristics, having weights of about ten tons and top speeds of thirty to forty-five miles per hour. Older models carried machine guns only, whereas later versions, including the M3, also mounted a 37-mm. gun.[20]

In addition to procuring tanks, the Armored Force also had to obtain the means of transporting its infantry and artillery any-where the tanks could go if the armored division was expected to function as a unit. The solution to transporting riflemen was the halftrack, a trucklike vehicle with driving treads behind and steer-able front wheels. The Army had tested more than a dozen proto-types by 1940, two of which were ready for production as the M2 and M3 in September.[21] Ideally, armored artillery would consist of self-propelled weapons utilizing tanklike chassis, but although the Army had experimented with some prototypes in 1939 and 1940, no production orders were forthcoming. Throughout 1941, the ar-mored divisions would make do with standard artillery pieces towed by halftracks.[22]

In October 1940, General Chaffee announced that the 1st and 2d Armored Divisions had fulfilled his original training directive and that after a winter spent in remedial training of the individual and the small unit, they would be ready for combined training with corps and armies in 1941.[23] Between April and June 1941, the 2d Armored Division participated in air-ground tests at its home base, Fort Ben-ning, Georgia, while both it and the 1st at Fort Knox, Kentucky, car-ried out three months of regiment, brigade, and division training in preparation for the upcoming maneuvers season.[24] When corps and army maneuvers began that summer, the armored divisions, with some justification, would regard themselves as the Army's elite.

Another unit stationed at Fort Benning, the 4th Infantry Divi-sion, would play an important role in the development of armored doctrine. Armored forces plunging deep behind enemy lines are vulnerable to enemy counterattacks against their flanks and rear. The German solution to this problem was the motorized division, which was basically a truck-transported infantry division. During the French campaign of 1940, five such motorized divisions fol-lowed the panzer spearheads and protected their lines of commu-nication. In November 1940 the War Department announced that the U.S. Army would also have a motorized division. As originally conceived, this unit would differ from the standard triangular divi-sion only in its ability to move all of its troops, weapons, and sup-plies simultaneously, using its own organic motor transport. In battle the motorized division's function would be to accompany the armored spearhead, covering its flanks and rear so that the armored divisions could concentrate on continuing their advance.[25] The chief of the Infantry, General Lynch, stressed that the operations of the motorized division would be fundamentally defensive. He proposed an increase in the division's antitank and antiaircraft capabilities to bolster its strength on defense.[26]

The 4th Infantry Division, chosen to become the prototypical motorized division, began to reorganize in July 1941. By that time, however, the motorized division concept had undergone a complete revision. When it emerged from the transition process, the 4th no longer resembled a triangular division; rather, it had become essentially a light armored division. With 2 infantry regiments, 1 mechanized regiment, 2,600 vehicles, and 14,000 men, the 4th Motorized Division was not a defensively oriented support unit as originally conceived—it was a powerful, highly mobile offensive weapon in its own right.[27]

At a time when the Armored Force was attaining new levels of firepower and maneuver, and when even the Infantry was drawn to motorization, the Cavalry, traditional arm of mobility, found its very existence threatened. World War I provided ample evidence that the day of the mounted service had passed, and although General Pershing, himself a cavalryman, had claimed that "cavalry is as important today as it has ever been," he took only four cavalry regiments to France with the American Expeditionary Forces.[28] In 1931, Chief of Staff MacArthur made it clear to the Cavalry that the equestrian arm faced an uncertain future. "Modern firearms have eliminated the horse as a weapon, and as a means of transportation he has become, next to the dismounted man, the slowest means of transportation," he said.[29] "The time has therefore arrived when the Cavalry arm must either replace or assist the horse as a means of transportation, or else pass into the limbo of discarded military formations."[30] But with the exception of Chaffee's mechanized brigade, the Cavalry establishment clung tenaciously to the horse rather than embracing the "combat car" as a means of revitalizing the arm. *(Chart 4)*

In 1938 the Cavalry received as its new chief Maj. Gen. John K. Herr, who was more interested in the Cavalry's nineteenth century traditions than in modern realities. Herr never wavered in his love of the horse or in his conviction that German mechanization owed its success exclusively to the topography and road systems of Europe.[31] With Herr in control, the Cavalry's major concession to mechanization was the development of the horse-mechanized corps reconnaissance regiment. This curious formation included one

CHART 4—CAVALRY DIVISION (HORSE), 1941

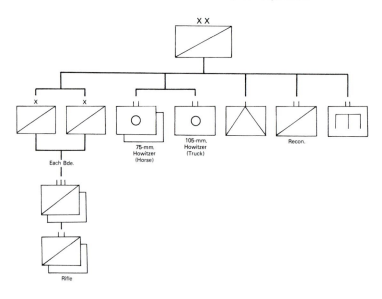

mechanized squadron mounted on motorcycles, scout cars, and (in 1941) Bantams, otherwise known as jeeps. The second squadron, which carried the designation horse-portee, rode its horses in action, but for long-distance moves the squadron loaded onto trailer-trucks, horses and all. General Herr claimed that a squad of eight troopers could embark its horses, forage, rations, machine guns, and equipment in five to eight minutes.[32] Out of twelve Regular regiments, the Cavalry adapted two to the horse-mechanized format. Eight were assigned to the 1st and 2d Cavalry Divisions. National Guard induction brought in two more all-horse regiments and seven horse-mechanized, which together with the two Regular horse-mechanized units made a total of nine, one for each army corps.[33]

With the activation of the Armored Force in July 1940, the Cavalry surrendered its claim to full partnership among the combat arms. Maj. Gen. Robert Grow later stated that Herr "lost mechanization for Cavalry and . . . Cavalry . . . lost a prestige that it can never regain again."[34] General Herr himself realized, at the onset of the 1941 maneuver season, that "the pressure was on from certain quarters to eliminate the mounted service."[35]

Even as mechanization eclipsed one arm, it gave rise to another. To wage decisive armored warfare, the Army needed a means of neutralizing hostile armored forces. Many officers, General McNair included, believed that finding a way to defeat armored operations

A 37-mm. antitank gun. *(National Archives.)*

was the Army's major problem.[36] As of 1940, even less progress had been made in the antitank field than in mechanization. The Army did not decide to develop a specialized antitank gun until 1936, and the 37-mm. weapon that finally appeared in 1939 was merely a direct copy of an obsolescent German weapon.[37] Sixty of these inadequate weapons, scattered among the infantry regiments and artillery battalions, were the triangular division's sole defense against armor at the end of 1940.[38] The chief of the Infantry, whose branch was charged with responsibility for antitank development, neglected it almost completely.[39] The Field Artillery, to which 40 percent of the Army's antitank forces belonged, summed up antitank warfare in just six pages of its basic instructional manual.[40]

General McNair was perhaps the Army's keenest student of antitank matters. He studied means of stopping the tank throughout the 1930s but received little encouragement from his superiors. In 1937 McNair had directed the field tests that helped persuade the General Staff of the need for regimental antitank companies.[41] During his subsequent tour as commandant of the Command and General Staff School he initiated a review of antitank measures that culminated in the publication of a tentative field manual, written for instructional purposes, in 1939.

This study, *Antimechanized Defense*, embodied the antitank concepts that McNair brought to General Headquarters in 1940. The most fundamental of these was the inaccurate notion that armored forces equated to massed tanks (as opposed to combined-arms task forces) and that antitank guns should likewise be pooled in order to defeat them. *Antimechanized Defense* proposed that each infantry division should possess a battalion of antitank guns to serve as a highly mobile antimechanized reserve in support of the regimental antitank companies. With enemy armor neutralized by its antitank elements, the division would be otherwise free to get on with offensive operations.[42]

McNair's elevation to the post of GHQ chief of staff in 1940 provided him with the podium from which to expound his views. A War Department training memo issued on 23 September 1940 bore the strong imprint of *Antimechanized Defense*: field units were advised to post a minimum of their antitank guns in frontline positions and to retain as many as possible in mobile reserve.[43] The field armies and corps, however, failed to take the initiative in developing their own antitank capabilities. Very few gun crews had ever seen a real tank in action; even fewer had fired a real antitank gun at a moving target.[44] The VI Corps and the Armored Force were the only headquarters to issue comprehensive antitank instructions to their troops.[45]

The hesitant manner in which the Army proceeded with antitank development was doubly unfortunate, for it reinforced an unreasonable fear of the tank that stemmed from the stunning German victories in Europe. The erroneous belief that the Germans possessed seventy-ton amphibious tanks gained wide currency.[46] Artillery officers abandoned the notion of providing antitank defense for the division and began thinking in terms of last-ditch fighting by isolated batteries.[47]

Finally, in April 1941, General Marshall decided that, as had been the case with armor, direct action by the General Staff would be necessary before any meaningful antitank development could be expected. He instructed the G–3 (Operations and Training) Section to study the feasibility of highly mobile antitank units, such as those proposed in *Antimechanized Defense*.[48] G–3 held a conference on 15 April at which the various branch representatives agreed with General Headquarters on the need to create mobile antitank units, but there was no agreement on which branch should control the new forces.[49] General Marshall promptly responded to this latest round of bickering among the arms by assigning antitank development directly to G–3. In less than two weeks G–3 produced a recommendation for the establishment of divisional antitank battalions to reinforce the regimental antitank companies, very much as proposed in *Antimechanized Defense*. Activation of the new battalions came on 24 June 1941.[50]

General McNair was already thinking in grander terms. Taking the principle of pooling to a higher level, he proposed the creation of an independent antitank arm that would control all antitank units in the Army with the power to assign them wherever they were needed.[51] Furthermore, both he and General Marshall expanded the concept of an active, mobile antitank defense to include actually taking the fight to the enemy armor. In assigning antitank development to G–3, Marshall stated that antitank units should possess an "offensive weapon and organization." [52]

General McNair's faith in the ability of mobile antitank forces to defeat armored operations was by no means universally shared. Generals Chaffee and Lynch, for instance, both believed that armored forces could be countered only by other armored forces.[53] But given the backing of Marshall and McNair, it was certain that the new antitank units would participate in the upcoming 1941 maneuvers, where both they and the new Armored Force would be put to the test.

Notes

1. Mary L. Stubbs and Stanley R. Connor, *Armor-Cavalry Part I: Regular Army and Army Reserve*, Army Lineage Series (Washington, D.C.: U.S. Army Center of Military History, Government Printing Office, 1969), pp. 42–49.

2. Quoted in Stubbs and Connor, *Armor-Cavalry I*, p. 50.

3. George A. Lynch, "Firepower . . . Manpower . . . Maneuver," *Infantry Journal*, Nov–Dec 39, pp. 498–505, 606.

4. For a complete analysis of American armor developments between the world wars, see Timothy K. Nenninger, "The Development of American Armor, 1917–1940," Master's thesis, University of Wisconsin, 1968.

5. Mildred H. Gillie, *Forging the Thunderbolt* (Harrisburg: Military Service Publishing Co., 1947), p. 118.

6. Stubbs and Connor, *Armor-Cavalry I*, p. 58; Gillie, *Thunderbolt*, p. 162.

7. Patton, a tank brigade commander in World War I, could have established himself as the Army's foremost tank advocate. When all tanks went to the Infantry in 1920, however, Patton returned to the Cavalry, where he devoted the interwar years to polo, equitation, and saber design. See Martin Blumenson, *The Patton Papers, 1885–1940* (Boston: Houghton Mifflin, 1972).

8. Gillie, *Thunderbolt*, pp. 163–65.

9. Richard M. Ogorkiewicz, *Armoured Forces* (New York: Arco, 1970), pp. 75–76, 84.

10. "AGF Study No. 27, The Armored Force, Command, and Center" (Historical Section, AGF, 1946), p. 15.

11. Ibid., p. 35.

12. U.S. Congress, House, Subcommittee of the Committee on Appropriations, *Hearings on the Military Establishment Appropriations Bill for 1942*, 77th Cong., lst sess., 1941, pp. 559–60 (Statement of Maj Gen Adna R. Chaffee).

13. Ibid.

14. Gillie, *Thunderbolt*, p. 175; House, *Hearings on the Military Establishment Appropriations Bill for 1942*, p. 559.

15. House, *Hearings on the Military Establishment Appropriations Bill for 1942*, p. 562.

16. Donald E. Houston, *Hell on Wheels: The 2nd Armored Division* (San Rafael, Calif.: Presidio, 1977), p. 41.

17. Stubbs and Connor, *Armor-Cavalry I*, pp. 58–59.

18. Gillie, *Thunderbolt*, pp. 175–77.

19. Ibid., p. 204.

20. Peter Chamberlain and Chris Ellis, *British and American Tanks of World War II*, 2d ed. (New York: Arco, 1975), pp. 84–89.

21. Christopher F. Foss, *Jane's World Armoured Fighting Vehicles* (New York: St. Martin's, 1976), p. 310.

22. "Armored Force Artillery in the Tennessee Maneuvers," *Field Artillery Journal*, Sep 41, p. 699.

23. "AGF Study No. 27," p. 50.

24. "17th Bomb Wing Report," 2 Jul 41, 353 Air-Ground, GHQ, U.S. Army, 1940–42 General Corresp, RG 337, Records of AGF, NA.

25. WD Training Cir 10, 26 Nov 40, sub: Employment of Motorized Divisions, General Files AG 353 (12–28–39), RG 94, Office AG Central Files 1926–39, NA.

26. George A. Lynch, "Motorized Divisions," *Infantry Journal*, Jan 41, pp. 2–5.

27. Ritchie Wolfe, "The New Motorized Division," *Field Artillery Journal*, Oct 41, pp. 715–23.

28. John K. Herr and Edward S. Wallace, *The Story of the U.S. Cavalry* (Boston: Little, Brown, 1953), pp. 243–44.

29. Quoted in Gillie, *Thunderbolt*, p. 48.

30. Quoted in Stubbs and Connor, *Armor-Cavalry I*, p. 55.

31. Herr and Wallace, *Cavalry*, pp. 252–54.

32. Ibid., p. 248. For information on the horse-mechanized regiment, see the Bruce Palmer, Jr., Papers, pp. 23–27, Oral History Collection, Military History Institute (MHI), Carlisle Barracks, Pa.

33. Stubbs and Connor, *Armor-Cavalry I*, pp. 70, 72.

34. Houston, *Hell on Wheels*, p. 34.

35. Herr and Wallace, *Cavalry*, p. 250.

36. Greenfield, Palmer, and Wiley, *Organization*, p. 74.

37. Watson, *Chief of Staff*, p. 43.

38. "The Triangular Division Today," *Infantry Journal*, Jan 41, p. 25.

39. Memo, G–3 for CofS, 19 Apr 41, sub: Creation of Additional Antitank-Antiaircraft Units, Andrew D. Bruce Papers, Organization of Tank Destroyer Command, MHI.

40. U.S. Army, Field Artillery School, *Field Artillery Gunnery* (Fort Sill, Okla.: Field Artillery School, 1941), pp. 138–43. See also Allerton Cushman, "Direct Fire—1941 Edition," *Field Artillery Journal*, Jan 41, pp. 11–13.

41. Greenfield, Palmer, and Wiley, *Organization*, p. 74.

42. Command and General Staff School (CGSC), *Antimechanized Defense (Tentative)* (Fort Leavenworth, Kan.: CGSS Press, 1939). See especially ch. 1.

43. Emory A. Dunham, "AGF Study No. 29, Tank Destroyer History" (Historical Section, AGF, 1946), p. 1.

44. O. F. Marston, "Fast Moving Targets," *Field Artillery Journal*, Jul–Aug 40, pp. 264–67.

45. Dunham, "AGF Study No. 29," p. 1.

46. "Artillery and the Tank," *Field Artillery Journal*, Jul–Aug 40, pp. 243–48.

47. Ralph Van Wyck, "Antitank Battery Training," *Field Artillery Journal*, Jan 41, pp. 6–10.

48. Memo for ACofS, G–3, 14 Apr 41, sub: Creation of Additional Antitank and Antiaircraft Units, Directives, Chronological, George C. Marshall (GCM) Research Library, Lexington, Va.

49. Memo, G–3 for CofS, 19 Apr 41, sub: Creation of Additional Antitank-Antiaircraft Units, Bruce Papers, MHI.

50. Dunham, "AGF Study No. 29," p. 2.

51. Memo, G–3 for CofS, 19 Apr 41, sub: Creation of Additional Antitank-Antiaircraft Units.

52. Memo for ACofS, G–3, 14 Apr 41, Bruce Papers, MHI.

53. C. M. Baily, "The Development of American Tank Destroyers in World War II," Thesis, U.S. Army CGSC, 1976, pp. 7–8; House, *Hearings on the Military Establishment Appropriations Bill for 1942*, p. 556.

CHAPTER 3

The Air-Ground Dilemma

The drive to create a battle-worthy Protective Mobilization Plan Army in 1941 involved air as well as ground forces. The airplane had come of age as a weapon of war in the preceding decade, attaining performance characteristics that pushed the limits of propeller-driven, reciprocating-engine design. The destructive capacity of the aircraft had also escalated, as symbolized by Guernica, Warsaw, Rotterdam, and Coventry. Even so, public perceptions of air power exceeded the real capabilities of contemporary air forces.

The Army Air Corps of 1939 numbered only 20,000 men and 1,700 aircraft.[1] On 16 May 1940, in response to German aggression in Europe, President Roosevelt called for a military air arm of 50,000 planes and a productive capacity of 50,000 planes per year.[2] (Astounding as this proposal seemed at the time, the Army air arm would procure 230,000 aircraft over the next five years.)[3] In July 1940, Congress authorized an air corps of 54 groups, totaling 3,149 combat aircraft. An 84-group, 7,799-plane force gained approval in March 1941.[4]

On 20 June 1941, at the urging of General Marshall, the War Department reorganized the Army air arm to reflect the growing role of air power in national strategy. The old Army Air Corps, equal in status to the Infantry, Cavalry, and Field Artillery, gave way to the Army Air Forces (AAF), an autonomous agency within the War Department. Maj. Gen. H. H. Arnold, named chief of the Army Air Forces, also functioned as deputy chief of staff for air, making him answerable only to the Army chief of staff. (As a de facto member of the Joint Chiefs of Staff, Arnold achieved parity with the chief of staff and the chief of naval operations.) All AAF combat elements came under the Air Force Combat Command, headed by Lt. Gen. Delos C. Emmons, with operational control being vested in four numbered air forces.[5] By this time the air service numbered 150,000 men.[6]

For all of the importance attached to the growing air arm, there was no consensus as to the actual function of an air force in war. Officially, the War Department maintained that an air force's primary function was to support the ground elements on the battlefield. This traditionalist interpretation classed the air service as but one of the combat arms, all of whose actions needed to be closely orchestrated to produce effective military operations. The War Department training directive for 1940–41 called for combined-arms teamwork among the Infantry, Cavalry, Field Artillery, and Air Corps.[7] Field Manual 1–5, *Employment of Aviation of the Army* (1940), assigned all aviation within a theater to the commander of field forces, who then assigned air units to specific corps and divisions for integration into the ground scheme of battle.[8] The subordination of air to ground units continued to hold sway among ground officers even after the creation of the Army Air Forces. General McNair was a prominent advocate of this arrangement.

By contrast, General Marshall held a much more liberal view toward air power. He encouraged air officers in their belief that air power represented such a radical departure in military affairs that it should be conducted on its own terms and not in lock step with the actions of ground forces. Air officers advocated a system under which air units, controlled by air officers, roamed the entire theater of war, striking at the most remunerative targets. They believed that air operations should first be directed against enemy air forces, and then against targets beyond the range of friendly artillery. Operations in the immediate vicinity of the front were held to be unacceptably dangerous and relatively unproductive.[9]

The ultimate expression of independent air power was the doctrine of strategic bombing, which gradually came to dominate discourse among airmen in the 1930s. The principal agent for converting the Air Corps to strategic bombing was the Air Corps Tactical School, an institution established to train air officers for high command. High-altitude precision strategic bombing first appeared in the school's curriculum in 1926. By 1930 strategic bombing formed the basis of instruction. As early as 1933, students undertook targeting studies that examined the potential impact of strategic bombing upon transportation networks, iron and steel industries, electric power grids, and the like. By 1935, "the full-blown theory of high-level daylight precision bombardment of pinpoint [strategic] targets was being taught at the Tactical School."[10]

Also in 1935, Boeing's experimental four-engine bomber, the superb Model 299, underwent trials for the Air Corps. In 1936 the Air Corps accepted two Model 299s under the military designation B–17, and, in the words of General Arnold, "from then on, the B–17 was the focus of our air planning."[11] Congress funded the B–17 on the understanding that it was "especially useful for coastal patrol," but the Air Corps knew the new airplane for what it was—a true strategic bomber.[12]

Left to its own devices, the Air Corps would have procured four-engine bombers to the virtual exclusion of other types. Doubters in the Congress and War Department, however, held the procurement of the B–17 and the B–24, a comparable type, to a trickle.[13]

Although strategic bombing was not yet feasible, preoccupation with it resulted inevitably in neglecting other manifestations of air power. As stated in the official Air Force history of the Air Corps Tactical School, "With the increase in emphasis on the strategic employment of the bomber, there was a decline in attention paid to air support of surface operations. Nevertheless, this phase of air force activities was never completely neglected; throughout the history of the school, instructors recognized that air operations in support of ground forces might be required."[14] The Air Corps' true attitude towards ground support was unmistakable: "The idea of employing both ground forces and the GHQ AF only against opposing ground forces, and thereby defeating the enemy in detail, was . . . an alluring but false doctrine."[15]

Such attitudes meshed poorly with the 1940–41 strategic situation, which called for hemispheric defense, not the bombing of an enemy's homeland. They also flew in the face of reports from the European war, where the German *Luftwaffe* proved conclusively that air forces operating in the ground-support role played an important, if not decisive, role in mechanized warfare.

Designed specifically for ground-support operations, the *Luftwaffe* opened hostilities in the 1939 and 1940 campaigns by destroying enemy aircraft on the ground and crippling maintenance and production facilities, thus securing air superiority. Next, German dive bombers, acting as highly mobile heavy artillery, smashed enemy strongpoints obstructing the deep thrusts of the panzer forces. The *Luftwaffe* provided flank security for those forces by interfering with the enemy's attempts to organize counterattacks. German air power also isolated the battlefield by methodically attacking lines of communication, thus preventing enemy reserves from moving forward and disrupting the retreat of beaten units. Finally, the Germans utilized terror bombing of civilians to browbeat enemy governments into prompt capitulation.[16]

Understandably, General Marshall wanted an air service that could replicate the remarkable accomplishments of the *Luftwaffe*. Although General Arnold claimed that *Luftwaffe* operations conformed with doctrine taught at the Air Corps Tactical School, the American air arm was not capable of performing all of these functions.[17] It is true that American doctrine stressed air superiority as a first priority. The Air Corps was also doctrinally prepared to disrupt enemy counterattacks and to isolate the battlefield.[18] Events would prove that American bombers were capable of dealing devastating blows against population centers. But missing from the American repertoire was the heavy artillery function—the selective hammering of enemy strongpoints on the immediate battlefield. This mission appeared in doctrine but was underrepresented in aircraft procurement and in training programs.[19]

Such had not always been the case. Between 1932 and 1936, the Air Corps had purchased 156 single-engine attack aircraft intended specifically for ground support. They mounted four to five forward-firing machine guns and carried an assortment of fragmentation, demolition, and chemical bombs. But in 1939 the Air Corps phased out the attack plane category and in 1940 began replacing its single-engine attack plane with a twin-engine light bomber, the A–20.[20]

The 54-group expansion program authorized in 1940 included only 7 ground-attack groups totaling 438 light bombers. The 84-group plan of 1941, which called for 7,799 aircraft, included just 770 light bombers in 13 ground-attack groups. General Marshall refused to approve the 84-group proposal until it included aircraft similar to the German Ju–87 Stuka dive bomber. Under this pressure, the Air Corps agreed to designate 12 of the 13 ground-attack groups as dive-bomber units, even though the Air Corps did not possess a single dive bomber and had not even approved a model for production.[21] Three months later, in June 1941, Assistant Secretary of War for Air Robert A. Lovett took the air service to task for continuing to neglect dive-bomber procurement.[22] Only then did the Army Air Forces accept its first dive-bomber design, the A–24.[23] This aircraft, which was simply an Army designation for the Navy's Douglas SBD Dauntless dive bomber, had only two light machine guns in forward-firing mounts, a feature that limited its effectiveness in the ground-support role. Many more months would pass before the AAF training program produced even one fully qualified dive-bomber pilot.[24]

Indeed, the training of aircrews in ground-support operations raised an array of new obstacles. Logically, such training required the participation of both air and ground units, but General McNair, responsible for joint air-ground training, had no authority over AAF training schedules. Nor could the air service attempt the

The A–24 attack aircraft, the Army's version of the Navy SBD Dauntless dive bomber. *(DA photograph.)*

complex problem of air-ground coordination until proficiency in
basic skills had been attained. As stated in the Air Corps training
directive for 1940–41, "because of the current Air Corps expansion, individual training must be given first priority," although
"every advantage must be taken for training in tactical cooperation
with the other arms." [25]

In January 1941, General Headquarters issued instructions and
schedules for upcoming corps and army training in which the Air
Corps was conspicuous by its absence.[26] However, the Air Corps was
able to provide one bomber wing for the air-support tests conducted
under the direction of IV Corps at Fort Benning between February
and June 1941. Elements of the 17th Bombardment Wing (Light)
carried out nine joint exercises with the 4th Division, 31st Division,
and 2d Armored Division, in the course of which the airmen developed procedures for establishing command posts and communications systems for ground-support units. The tests also provided data
on identification problems between ground and air, and on minimum safe distances between targets and friendly ground units.[27]
Beneficial as the tests were, they only began to address the intricate
problems inherent to large-scale ground-support operations.

Aside from the Fort Benning tests, field training in the spring of 1941 began without the significant participation of the Air Corps. Although all troops would have benefited from the participation of aircraft in the combined-arms training program, those most seriously affected by the lack of significant air-ground cooperation were the members of the Army's new parachute force. The 501st Parachute Battalion, established in October 1940, began training in early 1941 with only twelve transport aircraft—enough to drop one company at a time.[28] After German airborne operations in 1940 and 1941 had demonstrated the potential of such forces, the Army laid plans to greatly expand its parachute and air-transport programs. To ease the shortage of transports for the airborne force, General Marshall even proposed the conversion of commercial aircraft to military use.[29]

Joint training of any sort between air and ground units had yet to begin in earnest even as the 1941 maneuvers season got under way. The War Department training circular for 1941–42 implicitly relegated ground support to third place on the Army Air Forces' scale of priorities, ordering that "the air forces, directed by the Chief of Army Air Forces, develop their triple mission as a separate [i.e., strategic] striking force, as an element of regional air defense and as a component of combined arms in close support of ground operations." [30] Echoing these priorities was the Army Air Forces' own training directive for 1941–42: "Emphasis will be placed on training and operations at altitudes above 20,000 feet, including combat maneuvers, visual and photographic reconnaissance, aerial gunnery and *bombing* at or near the *service ceiling* of the aircraft." [31]

The air arm's accomplishments from 1939 to 1941 were remarkable. It succeeded in expanding sevenfold and in modernizing simultaneously. Virtually every aircraft type that it would use in World War II was either under design or in production. With the establishment of the Army Air Forces, airmen attained representation in formulating national strategy. They developed a doctrine of strategic bombing that raised prospects of air power alone winning wars. In the midst of all this activity, ground-support aviation lost the limelight, and would remain the stepchild of American air doctrine for the foreseeable future.

Notes

1. Wesley F. Craven and James L. Cate, eds., *Plans and Early Operations, January 1939 to August 1942,* The Army Air Forces in World War II, vol. 1 (Chicago: University of Chicago Press, 1948), p. 104.

2. Michael S. Sherry, *The Rise of American Air Power: The Creation of Armageddon* (New Haven: Yale University Press, 1987), p. 91.

3. R. Elberton Smith, *The Army and Economic Mobilization,* U.S. Army in World War II (Washington, D.C.: U.S. Army Center of Military History, Government Printing Office, 1959), p. 27. See Table 11.

4. Robert F. Futrell, *Ideas, Concepts, Doctrine: A History of Basic Thinking in the United States Air Force* (Maxwell AFB, Ala.: Air University, 1971), p. 55.

5. Craven and Cate, *Plans and Early Operations,* p. 115.

6. Ibid., p. 110.

7. WD Training Directive 1940–41, 2 Mar 40, General Files AG 353 (12–28–39), RG 94, Office AG Central Files 1926–39, NA.

8. U.S. War Department, *Air Corps Field Manual: Employment of Aviation of the Army,* FM 1–5 (Washington, D.C.: Government Printing Office, 1940). See especially pp. 5, 10, 13, 21–22.

9. Thomas H. Greer, *The Development of Air Doctrine in the Army Air Corps,* USAF Historical Study 89 (Maxwell AFB, Ala.: USAF Historical Division, Research Studies Institute, Air University, 1955), p. 67.

10. Robert T. Finney, *History of the Air Corps Tactical School,* USAF Historical Study 100 (Maxwell AFB, Ala.: USAF Historical Division, Research Studies Institute, Air University, 1955), pp. 27–33.

11. H. H. Arnold, *Global Mission* (New York: Harper and Brothers, 1949), p. 156.

12. Ibid., p. 157.

13. Greer, *Air Doctrine,* p. 91.

14. Finney, *Tactical School,* p. 36.

15. Ibid.

16. See Robert M. Kennedy, *The German Campaign in Poland,* DA Pamphlet 20–255 (Washington, D.C.: Department of the Army, 1956), pp. 78–112.

17. Greer, *Air Doctrine,* p. 109.

18. FM 1–5 (1940), pp. 2, 23.

19. Ibid., p. 22.

20. Futrell, *Ideas, Concepts, Doctrine,* p. 44; Greer, *Air Doctrine,* pp. 67–68, 122; Craven and Cate, *Plans and Early Operations,* p. 109.

21. Futrell, *Ideas, Concepts, Doctrine,* p. 55. In all fairness to the Air Corps, it must be noted that the Stuka was even then nearing obsolescence.

22. Greer, *Air Doctrine,* p. 122.

23. Craven and Cate, *Plans and Early Operations,* p. 748.

24. Lewis H. Brereton, *The Brereton Diaries* (New York: William Morrow, 1946), p. 7.

25. "Air Corps Training, 1940–41," General Files AG 353 (12–28–39), RG 94, Office AG Central Files 1926–39, NA.

26. CofS GHQ to Army Commanders, 14 Jan 41, sub: Combined Training, 353 Training Directives, GHQ, U.S. Army, RG 337, Records of AGF, NA; CofS GHQ to Army Commanders, 15 Jan 41, sub: Corps and Army Training, 353 Training (General), RG 337, Records of AGF, NA.

27. "17th Bomb Wing Report," 21 Jul 41, 353 Air-Ground, GHQ, U.S. Army, 1940–42 General Corresp, RG 337, Records of AGF, NA.

28. Greenfield, Palmer, and Wiley, *Organization*, p. 94.

29. Memo, CofS for Gen Arnold, 25 Jun 41, Directives, Chronological, GCM Library.

30. WD Training Directive, 1941–42, 19 Aug 41, AG 353 (6–16–41), MT M–C, RG 407, Army AG Decimal File 1940–45, NA.

31. GHQ AF Training Directive, 1941–42, 1 Jun 41, AF 353, RG 407, NA.

CHAPTER 4

Planning the GHQ Maneuvers

The objective of all training for the period July 1, 1941 to June 30, 1942, is to prepare the Army of the United States for combat under whatever conditions the defense of our country and its possessions may require.[1]

Preliminary planning for an army-versus-army exercise of some sort, to be held in 1941, began as early as December 1939. By November 1940 General McNair and his deputy, Lt. Col. Mark W. Clark, had begun formulating concrete plans for the next year's training activities, which they hoped would transform a heterogeneous assemblage of military manpower into a battle-worthy Protective Mobilization Plan Army. By July 1941 the Army would consist of 1.4 million men organized into 4 field armies, 9 traditional corps and 1 armored corps, 27 infantry divisions, 4 armored divisions, 2½ cavalry divisions, 54 authorized combat aircraft groups, and 6 groups of transport aircraft.[2] The Army had to complete its training without fail in the summer of 1941 because demobilization of the National Guard was due to begin on 15 September, and the first draftees would go home in November as their year of federal service expired. The Army would not be able to replace the 250,000 Guardsmen and their 18 divisions; instead, the recently created corps and army troops would be skeletonized to help provide manpower for a 21-division Army.[3]

On 15 January 1941, General Headquarters sent a directive to the four field army commanders outlining corps and army training for the year. It called for one to two months of corps-level training to begin after the completion of divisional combined training. Corps training was to culminate in corps-versus-corps or corps-versus-division maneuvers before 30 June 1941. After corps training, and a similar period of field army training, two enormous army-versus-army maneuvers would take place under GHQ direction. August 31 was the target date for the end of the maneuvers and for the attainment of combat readiness for the PMP Army.[4]

As originally conceived, the first GHQ maneuver would match First Army against IV Corps (borrowed from Third Army) at some unspecified location. To offset First Army's size advantage (two corps of five divisions), the 2d Armored Division would reinforce IV Corps' two infantry divisions. After that exercise, General Headquarters planned to direct a maneuver between Second Army and Third Army in the vicinity of Camp Beauregard in Louisiana. Second Army's sole corps (four divisions), augmented by the 1st Armored Division and 2d Cavalry Division, would oppose Third Army's two corps (six infantry divisions) with the 2d Armored Division and 1st Cavalry Division attached. Fourth Army's two corps and three divisions would have to be content with a coast-defense exercise in Washington State against a theoretical enemy.[5]

By March, General Headquarters knew that its timetable had been overly optimistic. Corps training could not even begin until 24 May, and only four of the nine corps would finish their corps maneuvers by the end of June. General Headquarters scheduled further corps training in August and October for the other five corps. It also postponed the Second Army–Third Army GHQ maneuvers until September and moved the First Army–IV Corps maneuvers to November, even though several National Guard divisions would have left federal service by then unless terms of service could be extended.[6] Later alterations in the maneuvers schedule allowed I Armored Corps (1st and 2d Armored Divisions) to operate as a unit in at least part of both maneuvers. General Headquarters also ordered IV Corps to participate in the Second Army–Third Army exercises before its November confrontation with First Army.[7]

While the 1941 maneuver schedules underwent final revisions and the troops prepared for corps and army training, General Headquarters began laying the groundwork for the great army-versus-army maneuvers. The fundamental goal was to make the maneuvers as much like real war as possible in order to test and train under near-battle conditions. Given the smallness of the GHQ staff (only twenty-nine officers and sixty-four enlisted men as of June 1941), General McNair himself became closely involved with the myriad details of organizing the maneuvers.[8] One aspect of the preparations that McNair supervised personally was writing a new umpire manual. Poor umpiring had contributed greatly to the problems encountered in earlier maneuvers, and General McNair counted on the GHQ *Umpire Manual*, first published in February 1941, to assure the realistic play of battle in the maneuvers.

General McNair predicated the new manual on the principle of free maneuvers. There would be no elaborate, prewritten scenarios dictating the action in the GHQ maneuvers, and only a minimum of artificial constraints. Just as in a real war, General Headquarters, acting as high command for both sides, would give the opposing commanders basic intelligence about their adversaries and assign each a general mission to accomplish in his own manner. The maneuver would be continuous, day and night (except that nighttime mechanized combat was proscribed for safety reasons) until one or the other prevailed. Thereupon General Headquarters would immediately issue a critique, commenting upon the action and pointing out mistakes and shortcomings.[9]

Just as in real war, the success or failure of campaigns and battles rested upon the outcome of small-scale engagements, as determined by designated umpires. These officers would travel with the frontline units for the purpose of imposing the effects that would have resulted from real combat. According to the manual, General Headquarters would provide one umpire for each rifle company, plus an umpire at battalion headquarters. Thus a division would have about thirty-six umpires to monitor its infantry units, plus another fourteen or so with the artillery and engineers.[10]

Whenever opposing forces met and engaged in simulated battle, the umpires' principal function would be to determine which force could advance and which should give ground. Umpires would decide this by comparing the two units' effective firepower, which was derived numerically as follows: each rifle counted for 1 point, each .30-caliber machine gun 6 points, each .50-caliber machine gun 10 points, and each 81-mm. mortar 15 points. When two units became fully engaged, the umpires from each side would display white flags, the sign for all forward movement to cease. The two groups of umpires would then meet in no man's land and compare firepower levels, as modified by terrain and position. Depending upon circumstances, the side with a three-to-one or greater firepower advantage would win the decision. The umpires from the stronger force would then display red flags; those from the weaker, blue flags. This would signal permission for the stronger force to advance, whereupon the weaker unit would be required to retreat to a new position. If, in the opinion of the umpires, neither side mustered the requisite firepower advantage, then both umpire groups would display red flags and neither side could advance. The opposing commanders would thus be encouraged to maneuver their units so as to gain superiority in another manner.[11]

The manual also provided umpires with a means of assessing combat casualties. Depending upon the severity of the fighting and the degree of exposure to hostile fire, an infantry unit could expect to sustain 1 to 3 percent casualties every hour, with a rule of thumb maximum of 15 percent casualties per day. Individual soldiers were not designated as casualties unless evacuation squads were to be given practice; instead, the umpire would simply reduce his unit's fire-power in proportion to its accumulated casualties, thus allowing all soldiers to remain with their units for the duration of the maneuver.[12]

General Headquarters discouraged taking prisoners, inasmuch as soldiers would receive no useful training while sitting in pris-oner of war (POW) stockades. But since some prisoners would in-evitably be taken, GHQ devised an ingenious method of dealing with them. Captors were to take their prisoners to the field army replacement depot for interrogation and feeding. Once a day, GHQ would arrange the transfer of prisoners, who would then be taken to their own army's replacement depot and processed as if they were combat replacements for their original units.[13] Even the news correspondents covering maneuvers were liable to capture: each reporter would be assigned to one of the opposing armies, and if enemy forces captured him he would be held for twenty-four hours and prohibited from filing copy until exchanged.[14]

Included in the umpires' duties was the supervision of activities that, of necessity, had to be simulated in the maneuvers. Artillery fire, in particular, involved a rather intricate simulation scheme. One umpire, attached to the artillery battalion, would observe the laying of guns and then radio the target coordinates to a mobile fire umpire, whose function was to mark the impact area with flags. Unit umpires within the area would then assess the effects of the ar-tillery fire. On the average, a unit could expect to suffer 1 to 2 per-cent casualties from a well placed barrage, although higher losses would be imposed upon units caught on the road in column.[15]

Umpires also supervised the construction of obstacles and the execution of demolitions. Since General Headquarters considered it impractical actually to block roads and blow up bridges, engineer units were required instead to simulate such operations in detail. In the case of roadblocks, real obstacles were to be constructed at road-side. To demolish a bridge, GHQ required the engineers to assem-ble the necessary materials and to place simulated charges on the span. Bridge replacement involved the actual construction of a new bridge beside the theoretically destroyed one. The umpire who watched over demolitions was required to leave with a sentry a signed declaration stating that the bridge had been properly de-stroyed so that umpires with other units encountering the obstacle could then prescribe appropriate repair measures.[16] Col. Dwight D. Eisenhower related the following tale involving such simulations:

An umpire decided that a bridge had been destroyed by an enemy attack and flagged it accordingly. From then on, it was not to be used by men or vehicles. Shortly, a corporal brought his squad up to the bridge, looked at the flag, and hesitated for a moment; then resolutely marched his men across it. The umpire yelled at him:

"Hey, don't you see that that bridge is destroyed?"

The Corporal answered, "Of course I can see it's destroyed. Can't you see we're swimming?" [17]

The participation of air and mechanized forces in the 1941 maneuvers created serious difficulties for the writers of the *Umpire Manual*. In the case of air-ground engagements, there obviously would be no way for opposing umpires to meet face to face, and there was little chance that radio equipment could be spared for air-ground umpire communications. The manual could only suggest that casualty rates of 1 to 10 percent be assessed among ground units attacked by "an appropriate number (one airplane against a company or less) of low-flying airplanes," but ground umpires alone might be hard pressed to decide what actually constituted an effective air attack.[18] In some cases, aircraft would be dropping flour-bag bombs, but in others it would be up to the umpire on the spot to determine whether his troops had been attacked. Likewise, air umpires could assess losses from antiaircraft fire (one-half to one airplane per minute) only if they happened to notice the appropriate antiaircraft flags being displayed thousands of feet below.[19]

The section of the *Umpire Manual* dealing with tank-antitank combat raised even deeper concerns about realism and fairness. Antitank advocates objected to the rule under which any and all infantry troops within 100 yards of a hostile tank were to be considered neutralized, and assessed a firepower value of 0, as long as the tank remained. This meant, for example, that if a Red tank should happen to blunder into an infantry engagement, all Blue infantry in the area would automatically become helpless against any enemy action. Although antitank guns could, of course, operate in the presence of hostile tanks, friendly infantry would be unable to assist or protect them. What is more, any tanks destroyed would be out of action only for that day and could then return to their units for the rest of the maneuver.[20]

Although antitank proponents had some valid objections to the *Umpire Manual*, armor advocates had even better reason to complain. In a fair fight between tank units, losses were to be inversely proportional to the number of tanks involved—20 Red tanks fighting 30 Blue tanks would lose 3 tanks to the Blue's 2.[21] But when fired upon by antitank guns, armored units could lose up to 1 tank per gun per minute.[22] The tanks, on the other hand, could not knock out antitank guns with gunfire at all, but only by charging and overrunning them—a difficult task indeed, given antitank weapons'effectiveness.[23]

Armor also objected to the list of weapons that the *Umpire Manual* (and subsequent revisions) designated as being effective against tanks. The .50-caliber machine gun could destroy light tanks at a range of 1,000 yards, despite the fact that the .50-caliber was no longer considered to be a real antitank weapon. (General Headquarters ordered that it be replaced by "effective" antitank guns wherever possible.) [24] Similarly, GHQ accorded the 37-mm. antitank gun a range of 1,000 yards against light tanks and 500 yards against mediums, even though the Ordnance Department insisted that the 37-mm. gun had been obsolete from the day it was accepted.[25] In June 1941, *Time* magazine reported on an ordnance test in which the 37-mm. failed to penetrate even one inch of tank armor at 100 yards.[26] (The M3 light tank carried a maximum of 1.5 inches of armor.) [27] General McNair's close involvement with both antitank development and the writing of *Umpire Manual* did nothing to quiet the Armor branch's protests.

But at least both sides in the debate could take comfort in the knowledge that there would be more real equipment and less simulation in the 1941 maneuvers than had been the case in previous years. General McNair was reported as saying that he wanted no more maneuvers in which "one man with a flag is a tank." [28] The first M3 medium tanks, 105-mm. howitzers, halftracks, jeeps, and modern combat aircraft became available in time for the 1941 maneuvers. To encourage experiments with light liaison airplanes, the firms of Piper, Aeronca, and Taylor offered the free use of eleven Cub-type sport planes for the maneuver season.[29] Even with the weapons that still had to be simulated, General Headquarters imposed as much realism as possible. Simulated weapons would count only if their crews were present and properly trained, and if the weapons were realistically sited, served, and supplied.[30]

The supply of blank ammunition, while still below the Army's needs, had improved over the previous year. For calendar year 1941, the adjutant general authorized the expenditure of .5 million .50-caliber blanks, the same number of 37-mm. antitank blanks, 45,000 75-mm. blanks, and 10,000 practice land mines.[31] For August and September alone, Third Army received 4 million .30-caliber blanks and 170,000 antitank rounds.[32] To make the sound of battle even more realistic, the Army authorized $15,000 for the construction of seven loudspeaker-equipped sound trucks to broadcast prerecorded battlefield noises.[33]

Free maneuvers at the army-versus-army level required huge areas of ground for off-road maneuver. Nothing would so utterly ruin realism as "No Trespassing" signs. Accordingly, in 1941 the Army, operating through state and local governments, set about leasing land where necessary and obtaining trespass rights where possible. In Louisiana, where the Second Army–Third Army maneuvers were scheduled to take place, Third Army already possessed maneuver rights to 3,404 square miles (including 405 square miles of the Kisatchie National Forest and 600 square miles across the Sabine River in Texas).[34] By September 1941, the enlarged maneuver area consisted of 30,000 square miles that extended from Shreveport south to Lake Charles and from Jasper, Texas, to the Mississippi River.[35]

General Headquarters selected a 9,375-square-mile area straddling the North Carolina–South Carolina border for the First Army–IV Corps maneuvers. Irregularly oblong in shape, the area fell generally within a triangle marked by Charlotte, North Carolina, on the northwest; Fayetteville, North Carolina, on the east; and Columbia, South Carolina, on the south.[36] Although some landowners still posted their property "Off Limits to Troops," in general the citizens of Louisiana and the Carolinas granted trespass rights readily.

By June 1941, GHQ's one outstanding requirement for the conduct of successful army-versus-army maneuvers was money. Field maneuvers are an expensive form of training because of the property, transportation, and materiel involved. In the past, some congressmen had been highly critical of maneuvers, particularly because the Army usually had failed to make a very satisfactory showing.[37] But in the spring of 1941 Congress was in no mood to quibble over defense expenditures, particularly for training.

On 2 May 1941, Brig. Gen. Harry L. Twaddle, General Staff G–3, appeared before the military subcommittee of the House Appropriations Committee to justify the Army's request for $136 million in training funds for fiscal year 1941. Funding for the GHQ maneuvers came under a $28,587,000 item for field exercises, which General Twaddle defended at some length:

I cannot emphasize too strongly the importance of the training for which these funds are requested. The great expansion of the Army, which has occurred since last fall, has produced numerous new headquarters from battalion to Army, staffed with officers who, as yet, have had little opportunity to acquire by first hand experience the knowledge necessary in moving, supplying, and controlling large concentrations of troops and maneuvering them in the field. Such knowledge cannot be gained by study alone. Actual experience is essential. This need, and the need to give the men themselves training in meeting the increased physical demands to be encountered in maneuvers, make necessary the schedule of large maneuvers which has been prepared. It is also essential that all units be practiced in new methods and material developed as a result of European experience.

The Congress has provided very large sums for shelter, clothing, equipment, and food to build a strong national defense structure. The funds which we request here serve as a capstone to that structure, by providing for the necessary extension of training activities.[38]

After a perfunctory discussion, Chairman Buell Snyder's only comment was, "We want you to have every penny necessary for this kind of training, but we do expect you to exercise all reasonable economies."[39]

The House Appropriations Committee approved the entire training budget, which the House passed without amendment except to add $7,682,000 left over from the field maneuvers section of the 1941 budget. The military appropriation bill encountered no serious difficulty in the Senate, and at 6:20 p.m. on 30 June 1941, the Military Appropriation Act of 1942 became law. It totaled nearly $13 billion and included the Army's entire request for maneuvers funds.[40] The Army, confident of passage, had already approved the expenditure of $19 million on corps and army training.[41]

The great controversy that summer was not over money, it was over manpower—specifically, the War Department's attempt to extend the term of military service for its citizen-soldiers. The issue was so politically sensitive that, as late as 28 April 1941, General Marshall told Congress that the War Department had no contingency plans for retaining selectees and Guardsmen longer than the original twelve-month term.[42] In reality, the War Department had considered that possibility throughout the process of formulating training schedules for 1941.[43] From the outset, plans for the GHQ maneuvers tentatively included the participation of National Guard units entitled to release from federal service on the opening day of the Louisiana exercises.[44]

The Army's caution was well founded. When the extension bill was submitted to the House, it met not only with the violent opposition of pacifists and isolationists but also came under attack from partisan opponents of the Roosevelt administration (many of whom supported the bill in principle) and from legislators who simply disliked the idea of inducting some men for one year and then keeping them longer while millions of others escaped service altogether. The bill came to a vote on 12 August and passed 203 to 202, raising the overall term of military service from twelve months to two and a half years for selectees, Guardsmen, and Reservists.[45] The extension of service meant that General Headquarters could carry out its great maneuvers with the knowledge that the Protective Mobilization Plan Army would remain intact long enough to justify the effort and expense of training it.

Meanwhile, the Army's field forces spent the spring and summer undergoing corps and army training. On 24 May, 60,000 men from three divisions began field training under IX Corps and Fourth Army on the west coast. These corps exercises culminated a month later in a field maneuver pitting 7th Division against IX Corps, and in September Fourth Army opposed IX Corps in the final west coast maneuver of the year. (The Fourth Army maneuvers showcased the talents of 7th Division's commander, Maj. Gen. Joseph W. Stilwell.)[46] On 1 June, Third Army's VIII Corps with three divisions began two weeks of training in Texas, and the next day VII Corps of Second Army entered upon three weeks of field training in Tennessee. The 2d Armored Division joined VII Corps' three divisions for the climactic corps maneuvers.[47]

GHQ observers, in their critiques of the June maneuvers, noted that many units had progressed to corps training before they had mastered basic training.[48] Col. J. Lawton Collins, VII Corps chief of staff, felt that "we were cramming too much, too soon, in these early exercises."[49] Nonetheless, there was no denying that the Army had made considerable progress already in 1941, and that with remedial basic and small-unit training, the troops could be made ready for the GHQ army-versus-army maneuvers that autumn.

During the June maneuvers in Tennessee, the Army's new tank, antitank, and (to a lesser degree) air forces made their combined training debut. The tank and antitank elements quickly developed a rivalry that would become increasingly pronounced as the maneuver season progressed. General McNair himself set the tone in a warning to all antitank units: "The Armored Force is looking forward to the approaching corps and army maneuvers with confidence and enthusiasm. Such units in the current European war have achieved an unbroken succession of successes. Our Armored Force is not concealing its expectation of repeating such successes during the maneuvers."[50]

Despite General McNair's exhortations for aggressive antitank combat, the 2d Armored Division, under the irrepressible Maj. Gen. George S. Patton, ran roughshod over its opponents during the Tennessee maneuvers. In three of the four exercises in which it took part, the 2d Armored Division defeated the opposition and ended the maneuver, in one case within three hours.[51] In the opinion of

General McNair, antitank defense was still too passive, although anti-tank guns did embarrass the tankers on several occasions.[52] The greatest problems that 2d Armored Division encountered, however, were internal. Reconnaissance was often inadequate, tactics were often too headstrong, and the staff failed to keep the division's various elements coordinated.[53]

The Armored Force undertook to correct some of the problems revealed in Tennessee, but it had to do so without the guidance of its founder. General Chaffee, chronically ill, stepped down as chief of the Armored Force on 1 August. Three weeks later, he died. His successor, Maj. Gen. Jacob L. Devers, took up the task of preparing the Armored Force for the GHQ maneuvers.[54] Remedial training emphasized small-unit tactics, coordination between tanks and artillery, and increased staff efficiency. In particular, division headquarters worked on streamlining the process of formulating and issuing its orders.[55]

The Armored Force also reviewed its tactics, particularly those dealing with antitank defense. One memorandum, circulated by lst Armored Division, described a method of attacking an antitank position that involved a regimental advance on a 1,000-yard front. Tanks, artillery, and engineers were to be carefully coordinated, but, significantly, there was no mention of infantry.[56] In such tactics lay the seeds of future difficulties for armor and future victories for antitank proponents, because the terrain of Louisiana and the Carolinas was seldom conducive to mechanized advances on 1,000-yard fronts. Furthermore, by neglecting the close coordination of infantry and tanks, the Armored Force denied itself one of the two economical methods of eliminating antitank guns as allowed by the *Umpire Manual*—infantry assault (artillery fire was the other).

The June maneuvers also prompted antitank advocates to reappraise their organization and tactics. The 5th Division's antitank unit, which had taken the brunt of several tank attacks in Tennessee, issued its own training memorandum, which Second Army reprinted and distributed widely. It urged antitank battalions to practice the techniques of identifying enemy armor and transmitting tank information among friendly units so that armored attacks would lose the advantage of surprise. The 5th Division stressed the need for mutual support among units and the employment of enfilade fire from concealed positions.[57]

General McNair, however, preferred to see a more aggressive style of antitank combat than the divisional battalions seemed capable of offering. The antitank battalion, aside from being a rather small force to attack an armored column, had as its first job the protection of the division. On 8 August, McNair ordered Lt. Gen. Ben Lear, commander of Second Army, to convert two field artillery brigades into nine antitank battalions and turn them over to Lt. Gen. Walter Krueger, Third Army, for use in the Louisiana maneuvers. McNair instructed Krueger to organize the nine battalions into three antitank groups (regiment-size forces), each consisting of three antitank battalions plus an infantry company, an engineer company, a platoon of scout cars, and a flight of reconnaissance aircraft. These groups were to be highly mobile, relatively self-sufficient, and designed to serve as an aggressive army-wide antitank reserve.[58] *(Chart 5)*

McNair emphasized that these antitank groups were to employ offensive tactics in the upcoming maneuvers. They were to locate hostile tanks with vigorous reconnaissance, and, utilizing their high mobility, rush to the scene and engage with massed antitank fire before the tanks had a chance to deploy into fighting formations. When a defensive posture was unavoidable, McNair told Krueger that he should pull the antitank groups back and let the divisions and their provisional antitank battalions channel the enemy's tank attack. Once the principal armored thrust had been ascertained, the antitank groups were to launch decisive counterattacks on its flanks.[59]

General Krueger organized the antitank groups as ordered and prepared them to face I Armored Corps (1st and 2d Armored Divisions) in the Louisiana GHQ maneuvers. He trained them to conduct constant, rapid reconnaissance and to communicate efficiently within the group and with other units. Of particular importance was the training received in moving rapidly from one position to another, deploying the guns in favorable positions, and delivering fast and accurate fire.[60]

Although the antitank groups would enter the GHQ maneuvers untested, antitank advocates hoped that they would provide the key to reversing the Armored Force's string of maneuvers victories. The proponents of armor, on the other hand, believed that the I Armored Corps, operating as a unit in Louisiana for the first time, would sweep all before it. Events abroad that summer heightened the tank-antitank drama by providing both sides with encouraging evidence. On one hand, German panzer divisions utterly dismembered the Soviet Army; on the other, German antitank units in North Africa proved to be more than a match for British armor. The tank-antitank issue assumed so much significance that General McNair summarized the upcoming Louisiana maneuver as being ". . . a test of tank warfare and antitank defense . . . we are definitely out to see . . . if and how we can crush a modern tank offensive."[61]

CHART 5—GHQ ANTITANK GROUP, 1941 MANEUVERS

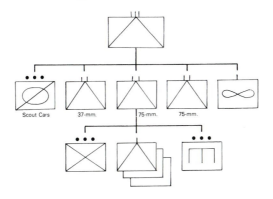

Predictably, the Army Air Forces was less enthusiastic about participating in the GHQ maneuvers than either the tank or the antitank elements; nonetheless, the air arm experienced a remarkable transformation of attitude in the summer of 1941. The initial plans for the GHQ maneuvers made no reference to large-scale air participation,[62] and as of 1 June the airmen promised only four squadrons for Louisiana and four for the Carolinas.[63] But on 18 June, when AAF autonomy and the official sanctioning of strategic bombing were close at hand, General Arnold reversed the air service's traditional reluctance to become involved in ground training. He offered no less than 600 combat aircraft, organized into 4 bombardment groups and 4 fighter groups, plus additional noncombat aircraft, for participation in each of the GHQ maneuvers.[64]

General Arnold's generosity prompted General Emmons, head of Army Air Forces Combat Command, to send off a sharp protest that reflected traditional air force attitudes. General Emmons pointed out that to assemble 8 operational groups, 39 groups would have to be stripped of their experienced personnel and modern equipment. Furthermore, he claimed that participation in the maneuvers on such a scale would cost the Army Air Forces four months of the best training weather, which was needed for such fundamentals as coastal air defense, bombing, gunnery, and navigation. Emmons protested that the maneuvers were being held in areas unlikely to be the scene of real operations in the event of invasion, and that the facilities there were accordingly poor. But the crux of his argument was clearly that "we are fighting for an opportunity to develop *Air Power* but we are devoting four extremely important months to the creation of *Ground Power*." [65] As an alternative, Emmons proposed sending just 1 light bomber group to each

GHQ maneuver, and perhaps executing some long-range missions with other units.[66]

General Arnold, however, overruled Emmons and stood behind the 8-group offer. In mid-August he designated the air units that were to take part in the GHQ maneuvers: 2 medium bomber groups of twin-engine B–25 and B–26 aircraft, 2 light bomber groups flying twin-engine A–20 attack planes and single-engine A–24 dive bombers, and 4 pursuit groups of single-engine P–39, P–40, and P–43 aircraft as well as some twin-engine P–38 interceptors.[67] All of these types, with the exception of the P–43, were modern enough to eventually see extensive service in World War II, and some were already in action with the Allies.

But General Arnold could not rectify by fiat the air service's long-standing neglect of ground-support aviation. To secure an adequate number of dive bombers for the maneuvers he was forced to ask Admiral Stark for the loan of 2 dive-bomber squadrons to supplement the Army Air Forces' few A–24s.[68] Stark did even more—he provided 3 fighter squadrons, 4 dive-bomber squadrons, and 1 torpedo squadron for participation in both GHQ maneuvers.[69] These Navy and Marine Corps air units raised the number of combat aircraft by the equivalent of 2 groups. (Stark's apparent interest in the GHQ maneuvers prompted General Marshall to invite the lst Marine Division's participation. The admiral declined, citing the need for higher priority small-unit and amphibious training among Marine Corps units.) [70]

With the addition of naval air units, aircraft in the maneuvers would not only be relatively modern, they would also be present in meaningful numbers. The Germans had attacked Poland in 1939 with 60 divisions and 36 groups of combat aircraft, for a ratio of 1 group to 1.6 divisions. The forces in Louisiana would consist of 18 divisions and 10 groups (1 to 1.8), and those in the Carolinas would include 14 divisions and 10 groups (1 to 1.4). By comparison, the 22 American divisions fighting in Normandy during the summer of 1944 were supported by no fewer than 29 fighter and bomber groups of the Ninth Air Force, yielding 1 group to .8 divisions.[71]

The participation of large air forces in the GHQ maneuvers suddenly pushed to the fore the issue of command and control over tactical air units. Although published doctrine provided some very general guidance on coordinating air and ground units, aside from the recent Fort Benning tests, the entire issue resided in the realm of theory. The problem was particularly delicate because it revived the touchy subject of independent versus subordinate air power. Ground commanders understandably wanted direct control over the air units supporting their operations. They claimed that prompt delivery of air support depended upon subordinating specific air units to each corps or division and cited the principle of unified command in support of their position. The air officers could plead a principle of war, too—concentration of effort—in their insistence that air units should be unified under the control of one air commander.[72]

In July 1941 the War Department struck something of a compromise when it ordered that each field army should gather all of its aviation together into an air support command (ASC). Although air units were thus centralized to a degree, the command remained under the authority of the field army commander. Nonetheless, General McNair spoke for many ground commanders when he said that the air support command was ". . . one more step in the separation of the air from the rest of the Army. What may be the result is hard to predict, but it seems quite unlikely that it will facilitate the interworking of air and ground."[73] For the Louisiana maneuvers the Army Air Forces created one air task force (a temporary organization analogous to the air support command) for each side, and named Maj. Gen. Herbert A. Dargue and Maj. Gen. Millard F. Harmon to command them.

Ground-support operations in the maneuvers would be closely controlled by air task force (ATF) headquarters. Frontline troops desiring battlefield air support would find their requests relegated to the broader missions of the air task force, which generally involved air superiority and interdiction. To obtain air support, ground units were to pass their requests up the ground chain of command to corps headquarters (division headquarters in armored formations) where an air support demand unit composed of AAF liaison officers would screen requests and transmit those deemed appropriate to air task force headquarters. Only when this headquarters concurred in the ground request would aircraft be dispatched to fulfill it. Communication between the ground unit being supported and airborne aircraft could take place only through the air support demand unit. Moreover, the chances of ground requests for frontline support being met were not great, for the air task force would much prefer to execute missions of its own choosing in accordance with its general directives. According to prevailing air doctrine, ground-support missions should never be flown within the range of friendly artillery.[74]

A shortage of transport aircraft in the Army Air Forces continued to hamper the training of airborne troops and even militated against their participation in the GHQ maneuvers altogether. Originally, General Headquarters had no plans to employ parachute troops in

Louisiana at all but did expect the 502d Parachute Battalion to participate in the Carolina maneuvers. Not until 29 August did the 502d Battalion receive orders to send one company to Louisiana, for which the Army Air Forces provided thirteen transport planes. General Headquarters announced that the parachutists would secretly be made available to each side in succession, but clearly there would be no realistic test of airborne warfare in Louisiana.[75]

The parachute company was the last unit designated for participation in the Louisiana maneuvers. As the summer of 1941 neared its end, a great convergence on Louisiana began. Among the first to arrive were engineers who constructed runways, established train and truck unloading facilities, repaired roads, strengthened bridges, and arranged telephone and telegraph communications. While the engineers labored, the staffs of Second and Third Armies organized supply networks sufficient to sustain 400,000 men in the field. Second Army drew its supplies from Camp Robinson, Arkansas, whereas Third Army's plans called for 100 carloads of supplies a day from New Orleans. Along with the supply routes, evacuation systems for real and simulated casualties were necessary. The Army anticipated 136 deaths and 40,000 hospitalizations during the two weeks of maneuvers.[76]

GHQ established its headquarters at Camp Polk, Louisiana, near the center of the huge maneuver area. General. McNair, director of the maneuvers, and Brig. Gen. Mark W. Clark, his deputy director, led a contingent of approximately thirty GHQ staff officers, who were to serve as headquarters staff for the maneuvers, liaison officers with combat units, and special observers of the action.[77] Camp Polk also made arrangements to accommodate the scores of VIPs who wanted to witness the great maneuvers first-hand. Among the visitors were Undersecretary of War Robert P. Patterson; General Marshall; five congressmen, including Buell Snyder; the chiefs of the arms and services; eighteen British officers (including one air vice marshal); the Polish military attache; and four members of the Harvard Business School who sought information on Army logistics in the field.[78]

Furthermore, General Headquarters expected 200 civilian photographers and correspondents to descend upon Louisiana for the maneuvers. Such figures as Hanson W. Baldwin, Richard C. Hottelet, and Eric Sevareid would represent the major newspapers, magazines, and wire services. Each was to be given an officer's uniform, maps, and transport.[79]

In late August the participating field units themselves began to gather on the Louisiana maneuver grounds. General Krueger's Third Army, already in the maneuver area, administered a final round of corps training and then rehearsed the upcoming confrontation by maneuvering V Corps and VIII Corps against IV Corps. General Krueger then brought his ten divisions into the Blue assembly area north of Lake Charles.[80]

General Lear's Red Second Army conducted last-minute corps training, which included practice river crossings, in Arkansas. As a final exercise, Second Army's principal component, VII Corps, conducted a 185-mile withdrawal into Louisiana, pursued from delaying position to delaying position by a provisional corps. At the end of the problem, Lear's six divisions occupied the Red assembly area between Shreveport and Alexandria, north of the Red River.[81]

The much-publicized armored divisions arrived in Louisiana in time to participate in the last corps-versus-corps exercises. The 2d Armored Division traveled over 600 miles from Fort Benning, Georgia, and 1st Armored Division loaded 20 trains with armored vehicles and marched over 700 miles from Fort Knox, Kentucky, to the Red army area, where I Armored Corps assumed control of the two armored divisions.[82] From around the country approximately one thousand combat, observation, and transport aircraft gathered at air bases in Louisiana, Texas, and Mississippi.[83] By 14 September, a total of 472,000 troops were on hand in what was the densest military concentration in United States history.[84]

The GHQ maneuvers about to begin transcended the realm of training. The great maneuvers would be a critical testing ground for new tactical elements, for new weapons and equipment, and for the men who used them. To the individuals involved, the maneuvers meant many different things. Some enlisted men regarded them as but the latest of the many injustices perpetrated by the Army. The extension of service which had passed Congress the previous month seriously depressed morale. Although the Army officially believed that "morale ranged from fair to very good," civilian correspondents had no trouble locating hundreds of soldiers who expressed the intention to desert when their first year of service expired.[85] Their slogan was OHIO—"over the hill in October."

On the other hand, to many officers the upcoming maneuvers represented a means of professional advancement. Those who feared the summons of the removal board or who faced retirement due to age in grade knew that an outstanding performance in the maneuvers might win them a reprieve.

Excellent younger officers anticipated the opportunity to display their talents in the field and thus rise in the ranks. Antitank and armored officers hoped to prove the ascendancy of their arms, whereas dedicated horse cavalrymen knew that a poor showing by their beloved equestrian units would likely bring total mechanization upon them.

At the GHQ director's headquarters, the maneuvers represented an opportunity to analyze the effectiveness of the preceding year's training and to detect the areas in need of further attention. But to the Army's top command and to the nation's civilian leadership, the maneuvers would provide an answer for the most vital of questions: did the United States indeed possess a Protective Mobilization Plan Army capable of defending the nation's frontiers?

Notes

1. WD Training Directive, 1941–42, 19 Aug 41 (6–16–41)–(6–20–41), RG 407, Army AG Decimal File 1940–45, NA.

2. U.S. Congress, House, Subcommittee of the Committee for Appropriations, *War Department Military Establishment Bill FY 1942, Hearings,* 77th Cong., 1st sess., 1941, pp. 10–11.

3. Ibid.

4. CofS GHQ to CGs, 15 Jan 41, sub: Corps and Army Training, Binder 2, 353 Training (General), RG 337, Records of AGF, NA.

5. Ibid.

6. Memo, CofS GHQ for ACofS, G–3, 7 Mar 41, sub: Corps and Army Maneuvers in Summer and Fall, 1941, 354.2, Maneuvers Binder 1, RG 337 57, HQ AGF, GHQ, NA.

7. "Army Training, FY 1942," 1 Jun 41, Tab 1, Current Maneuvers File, RG 337 57D, HQ AGF, GHQ GS G–3, Subject File 1940–Mar 9, 1942, NA.

8. Greenfield, Palmer, and Wiley, *Organization,* p. 24.

9. General Headquarters, U.S. Army, *Umpire Manual* (Reproduced by CGSS, 17 Feb 41), p. 7.

10. Ibid., pp. 23–24.

11. Ibid., pp. 10–13.

12. Ibid., pp. 13–15.

13. CofS GHQ to CG, Second and Third Armies, 11 Aug 41, sub: Combat Replacements, GHQ Directed Maneuvers, Tab 20, Current Maneuver File; AG GHQ to Army Commanders, 15 Aug 41, sub: Prisoners of War During GHQ Maneuvers, Tab 16, Current Maneuver File. Both in RG 337 57D, NA.

14. CofS GHQ to Army Commanders and Commander, IV Corps, 17 Jul 41, sub: Press Relations, GHQ Directed Maneuvers, Tab 15, Current Maneuver File, RG 337 57D, NA.

15. *Umpire Manual,* pp. 14–15, 20–21.

16. GHQ ltr, 9 Apr 41, sub: Obstacles in Maneuvers, 354.2, Maneuvers Binder 1, RG 337 57, NA; *Umpire Manual,* pp. 18–19.

17. Dwight D. Eisenhower, *At Ease, Stories I Tell To Friends* (Garden City, N.Y.: Doubleday, 1967), pp. 243–44.

18. *Umpire Manual,* pp. 14–15.

19. *Umpire Manual,* pp. 16–18; "Blue Forces Gain in Carolina War," *New York Times,* 18 Nov 41.

20. *Umpire Manual,* pp. 13–15.

21. Ibid., pp. 20–21.

22. Ibid., pp. 16–17.

23. Ibid., p. 17.

24. AG GHQ to CGs, 15 Jul 41, sub: Changes, GHQ Umpire Manual, enclosed in the MHI copy of *Umpire Manual.*

25. AG GHQ to CGs, 10 Jun 41, sub: Changes, GHQ Umpire Manual, enclosed in the MHI copy of *Umpire Manual*; Constance M. Green, Harry C. Thomson, and Peter C. Roots, *The Ordnance Department: Planning Munitions for War,* U.S. Army in World War II (Washington, D.C.: U.S. Army Center of Military History, Government Printing Office, 1955), p. 184.

26. "Is It Good Enough?" *Time,* 16 Jun 41, pp. 19–20.

27. Foss, *Jane's World,* p. 119.

28. "No More Phony Maneuvers," *Time,* 16 Jun 41, p. 19.

29. Laurence B. Epstein, "Army Organic Aviation: The Founding Fathers," *U.S. Army Aviation Digest,* Jun 77, pp. 2–17.

30. AG GHQ to CGs, 16 Jul 41, sub: Assumed and Simulated Weapons During GHQ Directed Maneuvers, Current Maneuver File, RG 337 57D, NA.

31. TAG to CofS GHQ, 7 Aug 41, sub: Maneuver Ammunition, sec 1, 353 (5–15–41), RG 407, NA.

32. "Report of Ordnance Operations During Third Army Maneuvers August–September 1941," 10 Dec 41, sec 4–C, 353 (5–15–41), RG 407, NA.

33. ACofS for TAG, 22 Jul 41, sub: Purchase of Sound Truck Equipment in Connection With Army Maneuvers, sec 1, 353 (5–15–41), RG 407, NA.

34. Francis G. Smith, "AGF Study No. 17, History of the Third Army" (Historical Section, AGF, 1946), p. 7.

35. Jean R. Moenk, *A History of Large-Scale Army Maneuvers in the United States* (Fort Monroe, Va.: HQ, USCAC, 1969), p. 53.

36. Moenk, *Army Maneuvers,* pp. 13–15.

37. Pogue, *Marshall,* p. 89.

38. House, *War Department Military Establishment Bill FY 1942, Hearings,* p. 241.

39. Ibid.

40. U.S. *Statutes at Large,* LV, Part 1, p. 367.

41. TAG to Chief of the Armd Force; TAG to CG, Second Army; TAG to CG, Third Army; TAG to CG, Fourth Army. All 27 Jun 41, sub: Corps and Army Maneuvers, FY 1942, sec 1, 353 (5–15–41), RG 407, NA.

42. House, *War Department Military Establishment Bill FY 1942, Hearings,* p. 41.

43. Pogue, *Marshall,* p. 146.

44. "Army Training, FY 1942," Current Maneuver File, RG 337 57D, NA.

45. Pogue, *Marshall,* pp. 152–54.

46. "Corps Training, FY 1941," Current Maneuver File, RG 337 57D, NA; "Comments on the Fourth Army Maneuvers 6/20–30/41," 7 Jul 41, sec 5–C, 353 (5–15–41), RG 407, NA.

47. "Corps Training, FY 1941," Current Maneuver File, RG 337 57D, NA.

48. AG GHQ to CGs, 7 Jul 41, sub: Review of Training Prior To Further Corps and Army Training, Current Maneuver File, RG 337 57D, NA.

49. J. Lawton Collins, *Lightning Joe* (Baton Rouge: Louisiana State University Press, 1979), p. 109.

50. CofS GHQ to CGs, 15 May 41, sub: Antitank Defense, Binder 2, 353 Training Directives, GHQ, RG 337 57, NA.

51. Houston, *Hell on Wheels,* pp. 61–71.

52. Greenfield, Palmer, and Wiley, *Organization,* p. 80.

53. Houston, *Hell on Wheels,* pp. 61–71.

54. Gillie, *Thunderbolt,* pp. 205–08.

55. "1941 Training Memoranda, Performance of Antitank," RG 337 57D, NA.

56. Training Memo 64, I Armd Bde, 4 Aug 41, Armored Forces Training 1941, RG 337 57D, NA.

57. Training Memo 47, 5th Div, 7 Aug 41, sub: Antitank Training and Operation, Armored Forces Training 1941, RG 337 57D, NA.

58. AG GHQ to CG, Third Army, 8 Aug 41, sub: GHQ Antitank Units in GHQ-Directed Maneuvers, Binder 2, 353 Training Directives, GHQ, RG 337 57, NA.

59. Ibid.

60. Ibid.

61. "Gale Holds Back War Game Start," *New York Times,* 15 Sep 41.

62. CofS GHQ to CGs, 15 Jan 41, sub: Corps and Army Training, Binder 2, 353 Training (General), RG 337, NA.

63. "Army Training, FY 1942," Current Maneuver File, RG 337 57D, NA.

64. Memo, ACofS for TAG, 18 Jun 41, sub: Increased Participation of Air Force Units in 1941 Maneuvers, sec 1, 353 (5–15–41), RG 407, NA.

65. Memo, Lt Gen Emmons for Chief AAF, 24 Jun 41, 353 Air Force Combat Command, RG 337 57, NA.

66. Ibid.

67. Chief AAF to CG Air Force Combat Command, 19 Aug 41, sub: Amendment of Letter 7/16/41, 353 Air Force Combat Command, RG 337 57, NA.

68. Deputy CofS to CNO, 19 Jun 41, sub: Dive Bomber Participation in Army Maneuvers, sec 1, 353 (5–15–41), RG 407, NA.

69. CNO to CofS, 21 Aug 41, sub: Army Maneuvers—Participation In; Acting CofS to CNO, 25 Aug 41, sub: Participation of Fleet Aircraft in Army Maneuvers. Both in 354.2 Maneuvers Binder 2, RG 337 57, NA.

70. CofS to CNO, 9 Sep 41; CNO to CofS, 11 Sep 41. Both in Maneuvers Memoranda, General Corresp, RG 337 57, NA.

71. Robert M. Kennedy, *The German Campaign in Poland,* Department of the Army Pamphlet 20–255 (Washington, D.C.: Department of the Army, 1956), p. 69; U.S. Air Force, Office of Air Force History, *Condensed Analysis of the Ninth Air Force in the European Theater of Operations,* USAF Warrior Studies (Washington, D.C.: Office of Air Force History, 1984 [reprint]), charts following p. 92.

72. Greenfield, Palmer, and Wiley, *Organization,* p. 113.

73. Ibid., p. 108.

74. See "Letter of Instructions No. 1. Plan of Air Support of Second Army by Second Air Task Force," 353d Air Ground, RG 337, NA.

75. "Provisional Parachute Group," *Army and Navy Journal,* 13 Sep 41, p. 43.

76. "There Will Be Casualties," *Time,* 22 Sep 41, p. 32.

77. Greenfield, Palmer, and Wiley, *Organization,* p. 26.

78. "British to See Maneuvers," *New York Times,* 5 Sep 41. See also sec 1–A, 353 (5–15–41), RG 407, NA.

79. "Lesson in War Reporting," *Time,* 29 Sep 41, pp. 52–53.

80. Smith, "AGF Study No. 17," p. 19.

81. Bell I. Wiley and William P. Govan, "AGF Study No. 16, History of the Second Army" (Historical Section, AGF, 1946), p. 23.

82. "Maneuvers Widespread," *Army and Navy Journal,* 6 Sep 41, p. 27.

83. Moenk, *Army Maneuvers,* pp. 52–53.

84. "Army Training, August–November 1941," GHQ Binder 2, 353 Training Directives, RG 337, NA.

85. Memo, ACofS for CofS, 15 Sep 41, sub: Report of Visit to the Field, sec 4–C, 353 (5–15–41), RG 407, NA.

CHAPTER 5

Louisiana Phase 1
The Battle of the Red River

My God, Senator, that's the reason I do it. I want the mistake [made] down in Louisiana, not over in Europe, and the only way to do this thing is to try it out, and if it doesn't work, find out what we need to make it work.[1]

General George C. Marshall

The directive governing Phase 1 of the Louisiana maneuvers came from the pen of General Clark, the deputy director for GHQ maneuvers. General McNair, as director, told Clark to "keep the directive as simple as possible." Clark took a roadmap of Louisiana and on it marked an assembly area for Red Second Army east of the Red River, and for Blue Third Army an area between Lake Charles and De Ridder. He then composed a set of general instructions for each commander, worded in the manner of an actual wartime directive from General Headquarters, that would bring the two armies into conflict. These instructions determined the nature of the battle about to be fought. By giving each army an offensive mission, General Headquarters orchestrated a great meeting engagement to take place in the area between the Red and Sabine Rivers.[2]

On 12 September, General Lear, commander of Red Second Army, received the following instructions:

War will be declared at 12:00 Noon, 15 September. Move your army secretly into position, under cover of darkness, the night of 14/15 Sept. (movement to commence at 7:P.M., 14 Sept.) for invasion of Blue territory beginning at 5:00 A.M. 15 Sept. At that hour your troops will begin to cross the Red River. Destroy enemy now concentrated in vicinity of Lake Charles. Important you conceal preliminary movements toward frontier and that river crossing be accomplished as expeditiously as possible.[3]

This was an ambitious mission, for Lear's army consisted of only two corps, the VII and the I Armored. The VII Corps, commanded by Maj. Gen. Robert Richardson, controlled the 27th and 33d Divisions (square), the 6th Division (triangular), and the 107th Cavalry Regiment (horse-mechanized). The two square divisions were well-trained maneuvers veterans, but the 6th Division included a large number of troops just out of basic, and did not have its full allotment of motor transport.[4]

The Red army's best chance of victory rested on the mobility and striking power of its armored force. For the first time, the 1st and 2d Armored Divisions, commanded by Generals Magruder and Patton, would operate side by side under the control of I Armored Corps, commanded by General Scott. General Lear also attached his equestrian units, the 2d Cavalry Division and 4th Cavalry Regiment, to Scott's command, further augmenting Red army's corps of maneuver. In army reserve General Lear retained the 5th Division (triangular), minus one regiment en route to Iceland, and 35th Division (square). His air arm, the 2d Air Task Force, consisted of the 17th Bombardment Wing and 6th Pursuit Wing, plus four squadrons of fighters and dive bombers provided by the Navy. Commanded by General Harmon, the 2d Air Task Force brought over 300 combat aircraft to the maneuver.[5] *(Map 1)*

Although the armored force would probably determine Second Army's fate, General Lear, a meticulous and methodical soldier, was not conspicuously suited to the conduct of dashing, highly mobile operations. Sixty-two years old in 1941, his 43-year career had been divided among infantry and cavalry commands and staff assignments. Never popular with the troops, Lear had the reputation of being a stickler for spit and polish who criticized freely and abrasively. Lear had never been closely associated with the development of the armored force, and his philosophy of armored warfare was anything but daring: "It seems to me that many of you have the impression that an armored force can go busting into battle at a very high rate of speed. Quite the contrary. An armored force the size of a division requires a great deal of time for its deployment for battle."[6]

While this conviction was fundamentally true, General Lear was to carry it to the extreme. His plan of operations for the first Louisiana maneuver was sound, and even imaginative, if one discounts the time factor. Second Army was to cross the Red River along an eighty-mile front between Shreveport and Montgomery, with I Armored Corps leading the way. The armored force had orders to sweep all the way to the Sabine River near Many before facing south, where it would be in a position to launch a decisive flank attack against Blue Third Army advancing north. However, the

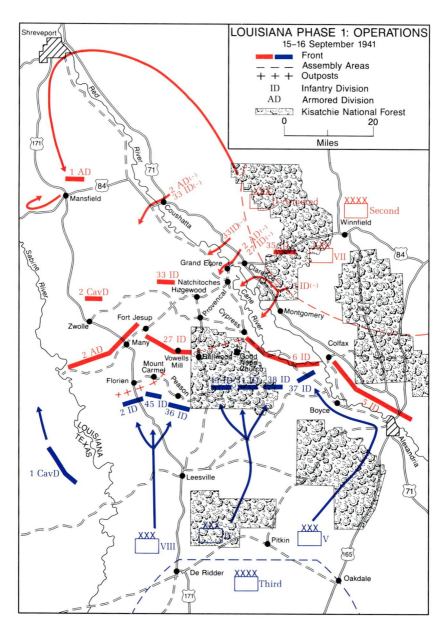

LOUISIANA PHASE 1: OPERATIONS
15–16 September 1941

Front
Assembly Areas
+ + +   Outposts
ID   Infantry Division
AD   Armored Division
Kisatchie National Forest

0   20
Miles

MAP 1

great armored attack was not to take place until VII Corps had also crossed the Red River and occupied a crescent-shaped line running from Fort Jesup to Colfax on the Red River. This would involve a delay of one full day, during which time the larger Third Army would possess the initiative.[7]

Lear's opponent, General Krueger, received instructions from General Headquarters that actually played nicely into Lear's hands:

> Reliable reports of Red movements in strength toward Red River indicate strong probability of early attack. Previous restrictions on movement and reconnaissance are removed, effective at 5:30 A.M., 15 Sept., at which hour you will advance toward the frontier, destroy any enemy forces south thereof and push into Red territory in the direction of Monroe.[8]

An advance on the axis Lake Charles–Monroe would leave General Krueger's large force of three corps (ten divisions) vulnerable to Lear's planned flank attack from the northwest. But despite the size of his army, Krueger was not inclined to play the role of the ponderous bear.

Krueger's Army career had begun in 1898, at the rank of private. While he worked his way through the ranks, Krueger kept pace with the changes in the art of war, and in fact became one of the Army's best educated and most perceptive officers. In 1939 Krueger commanded the 2d Division, the Army's prototype triangular division. In the course of testing the capabilities of the new formation, Krueger gained considerable proficiency in the use of motor vehicles for tactical maneuver. (His enthusiastic troops called themselves Blitzkruegers.) In 1941, at the age of sixty, he remained tough and physically active. Krueger was a soldier's soldier, and he enjoyed a much better relationship with the National Guard component than most other Regulars of high rank, including General Lear.[9] Anything but the pedant in his military philosophy, General Krueger was capable of dispensing with doctrine so long as his army conducted its operations with speed, forcefulness, and determination.[10]

With the able assistance of his chief of staff, Colonel Eisenhower, General Krueger formulated a simple and direct plan of operations that he issued orally to his subordinates the day before "hostilities" began. At zero hour Third Army would lunge forward from its restraining line just north of De Ridder–Oakdale and describe a great pivot toward the northeast, three corps abreast, that he hoped would trap the Red army against the Red River between Natchitoches and Alexandria. The V Corps, commanded by Maj. Gen. Edmund Daley, would form the eastern wing and the anchor for Third Army's pivot. General Krueger ordered Daley's force, which consisted of the 32d, 34th, and 37th divisions (square) and the 106th Cavalry Regiment, to

Mark W. Clark, Harry J. Malony, Dwight D. Eisenhower, Ben Lear, Walter Krueger, and Lesley J. McNair in Louisiana. *(Courtesy of the Dwight D. Eisenhower Library.)*

capture Alexandria and seize crossings over the Red River. Maj. Gen. Jay L. Benedict's IV Corps would constitute Third Army's center. The 31st, 43d, and 38th Divisions (square), with the 6th Cavalry Regiment, were to drive northeast to the river town of Boyce and seize crossings also. The VIII Corps, with Maj. Gen. George V. Strong commanding, would travel the longest path on the outer (western) perimeter of Third Army's pivot. Composed of the 2d Division (Third Army's only triangular division), 43d Division, 45th Division (perhaps the best of the National Guard divisions), and 113th Cavalry Regiment, VIII Corps' orders were to swing through Leesville to Natchitoches, protecting the army's west flank.[11]

General Krueger's army reserve included the 1st Cavalry Division, which he ordered across the Sabine River into Texas, and the three experimental antitank groups, one of which accompanied the cavalry. The other two he kept in reserve, as he did the 1st Tank Group, which consisted of two battalions of light tanks.[12] The 3d Air Task Force, which included more than 300 combat planes of the 2d Bombardment Wing, 10th Pursuit Wing, and four naval squadrons, received the simplest orders of all. General Krueger told the air commander, General Dargue, to support the army and seek out the Red armored force.[13]

Both armies closed on their lines of departure at sunset on Sunday, 14 September, in the midst of a tropical storm. Red Sec-

The 107th Cavalry Regiment (Horse-Mechanized) in Louisiana.
(Armor magazine.)

ond Army moved up to concealed assembly positions along the
Red River while engineers started work on four ponton bridges.
While traveling to its crossing point at Shreveport, the 1st Armored
Division incurred the first four fatalities of the maneuvers in traffic accidents involving civilian motorists.[14] Approximately sixty
miles to the south, Blue Third Army drew up to the restraining
line running from De Ridder to Oakdale. West to east, VIII Corps,
IV Corps, and V Corps stood poised for the race to the Red River.
The inclement weather sent 3d Air Task Force's aircraft fleeing to
bases farther inland overnight, but they would return the next
morning for the start of the operation.[15]

     The first great Louisiana maneuver began as scheduled on
Monday, 15 September, in spite of cloudy skies and torrential rain
showers. At 0500 the 1st Armored Division rumbled across the Red
River bridge at Shreveport and turned southward towards bivouac
positions around Mansfield, there to await the great armored attack scheduled for two days hence. Farther south, the 2d Armored
Division's reconnaissance, artillery, and infantry elements crossed
the Clarence–Grand Ecore highway bridge north of Natchitoches
and raced to the west. Before the last units had cleared the bridge,

leading reconnaissance elements were already on the division's initial objective between Many and Fort Jesup. The armored division's tanks crossed at the Coushatta highway bridge midway between Shreveport and Natchitoches and lumbered toward their concealed assembly positions near Many, behind the division's reconnaissance screen.[16]

No sooner had operations begun than Second Army's plans began to unravel. Pilots of the Blue air force braved cloudy skies to attack columns of the 1st Armored Division on the roads leading south from Shreveport. The first planes appeared about 0820, and thereafter a continuous stream of Blue aircraft harassed the division.[17] Other pilots penetrated the Red fighter umbrellas over Second Army's vital bridges. At Coushatta, a Navy dive bomber collided with a defending Red P–40 at an altitude of 800 feet, and although the dive bomber landed safely, the fighter crashed, killing the pilot.[18]

Even more serious than Blue air activity was the unexpected discovery of Blue reconnaissance troops along Second Army's initial objective line. At Many, 2d Armored Division's reconnaissance battalion, the 82d, collided with a strong detachment of Blue cavalry from VIII Corps even before the division had completely cleared the Red River bridges. Not only had General Krueger's ground and air forces located both Red armored divisions at the very outset of the maneuver, but clearly the Third Army was moving much faster than Lear had expected.

Beginning at 0530, General Krueger's supposedly ponderous square infantry divisions had poured across their restraining line and pressed north, utilizing a procedure known as shuttling, in which troops alternately marched and leapfrogged ahead in quartermaster and artillery trucks. Red pilots, peering through the clouds and rain showers, spotted marching columns up to 36 miles long and convoys of 95, 300, and 400 trucks on the roads leading north.[19]

On Third Army's east flank, the Blue V Corps staged a textbook advance on Alexandria. With the 106th Cavalry Regiment in the lead, V Corps reached the city without encountering serious opposition and started crossing the Red River. The Red army having blown all bridges, 37th Division crossed three battalions (1,200 men) to the east bank by boat. In the center of Third Army's line, IV Corps encountered poorer roads but no opposition as it advanced two divisions abreast behind the 6th Cavalry.[20]

Much to his surprise, General Krueger discovered that the bulk of the Red army appeared to be in VIII Corps' zone on the western flank. The 113th Cavalry Regiment, which was the unit that had encountered 2d Armored Division's reconnaissance elements at Many, fought a steady covering action all day against a growing force of Red tanks, infantry, and cavalry from the I Armored Corps. By nightfall Red troops of the 2d Armored Division's 41st Infantry Regiment had pushed the Blue cavalry back through Florien on the Leesville-Many highway and had established outposts on the highlands to the east. But VIII Corps was near at hand, pounding north from Leesville with the 45th and 36th Divisions in the lead. Once he ascertained that the Red armored force was massed on the west flank, General Krueger attached the 1st Antitank Group to VIII Corps.[21]

Meanwhile, General Lear struggled to bring VII Corps across the river and into the center and eastern wing of Second Army's line. At the river crossings, harassment by Blue aircraft continued to disrupt operations. Accompanied by the 107th Cavalry Regiment, 27th Division followed 2d Armored Division across the Clarence–Grand Ecore bridge and pressed west toward a linkup with I Armored Corps. By 0900 27th Division's leading elements established contact with the 2d Armored Division's left flank, but it would take all day to clear the bridges and bring the infantry up in force. Meanwhile, VII Corps' 107th Cavalry Regiment swung south into the forest to cover 27th Division's march up to the front.[22]

On the eastern end of the line, the Red 6th Division had to await the completion of two ponton bridges before it could join I Armored Corps and 27th Division west of the Red River. For one of the bridges, Second Army engineers selected a site south of Natchitoches that had been improved and used in a previous maneuver. Consequently, it was completed by 1100 on 15 September, approximately sixteen hours after it was begun. The second bridge, located a short distance upstream, did not open to traffic until 1900 the following day.[23] Nonetheless, on the afternoon of 15 September, 6th Division began occupying its long, crescent-shaped sector that extended from 27th Division's east flank to the Red River at Colfax.

Later that day the bulk of 2d Cavalry Division and 33d Division crossed upstream of Natchitoches on pontons. Both divisions then entered corps reserve, the 2d Cavalry Division with I Armored Corps and the 33d Division with VII Corps, behind the 27th Division line. Two Red divisions remained east of the Red River. The 5th Division outposted the east bank from Colfax downstream through Alexandria, and the 35th Division entered army reserve across from Natchitoches.[24]

By nightfall of the 15th, the Red Second Army had reached the initial objective line Many-Colfax, although with incomplete and overextended units. In the 2d Armored Division sector, 2d Ar-

Light tanks cross the Red River on a Corps of Engineers ponton bridge. *(Armor magazine.)*

mored Brigade held approximately twenty miles of front from the Sabine River to Fort Jesup with a reconnaissance battalion, an infantry regiment, and one of the division's three armored regiments. These forces also held an outpost line that covered Mount Carmel and Florien, giving Second Army a vital toehold on Peason Ridge, the dominating terrain feature of the maneuver area. The 27th Division front extended from Fort Jesup to the vicinity of Provencal. The inexperienced and underequipped 6th Division held a line of no less than thirty miles from the 27th's left to the Red River at Colfax. The greater part of the Red army was either east of the river or in reserve, awaiting the general offensive, scheduled for 17 September.

On Tuesday, 16 September, Red Second Army consolidated its positions and brought up the last elements of I Armored Corps and VII Corps. Along most of the front, action was limited to patrolling and skirmishing. The only major Red initiative of the day was a feint by the 1st Armored Division and 4th Cavalry Regiment toward Teneha, Texas. The demonstration was uncoordinated and poorly executed, and apparently deceived nobody in Third Army except for some civilian journalists.[25]

The heaviest fighting of the day took place along the western end of the line, where the 2d Armored Division clung to the northern face of Peason Ridge and strove to expand jump-off positions on the highlands for the next day's scheduled armored attack. Blue resistance was stubborn, for although General Krueger had initially been surprised to find the Red armored force so far to the north and west, his reaction was swift and vigorous. Third Army completely reoriented its axis of advance. Instead of wheeling towards the northeast to come parallel to the Red River (and, in so doing, presenting its left flank to I Armored Corps), the Blue army had begun to pivot toward the northwest in a maneuver that would bring it face to face with the Second Army, the line of contact running perpendicular to the Red and Sabine Rivers.

The VIII Corps, facing the Red 2d Armored Division on the west flank, received orders to maintain pressure and make limited advances while the rest of Third Army pivoted on its position. General Strong, the corps commander, covered his front with mixed horse-mechanized teams of the 113th Cavalry Regiment as he brought the 2d, 36th, and 45th Divisions into line abreast. When the 2d Armored Division attempted to push reconnaissance elements in the direction of Leesville, the 45th Division halted the Red probes with antitank and artillery fire. The 45th Division then took the initiative and nearly pushed the 2d Armored Division from Peason Ridge altogether. By nightfall, VIII Corps forced 2d Armored Division to withdraw its covering force to Florien and Mount Carmel, with Blue patrols following close behind.[26] The retention of Mount Carmel was particularly vital to the Red army, for from there the upcoming armored offensive would be able to fan out into the large, cleared highlands of Peason Ridge. If VIII Corps could capture Mount Carmel, the Red tanks would face an uphill struggle, both literally and figuratively.

With VIII Corps providing the western anchor, General Krueger swung the rest of Third Army toward the northwest. In the center of the Blue line, he reinforced IV Corps with the 1st Tank Group and ordered it to attack vigorously. The IV Corps began constructing a ponton bridge over the Cane River west of Colfax that would open into the weakest part of the Second Army line. Opposite IV Corps, the 6th Division's intelligence section had incorrectly deduced that the flat, swampy land between the Cane and Red Rivers was impassable; consequently, that particular corridor to the northwest was not even under observation, leaving the 6th Division's flank in the air.[27] On Third Army's eastern flank, General Krueger ordered V Corps to break off its crossing operations at Alexandria and abandon the three battalions that had crossed the river. The Red 5th Division captured the crossing force and, finding itself ignored, could do nothing but waste blank ammunition by firing after V Corps as it pushed upstream to support IV Corps along the Cane River.[28]

From his field headquarters in Natchitoches, General Lear considered the prospects for the next day's armored attack in light of the reverses suffered by Second Army on 16 September. He received a reassuring but misleading memo from General Scott, commander of I Armored Corps: "According to all G–2 information which I have been able to obtain from all sources the situation is developing favorably for the execution of the main effort of the Second Army in accordance with the plan submitted . . . on September 14." [29] General Lear recognized, however, that Second Army was in no position to launch the attack as planned. Without secure footholds on Peason Ridge there would be no room to bring the 1st Armored Division out of bivouac and into the line of battle. Consequently, late on 16 September General Lear issued orders postponing the attack by one day. September 17 would be devoted to probing the Blue defenses and securing a better base from which to attack with the armored force the next day.[30]

But General Lear's decision to operate conservatively and postpone the decisive attack until conditions improved carried its own price. By surrendering the initiative on 17 September, he would allow Krueger's Third Army to complete its reorientation, a fact that Lear should have realized, for by this time he knew Third Army's dispositions in detail. Prisoners had revealed information freely, Blue maps and orders had been captured, and Third Army's movements were observed from the air with increasing ease as the weather improved. Lear knew, for example, that two powerful Blue corps were converging on the badly overextended 6th Division in the unprotective terrain of the Red River valley only twenty miles from his own forward headquarters.[31]

General Lear did not alter his plans to meet this dangerous situation. He chose not to dilute the impact of the planned armored attack by committing reserves for defensive purposes, despite the imminence of the Blue threat to the east flank. His orders for 17 September kept five of the eight Red divisions idle—the 5th and 35th Divisions east of the Red River and the 1st Armored Division, 2d Cavalry Division, and 33d Infantry Division in bivouac behind the center and westward flank. The 6th, 27th, and 2d Armored Divisions would not only have to withstand the Blue juggernaut by themselves on 17 September, but General Lear expected them to launch limited attacks as well.

By contrast, when night fell on 16 September, General Krueger's Third Army had eight of its nine infantry divisions in line. Blue troops held key terrain on both flanks, were closing on the enemy in the center, and possessed the initiative all along a front line that ran from the vicinity of Florien in the west to the Cane River near Colfax.[32]

Early on Wednesday, 17 September, the Red 2d Armored Brigade (2d Armored Division) launched a two-pronged assault aimed at shoving the Blue VIII Corps back and holding it at arm's length along the line Florien–Mount Carmel in preparation for the next day's general armored attack. This, the first major armored operation of the maneuvers, made little headway. The armored troops, which included the 41st Infantry Regiment, tanks of the 66th Armored Regiment (light), and artillery support, found the north-south roads thoroughly covered by Blue antitank guns. One column, finding Florien held by a large antitank force, made some progress by sideslipping west of the Many-Leesville road. But Blue antitank guns from the 2d Division stopped it after a few miles' advance.[33]

At Mount Carmel, the other 2d Armored Brigade column collided with antitank and infantry forces from the Blue 45th Division. In a seesaw battle that raged all day, tanks, scout cars, soldiers, and guns surged back and forth while aircraft roared overhead and sound trucks blared battle noises (much to the delight of journalists on hand). By nightfall, Blue troops had not only driven off the armor but had closed on Mount Carmel from three sides and established a tentative grip on the town. To the east, the Blue 36th Division overran open ground, drawing abreast of 45th Division.[34] For the Red armored force to attack as planned the next day, the tanks would have to first fight their way back onto Peason Ridge before reaching the open highlands to the south.

Red forces also lost valuable ground that day in the heavily forested center of the line. Blue IV Corps dispersed the 107th Cavalry and drove the 27th Division out of Bellwood. Later in the day, after losing several vehicles to 27th Division's antitank battalion, Blue forces pierced VII Corps' line and captured the forest crossroads village of Vowells Mill.[35] These acquisitions gave the Blue Third Army effective control over the sparse network of roads that laced through the Kisatchie National Forest, and provided jump-off positions for further attacks against the Red front.

The Blue army scored its greatest success of 17 September in the flat open ground on Second Army's eastern flank. The IV Corps advanced along the vital Natchitoches-Alexandria highway and pushed the overmatched Red 6th Division pell-mell fifteen miles back from its original position on the Red River. The Blue 37th Di-

Third Army soldiers man a simulated antitank gun near Mount Carmel, Louisiana. *(DA photograph.)*

vision of V Corps exploited the undefended ground between the Cane and Red Rivers, advancing another five miles behind 6th Division's flank before being discovered.[36] Troops of the 38th Division volunteered to swim the rain-swollen Cane River to join in 37th Division's advance. In the attempt, five soldiers of Company B, 150th Infantry, struggled and sank in the muddy waters. Umpires stopped the battle; Red and Blue combatants dropped their weapons, shed their packs, and dived into the river. Three men were rescued and revived; two others drowned.[37] General McNair was later to cite the incident in refuting claims that enlisted men were disinterested participants in large-scale maneuvers. "The death of these fine soldiers," he said, "was even more heroic than if it had occurred in battle, for such sacrifices are not expected in maneuvers."[38]

Another Blue force threatened Second Army's eastern flank from the rear. At 0930, 127 soldiers of Company A, 502d Parachute Battalion, jumped from 13 transports over the town of Clarence on the east bank of the Red River. In spite of barely adequate training and inadequate materiel (men and equipment had to be dropped from different aircraft), the parachutists made a well-executed jump and embarked on a daylong career of mayhem. They commandeered vehicles, blew a ponton bridge, and captured a number of startled Red troops. Two hours elapsed before Red forces, consisting of one antiaircraft battery, brought any significant resistance to bear. One party of parachutists even managed to raid Second Army's permanent headquarters at Winnfield. Although the parachute attack was a suicide mission that had little bearing on the ground battle (no attempt was made to link up with Blue forces to the south), the raid did succeed in distracting and embarrassing the Red army.[39]

By nightfall on 17 September, the Blue Third Army had completed its reorientation towards the northwest and was in full contact with Second Army from flank to flank. In the western sector, the 2d, 45th, and 36th Blue Divisions of VIII Corps presented a solid front to the 2d Armored Division from Florien through Mount Carmel. The IV Corps' 43d Division faced the Red 27th Division in the forests north of Bellwood. The 31st and 38th Divisions of IV Corps, aided by V Corps' 37th Division, coiled around the Red 6th Division in the Cane River valley. Curiously, General Lear's reaction to Second Army's predicament was to proceed with planning for the next day's armored attack, even though the events of 17 September had worsened its prospects considerably. The only alterations General Lear and I Armored Corps made in the plans for 18 September actually weakened the attack and made it even less likely to succeed. *(Map 2)*

The great armored attack was originally conceived as a powerful two-division thrust from the western end of Peason Ridge south and east into the rear of Blue Third Army. The 2d Cavalry Division was to hold the gaps between armored columns, and VII Corps' infantry divisions would follow and consolidate gains.[40] But as the bad news mounted on 17 September, General Scott of I Armored Corps began tinkering with the plan in a counterproductive effort to shore up the entire Red line. Owing to the loss of a position on Peason Ridge from which to launch the attack, Scott ordered 2d Armored Division to recapture Florien and Mount Carmel before driving south toward Leesville.[41] He ordered the 1st Armored Division to launch its attack farther to the east, passing through the lines of VII Corps and pushing south into dense forest towards Kisatchie. Late in the day, as it became clear that Blue forces were turning Second Army's flank on the Red River, Scott decided to send one regiment of the 1st Armored Division even farther to the east to aid the hard-pressed 6th Division. Later still, I Armored Corps issued amended orders that would send the bulk of the 1st Armored Division eastward on this mission and then return it to the main axis of attack towards Kisatchie.[42]

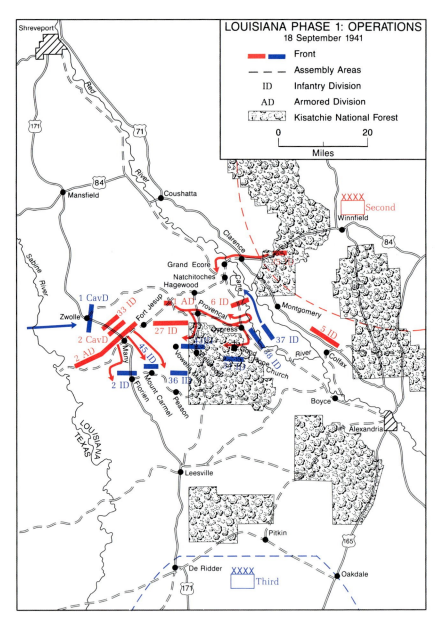

LOUISIANA PHASE 1: OPERATIONS
18 September 1941

Front

- - - Assembly Areas

ID   Infantry Division

AD   Armored Division

Kisatchie National Forest

0   20

Miles

Shreveport

Red River

Mansfield

Coushatta

Clarence

XXXX
Second

Winnfield

Grand Ecore

Natchitoches
Hagewood

Cane

Montgomery

84

Sabine River

1 CavD

33 ID

Fort Jesup

1 AD   6 ID

Provencal

5 ID

Zwolle

2 CavD

27 ID

Cypress

37 ID

River

Colfax

2 AD

45 ID

Vowells

48 ID

Many

36 ID

2 ID

Florien

Mount Carmel

Peason

Church

Boyce

LOUISIANA
TEXAS

Alexandria

Leesville

Pitkin

165

De Ridder

XXXX
Third

Oakdale

171

MAP 2

The prospects of success were not good. What had originally been planned as a concerted attack emerged as a series of diverging thrusts spattered across the entire Red front. The 2d Armored Division knew that it faced three alert Blue infantry divisions, one antitank group, and an estimated two hundred divisional antitank guns in the vicinity of Florien alone.[43] And because I Armored Corps did not complete its orders until 2030, the 1st Armored Division, which had been on alert since 1300, could not begin its movement out of reserve bivouacs until 2200. Once in motion the 1st Armored Division found some of its routes already crowded by troops of 33d Division, which was also moving up from reserve. As armored and infantry units became entangled in the darkness, 1st Armored Division's chances of launching its attack on time vanished. Sunrise on 18 September found the 1st Armored Division still struggling through traffic jams behind the Red lines. On one road, a signal truck laying wire for an infantry division blocked traffic in both directions and created a five-mile tie-up.[44]

On the western end of the line, however, the 2d Armored Division launched its two-pronged attack as scheduled at 0600 on 18 September. Elements of 2d Cavalry Division supported the flanks, and 33d Division of VII Corps advanced behind the armored columns to mop up. The 2d Armored Brigade led the western column, which consisted of the 66th Armored Regiment (light) and one of 41st Infantry Regiment's two battalions, towards Florien on the Many-Leesville highway. After advancing a few miles, the force collided with Blue antitank guns north of Florien and lost twenty of twenty-three tanks in the lead battalion before drawing back. With too little infantry and artillery to reduce the antitank positions, the 2d Armored Brigade left Florien in Blue hands and side-stepped west of the Many-Leesville highway before continuing its southward advance. Blue antitank guns deployed and redeployed in its path, finally bringing the column to a halt late in the day. At considerable cost, 2d Armored Brigade had advanced ten miles but had failed to secure any of its objectives.[45]

Meanwhile, 2d Armored Division's eastern column renewed the battle of Mount Carmel. The 68th Armored Regiment (light) with one battalion of infantry and with the 67th Armored Regiment (medium) in reserve, opened the battle by driving off a force of Blue infantry from the 45th Division that it encountered advancing north from the town. But the long, wooded defiles leading toward Mount Carmel from the west and north made ideal antitank gunnery ranges, and with only one battalion of infantry in support, the 68th Armored Regiment was unable to charge into the town.[46] In an attempt to envelop Mount Carmel from the rear, the armored regiment slipped a few tanks around the western edge of town and shifted the bulk of its forces about three miles to the east. Although this maneuver outflanked the 45th Division forces in Mount Carmel and brought the Red tanks closer to the strategic open ground near Peason, it also brought the 68th Armored Regiment up against a formidable concentration of Blue antitank guns. The crack 1st Antitank Group, eager to make its maneuvers debut, joined the 45th Division antitank battalion along a line roughly parallel to the Mount Carmel road. Elements of the 2d and 36th Divisions were nearby as well. This large but uncoordinated composite antitank force was the last Blue defense between the 68th Armored Regiment and the open ground leading to Leesville.[47]

The 68th Armored Regiment attacked the antitank line east of Mount Carmel at noon and, although it forced the Blue guns to yield some ground, failed to achieve a breakthrough after two hours of intense fighting. Without adequate artillery and infantry support, the Red tanks had little choice but to charge antitank positions head on and attempt to overrun them. After sustaining heavy casualties, the tanks withdrew and re-formed. They re-emerged from their assembly area about 1645 and resumed their ineffectual frontal assault against the wall of antitank guns. For its efforts, the 68th Armored Regiment succeeded in overrunning only 9 antitank guns at a cost of 31 tanks.[48]

While the 68th Armored Regiment spent itself along the Mount Carmel–Peason road, the 67th Armored Regiment (medium) probed into the forest even farther to the east searching for a gap in the Blue line between the 45th and 36th Divisions. The Red mediums drove a salient into the Blue line, pushing one 36th Division regiment a mile out of position and temporarily cutting off another, but once again Blue antitank guns turned the tide. A regimental antitank company from 36th Division knocked out 20 tanks along the forest tracks, one gun alone being credited with 11. Another antitank company set up an ambush at the end of a wooded defile that bagged so many Red vehicles and prisoners that the Blue gunners lost count.[49] When 2d Division's 9th Regiment arrived as reinforcements, the 36th Division restored its front and effectively ended the last Red threat to Peason Ridge.[50]

The tank-antitank battles around Mount Carmel were among the most bitterly fought of the maneuver. Soldiers on both sides became so caught up in the struggle that umpiring deteriorated. In their frustration, armored troops tried to override and bully the umpires accompanying the Blue antitank units. Some insisted that,

Blue infantryman *(foreground)* closes in on the unsuspecting crew of a mired Red tank during the Louisiana maneuvers. *(Field Artillery Journal.)*

under *Umpire Manual* rules, antitank guns as well as infantry were neutralized when within 100 yards of a tank. Others refused to be ruled out of action by antitank umpires, claiming that only a tank umpire could rule out a tank.[51] But the tankers' protests were unavailing, and when the umpires halted the battle of Mount Carmel at 1830, the 2d Armored Division had lost 98 light tanks, 17 medium tanks, and 98 other armored vehicles.[52] The division was spread out over a fifteen-mile front and, if anything, the Blue line was stronger than ever, because late in the day General Krueger had released the 2d and 3d Antitank Groups to VIII Corps.[53]

The 1st Armored Division met with even less success on the day. Because of I Armored Corps' decision to divert most of 1st Armored Division to aid the 6th Division, only one of the 1st's three armored regiments attacked directly along the primary axis of advance from Provencal toward Kisatchie. The 69th Armored Regiment (medium), minus one battalion, was late launching the attack because of traffic congestion. The Hagewood-Kisatchie road, the only direct north-south route through Kisatchie National Forest, provided superb targets for the Blue air force throughout the day as the Red columns snarled together in hopeless traffic jams. In a vain attempt to find an off-road route to the south, the 69th Armored Regiment plunged into the forest somewhere near Bellwood and became badly dispersed. Although it was only ten miles from its original staging area, the 69th lost contact with division headquarters and virtually disappeared from the battle.[54]

The second prong of 1st Armored Division's divergent effort was also late in attacking. The 1st Armored Regiment (light) was scheduled to make a dawn attack against the Blue forces closing in on Natchitoches but was not in position until 1015, by which time Blue antitank units were fully deployed to meet it. The tanks rumbled forward across flat, open ground directly at the antitank guns without any apparent artillery or air support. Umpires credited the Blue guns with 22 tanks by noon and declared an entire battalion destroyed shortly thereafter. The operation cost a total of 42 tanks without seriously threatening the Blue advance along the Red River.[55]

The third of 1st Armored Division's columns, operating under the direct control of 1st Armored Brigade, commanded by Brig. Gen. Orlando Ward, was the largest of the division's forces and suffered the most ignominious reverse. The 1st Armored Brigade, consisting of the 13th Armored Regiment (light), one battalion of mediums from the 69th Armored Regiment, plus infantry and artillery forces, began the day with a successful action against the Blue forces advancing north along the Alexandria-Natchitoches highway. About 1015 two squadrons of Red attack planes distracted the Blue defenders and allowed General Ward to launch a coordinated attack that caught the Blues by surprise. By 1030 Blue infantry was stampeding south. The Blue 38th Division deployed its antitank battalion and took credit for stopping the armored attack, but, in fact, General Ward had no intention of following up his success. Although the temptation to exploit his victory through the flat river valley must have been great, orders called for the 1st Armored Brigade to break off from the enemy, reenter the Kisatchie National Forest, and push southwest toward the main divisional objective beyond Kisatchie.[56] Thus, forfeiting a chance at decisive action in good tank country, the brigade turned and drove into the forest in the direction of Good Hope Church.

The road that 1st Armored Brigade followed may have looked promising on the maps at I Armored Corps headquarters, but it was in reality a one-lane mud track winding through some of the roughest terrain in the maneuver area. The steep, thickly forested hillsides and swampy lowlands precluded virtually all off-road vehicular movement. As the armored brigade pressed on, its units became badly strung out along the trail, and the medium tank battalion bogged down in mud and dropped out of action. To make matters worse, the brigade's route also ran directly along the Blue 31st Division's front. The Blue defenders quickly determined the armored brigade's intentions, since there was but one possible path the Red column could take, and deployed their antitank and infantry defenses accordingly.[57] Soon the woods were swarming with Blue troops. The 31st Division gave battle in the vicinity of Good Hope Church, a small chapel isolated in the midst of the forest. The fighting quickly grew in intensity and tempers began to flare. Blue soldiers began throwing handy objects at 1st Armored Brigade's tanks and soon discovered the pleasing effect that occurred when glass bottles filled with the acid used to manufacture smokescreens shattered against armored hulls. Six tank crewmen were burned badly enough to require medical attention.[58]

Officers were not immune to the increasing bellicosity. As the battle raged through the dense pines, commanders began arguing with the umpires and challenging their decisions. One confrontation became so ugly that, according to an umpire's report, "Col. Hasterly . . . was ruled out as a casualty to help the situation." [59]

As daylight waned, 1st Armored Brigade gave up its advance. General Ward ordered his command into an assembly area near Good Hope Church for the night. Blue infantry elements from 31st Division quickly surrounded the assembly, cut the Red supply line, and captured the gasoline train.[60]

Thus, the 1st Armored Division disintegrated as a fighting unit among the pines of the Kisatchie National Forest even as the 2d launched its last futile attacks against the antitank barrier at Mount Carmel. The 1st Armored Division headquarters, which had lost touch with most of its subordinate units, broadcast radio orders to them. The 69th Armored Regiment, believed to be somewhere in the forest west of Bellwood, received orders to cut its way through to Many the next day and attach itself to 2d Armored Division. Division ordered General Ward to leave his infantry and artillery behind and take the tanks of 1st Armored Brigade on a circuitous route back to friendly lines.[61]

September 18, the day that was to have been I Armored Corps' moment of glory, ended in the first major maneuvers defeat suffered by the Army's armored force. It also saw the rest of Second Army slide toward disaster. Once General Krueger had determined that the Red armored divisions were engaged and pinned down, he committed Blue Third Army's reserves in an all-out attack. After turning back the Red armored attacks south of Natchitoches, the Blue 37th and 38th Divisions broke the Red defense between the Cane and Red Rivers and captured virtually an entire regiment of the hapless 6th Division. A small Blue force pressed into Natchitoches itself, where General Lear had his field headquarters. Second Army hastily removed its headquarters to Mansfield, fifty miles distant, leaving a scratch force of airdrome defense units and miscellaneous air force personnel to defend the town.[62]

The disaster on the east flank finally forced General Lear to take the 35th Division out of army reserve, bring it across the Red River, and commit it to the defense of Natchitoches. The 33d Division, recently committed to the western end of the VII Corps line, also sent a regiment east to shore up the 6th Division zone.[63] But Blue pressure on the rest of the VII Corps front prevented any further reinforcement of the east wing. As small parties of Blue infantry infiltrated the Red lines, cut telephone lines, and blew bridges, the Blue 1st Tank Group spearheaded an attack against the Red center. After a running battle along the Hagewood-Kisatchie road, in which Red antitank gunners emulated their Blue counterparts by destroying 55 of the 65 tanks, the Blue attack reached Provencal, only five miles from VII Corps headquarters at Hagewood.[64]

In the western sector, another Blue force pushed through the woods to menace Fort Jesup, the western anchor of the VII Corps line. And after dark, the Blue 1st Cavalry Division crossed the Sabine River from Texas in the vicinity of Zwolle by fording and an improvised ferry. This audacious move planted the troopers directly in the 2d Armored Division's rear.[65]

The 13th Armored Regiment, 1st Armored Division, meets a black
cavalry unit near Zwolle, Louisiana. *(Field Artillery Journal.)*

General Lear, just before leaving Natchitoches for his new field
headquarters at Mansfield, reviewed Second Army's status and issued orders for 19 September. Red intelligence indicated that the
Blue Third Army could envelop either or both Red flanks. He was
especially worried about the loss of Natchitoches, which would isolate Second Army from its base of operations east of the Red River
and open the way for a Blue drive toward Monroe. Consequently, he
ordered the Red army to hold Natchitoches but to refuse its westward wing, occupying a line running from Natchitoches through
Provencal (already in enemy hands), Fort Jesup, and Zwolle "for the
purpose of reorganizing units and defending positions along the
line until it is expedient for this Army to resume the offensive." [66]
    Second Army's exhausted troops began their redeployment
during the night of 18–19 September. The 2d Armored Division
was in the most precarious position and had the farthest to retreat.
By the next morning, most of its units had broken contact with the
Blue defenders at Florien and Mount Carmel and had pulled back
to the line Many–Fort Jesup, where they paused before retreating
to Zwolle. The attack that the Blue VIII Corps launched on 19
September fell on air and turned into a desultory pursuit. Eight

Red tanks conducted a spoiling attack south of Florien that routed some Blue troops from 2d Division, but the major factor slowing the Blue pursuit was exhaustion, not fear of Red counterattacks.[67]

The main threat to the 2d Armored Division was from the Blue 1st Cavalry Division behind it. The Red 2d Cavalry Division, which helped cover the armored withdrawal, also had the difficult task of containing the Blue cavalry menace. Before dawn the Blue troopers, spoiling for action, burst out of their bridgehead near Zwolle with both horse and mechanized units. They destroyed a I Armored Corps railhead truck convoy, established roadblocks on the Leesville highway at three points, and gleefully captured a supply convoy destined for the 2d Armored Division.[68] When elements of the retreating 2d Armored Division reached Zwolle, they joined the 2d Cavalry Division in a battle against Blue cavalry for possession of the town. One attack, launched from the south and east, resulted in yet another embarrassment for the armored forces. Red cavalry and armored units became intermixed on the approach, and Blue attack aircraft strafed the tangled columns. As the confusion mounted, poor Red security allowed Blue cavalrymen to infiltrate among the Red forces, capture some mired tanks, and create something suspiciously like real panic. Red soldiers raced to their vehicles and drove heedlessly through marked artillery barrages to escape the Blue troopers.[69]

North of Zwolle, however, the remainder of 2d Armored Division strove to redeem its honor. Elements of the two light armored regiments and the infantry regiment, plus field artillery and cavalry support, conducted their best tank attack of the maneuver. Favored for once by the terrain, the Red forces laid down a smokescreen and charged west across the Leesville highway, dealing a severe blow to the 1st Cavalry Division. The Red armored units, however, still tended to charge at antitank guns rather than wait for artillery or infantry support, a practice that cost them 34 tanks.[70]

The center of the Red line was also the scene of armored action on 19 September as mechanized forces covered the withdrawal of VII Corps. The scattered elements of the 1st Armored Division (less the 69th Armored Regiment, which had joined the 2d Armored Division) reassembled behind the VII Corps line and then struck back at the advancing Blue troops. The 1st Armored Regiment (light) fought a daylong battle in the forest southwest of Provencal, disrupting the Blue advance and capturing 2 Blue infantry battalions, at the cost of 18 tanks. Farther south along the Hagewood-Kisatchie road, the 81st Reconnaissance Battalion of the 1st Armored Division traded losses with the Blue 43d Division and 1st Tank Group, sacrificing 7 light tanks but claiming 5 Blue tanks and 5 antitank guns.[71]

As on 18 September, the battles became bitter affairs and umpiring again broke down. Umpires reported that Blue officers joined in throwing smoke bottles at 1st Armored Division tanks. Furthermore, the division umpire from 1st Armored Division claimed that Blue umpires lost all pretense of impartiality and awarded unwarranted victories to Blue units. Every umpire conference became the scene of heated debate in which officers and soldiers participated. An unnamed Blue general refused to return some captured Red vehicles and men, saying, "I don't give a damn what the manual says." [72] Although the Red armored forces failed to effect a permanent recapture of Provencal, the inconclusive forest brawl succeeded in stabilizing Red Second Army's center, just as the battle of Zwolle helped steady the west flank. These armored actions demonstrated the counterattack potential that General Lear had forfeited for three days by keeping most of his armor in reserve.

Nothing, however, could shore up the Red east flank, which continued to crumble on 19 September. The Blue 37th and 38th Divisions continued their remorseless advance on Natchitoches and gained the eastern and southern approaches to the city by early afternoon. General Lear pulled the battered and disorganized 6th Division out of the fight for Natchitoches and turned the city over to 35th Division.[73]

Meanwhile, Second Army headquarters planned another major withdrawal by the center and west wing to a new defensive position anchored on Pleasant Hill. Natchitoches was to be held at all costs.[74] But before Second Army could implement the orders, word came from the GHQ director's headquarters to halt the maneuver at 1530.[75] Apparently, General McNair felt that the outcome of the battle of the Red River was no longer in question and that continuing the maneuver would serve no further training purpose. He may also have timed the recall to prevent fighting in the streets of Natchitoches during the Friday afternoon rush hour. Most importantly, the troops had to be rested and transported to their assembly areas in preparation for the second maneuver.

Soldiers greeted the end of the maneuver with relief. Although tired, they were reportedly in good spirits, with the possible exception of the armored troops, whom a civilian journalist described as being "cocky and brave" on Monday, but "silent and unhappy" on Friday.[76]

While the troops relaxed and moved to new assembly areas, interpretation of the first maneuver began. At the official critique conducted by the director's headquarters for the senior officers, General McNair expressed his satisfaction:

GHQ feels unqualified that the maneuver has been highly successful. All commanders and troops have a right to feel deep satisfaction. Both officers and men have shown themselves to be in prime physical condition— the first requisite of success in battle. In addition, upwards of half a million men have engaged in an entirely free maneuver, and have demonstrated their ability to move and fight soundly and effectively in accordance with a tactical situation which at times has been both difficult and complex. It is reasonable to regard the performance of troops in these maneuvers as an index of training progress during the past year, and the results are inspiring indeed.[77]

General McNair had special words of praise for the 2d and 3d Air Task Forces, for the ponton engineers who bridged the Red River, for the parachutists of the 502d Battalion, and for 1st Cavalry Division's skillful Sabine River crossing. However, he also noted a number of serious training deficiencies, especially with regard to the air threat: highways were constantly congested, few units practiced off-road dispersal or concealment, and the employment of antiaircraft units was generally unsatisfactory. Other errors included a reluctance to utilize maneuver in the attack or entrenchments in defense, and especially poor reconnaissance and security, which General McNair described as ". . . one of the most serious faults observed during the maneuver."[78]

In keeping with his belief that training deficiencies were but a symptom of leadership failures, General McNair reserved most of his criticisms for the commissioned ranks. At the highest levels he found that orders were too often complex, obscure, and late, sometimes arriving at subordinate commands after the hour they were to be executed. He also expressed dissatisfaction with the widespread inability of commanders to utilize all of the forces at their disposal, particularly the artillery. He cited instances of artillery orders arriving too late to allow survey and registration, of artillery immobilized because its transport was being used to shuttle infantry, and of commanders who simply allowed potentially useful artillery to remain idle.[79]

General McNair also criticized the officers at all levels for occupying excessive frontages. Though not faulting the Second Army by name, he gave instances of divisions covering fronts of twenty and twenty-seven miles and individual battalions deployed over several miles. "Under these conditions," he said, "control is difficult, if not impossible, and there can be no weight to the attack nor power to the defense." He blamed inadequate staff work for the incredible traffic jams and the occasional disruptions in the administration of supply.[80]

Aside from the general issues of training and leadership, the most important lesson of the first maneuver was undoubtedly the startling victory of antitank forces over tank. But what had actually been demonstrated, the soundness of antitank doctrine or the fallibility of armored doctrine? Not surprisingly, General McNair opted for the former interpretation: "An outstanding feature of the maneuver was the success attained in antitank defense due principally to guns." Although he acknowledged the influence of terrain in hampering armored operations, he stated further that ". . . the efforts directed to the solution of the [antitank] problem now are approaching definite form," although improvements were still needed in the antitank warning system, the coordination of command, and the use of mines.[81]

Sharing in McNair's accolades were the three mobile antitank groups: ". . . it seems clear that the mobile antitank gun defense now being developed gives promise of marked success . . . it is probable that additional antitank battalions—and perhaps larger units—will be formed." [82] However, an examination of antitank actions in the first maneuver reveals that the majority of tanks destroyed fell victim to the relatively passive divisional and regimental antitank units, not to the independent antitank groups. Seven divisional antitank battalions saw action, not to mention numerous regimental antitank companies and field artillery batteries. Among these, the various antitank units of the 43d Division received credit for 48 tanks, those of the 27th for at least 55, and those of the 45th Division for no less than 155.[83] By comparison, the 1st Antitank Group was the only one of the three groups to see action in all of Phase 1. Its only noteworthy contribution came at Mount Carmel on 18 September, when it knocked out 31 tanks of the 2d Armored Division.[84] The mobile antitank groups reaped more than their deserved share of praise for the antitank victory.

Moreover, some observers felt that the antitank victory had relatively little to do with antitank doctrine one way or the other. Many believed that Second Army's failure to appreciate the capabilities and proper role of its armored forces was responsible for armor's defeat. Among this group was the senior armored umpire, Col. William M. Grimes, who commented, "The I Armored Corps should have been used as the Army's spearhead—instead, the I Armored Corps was hamstrung by wrapping the VII Corps around its neck. Consequently the tempo of the Army was not the tempo of the armored corps but of the VII." [85]

In a report delivered at the Command and General Staff School, other observers also questioned the use of the 2d Armored Division to defend part of the line for three days when other reserve units were available. To them it seemed possible that, had the I Armored Corps kept rolling on 15 September instead of waiting for the rest of Second Army, Leesville might have been captured and Third Army's flank turned. But the most glaring error of the maneuvers was the dispersal of forces in the 18 September attack.[86]

Another body of criticism attributed the failure of the armored forces to their own doctrinal deficiencies. Many liaison officers in the field noted poor coordination within the armored divisions themselves. Tank regiments, infantry regiments, and artillery batteries tended to act independently. As a result, tanks often tried to attack alone, without waiting for support from the other elements. Even among and within tank units coordination was poor, and actions tended to be fought by individual tanks.[87] The failure to practice combined arms, in combination with the relative immunity from tanks accorded antitank guns under the *Umpire Manual*, made it almost inevitable that the armored forces would suffer much and accomplish little.

There was no time for tankers to ponder their sobering setbacks or for antitank forces to celebrate their victories. A full interpretation of the tank-antitank issue would have to wait, for Phase 2 of the Louisiana maneuvers was soon to put Second and Third Armies to the test again.

Notes

1. Pogue, *Marshall,* p. 89.

2. Mark W. Clark, *Calculated Risk* (New York: Harper and Bros., 1950), p. 15.

3. Quoted in "Second and Third Army Maneuvers, 1941," MHI Reference Collection, p. 4.

4. Edmund G. Love, *The 27th Infantry Division in World War II* (Washington, D.C.: Infantry Journal Press, 1949), p. 13; 33d Infantry Division Historical Committee, *The Golden Cross: A History of the 33d Infantry Division in World War II* (Washington, D.C.: Infantry Journal Press, 1948), pp. 8–9; [6th] Division Public Relations Section, *The 6th Infantry Division in World War II* (Washington, D.C.: Infantry Journal Press, 1947), pp. 14–16.

5. "Organization of Troops, GHQ Period, 14–30 September," 1st Phase Critique, RG 337 57D, HQ AGF, GHQ GS G–3, Subject File 1940–Mar 9, 1942, NA.

6. Bell I. Wiley and William P. Govan, "AGF Study No. 16, History of the Second Army" (Historical Section, AGF, 1946), p. 111.

7. "Second and Third Army Maneuvers, 1941," MHI Reference Collection, pp. 4–5.

8. Quoted in "Second and Third Army Maneuvers, 1941," MHI Reference Collection, p. 4.

9. Hill, *Minute Man,* pp. 392–95.

10. Dwight D. Eisenhower, *Crusade In Europe* (Garden City, N.Y.: Doubleday, 1948), p. 11; Smith, "AGF Study No. 17," pp. 14–15

11. "Report on Second and Third Army Maneuvers, 1941," CGSC Library, p. 1; Smith, "AGF Study No. 17," p. 20.

12. "Third Army Units," 1st Phase Critique, RG 337 57D, NA.

13. "Report on Second and Third Army Maneuvers, 1941," CGSC Library, p. 25.

14. Kingman to Gen Clark, 15 Sep 41, GHQ La. 1st and 2d Maneuvers Armd Forces, RG 337 57D, NA.

15. "Gale Holds Back War Game Start," *New York Times,* 15 Sep 41.

16. Telephone msg, Col E. A. Smith to Col Dumas, 14 Sep 41, GHQ La. 1st and 2d Maneuvers Armd Forces; "Report of Operations, 2d Armored Division," Annex 8. Both in RG 337 57D, NA.

17. Umpire Rpt, 1st Armd Div, Matter Reference Revision of Umpire Manual, RG 337 57D, NA; John Field, "With the Red Army," *Life,* 13 Oct 41, pp. 12–18.

18. "Tragedy Marks Army Field Game," *New York Times,* 16 Sep 41.

19. G–2 Rpt 19, VII Corps, 15 Sep 41, "Maneuver Report, VII Army Corps," RG 337 57D, NA.

20. "Second and Third Army Maneuvers, 1941," MHI Reference Collection, p. 6; "Report on Second and Third Army Maneuvers, 1941," CGSC Library, pp. 17–18; "Big Maneuvers Test U.S. Army," *Life,* 6 Oct 41, pp. 33–43.

21. Telephone msg, Col Smith to G–3 Dir Off, 15 Sep 41; Memo, J. A. Smith for Col Kingman, 15 Sep 41; Blakeney to G–3, GHQ Dir HQ, 15 Sep 41. All in GHQ La. 1st and 2d Maneuvers Armd Forces, RG 337 57D, NA. [Maj] McNair to Col Kingman, 15 Sep 41, GHQ La. 1st and 2d Maneuvers AT, RG 337 57D, NA.

22. Crittenberger to CG, 2d Armd Div, 15 Sep 41, GHQ La. 1st and 2d Maneuvers Armd Forces; "Report on Antitank Activities," 2d Cav Div, 9 Oct 41; "Maneuver Report, VII Army Corps." All in RG 337 57D, NA.

23. "Report on Second and Third Army Maneuvers, 1941," CGSC Library, pp. 11–12.

24. "Maneuver Report, VII Army Corps," app. II, RG 337 57D, NA; "Report on Second and Third Army Maneuvers, 1941," CGSC Library, pp. 12–18.

25. Umpire Rpt, 1st Armd Div, 15–16 Sep 41, Matter Reference Revision of Umpire Manual, RG 337 57D, NA; Edward K. Thompson, "With the Blue Army," *Life*, 13 Oct 41, pp. 18–25.

26. Memo, J. Smith for Col Kingman, 16 Sep 41, GHQ La. 1st and 2d Maneuvers Armd Forces, RG 337 57D, NA.

27. G–2 Rpt 22, VII Corps, 17 Sep 41, "Maneuver Report, VII Army Corps," RG 337 57D, NA; "Report on Second and Third Army Maneuvers, 1941," CGSC Library, p. 7.

28. "Second and Third Army Maneuvers, 1941," MHI Reference Collection, p. 6; AT Officer, 5th Div, to GHQ Dir HQ, 21 Sep 41, GHQ 1st and 2d Maneuvers AT, RG 337 57D, NA.

29. Maj Gen C. L. Scott to CofS, Second Army, 16 Sep 41, GHQ La. 1st and 2d Maneuvers Armd Forces, RG 337 57D, NA.

30. Operations Directive 3, Second Army, 16 Sep 41, "Maneuver Report, VII Army Corps," RG 337 57D, NA.

31. "Report on Second and Third Army Maneuvers, 1941," CGSC Library, p. 9.

32. "Second and Third Army Maneuvers, 1941," MHI Reference Collection, p. 6; FO 18, VII Corps, 16 Sep 41, "Maneuver Report, VII Army Corps," RG 337 57D, NA.

33. "Report of Operations, 2d Armored Division," Annex 8; AT Officer, 2d Div, to AT Dir, GHQ Dir HQ, 22 Sep 41, GHQ La. 1st and 2d Maneuvers AT. Both in RG 337 57D, NA. "Second and Third Army Maneuvers, 1941," MHI Reference Collection, p. 8.

34. D. C. McNair to Col Kingman, 17 Sep 41, GHQ La. 1st and 2d Maneuvers AT; G–2 Rpt 23, VII Corps, 17 Sep 41, "Maneuver Report, VII Army Corps." Both in RG 337 57D, NA. "Big Maneuvers Test U.S. Army," *Life*, 6 Oct 41, pp. 33–43.

35. G–2 Rpt 23, VII Corps, 17 Sep 41, and G–3 Rpt 17, VII Corps, 18 Sep 41, "Maneuver Report, VII Army Corps"; AT Officer, 27th Div, to AT Director, GHQ Dir HQ, 21 Sep 41, GHQ La. 1st and 2d Maneuvers AT. Both in RG 337 57D, NA.

36. "Report on Second and Third Army Maneuvers, 1941," CGSC Library, p. 7.

37. Factual Information on the Drowning Accident, 17 Sep 41, 354.2 Rpts 1941, RG 337 57, HQ AGF, GHQ, NA.

38. "General McNair's Comments," *Army and Navy Journal*, 4 Oct 41, pp. 136–37.

39. "Comments on First Phase Second Army vs. Third Army Maneuvers," 22 Sep 41, p. 12; "Report on Second and Third Army Maneuvers," p. 21. Both in CGSC Library. Greenfield, Palmer, and Wiley, *Organization*, p. 96.

40. Operations Directive 4, Second Army, 17 Sep 41, "Maneuver Report, VII Army Corps," RG 337 57D, NA.

41. FO 19, 2d Armd Div, 17 Sep 41, "Report of Operations, 2d Armored Division"; J. Smith to Col Kingman, 17 Sep 41, GHQ La. 1st and 2d Maneuvers Armd Forces. Both in RG 337 57D, NA.

42. Operations Directive 4, Second Army, 17 Sep 41, "Maneuver Report, VII Army Corps"; Lt Col Kingman, Armd Force and AT Dir to G–3 Dir, 17 Sep 41, GHQ La. 1st and 2d Maneuvers Armd Forces. Both in RG 337 57D, NA.

43. Summary of Intelligence, I Armd Corps, 17 Sep 41, GHQ La. 1st and 2d Maneuvers Armd Forces, RG 337 57D, NA.

44. Lt Col E. A. Smith to Lt Col A. F. Kingman, 20 Sep 41; Msg, Lt Col E. A. Smith, 18 Sep 41. Both in GHQ La. 1st and 2d Maneuvers, Armd Forces. Lt Col E.

A. Smith to Lt Col A. F. Kingman, "Notes Pertaining to 1st Phase," GHQ La. 1st and 2d Maneuvers AT. All in RG 337 57D, NA.

45. "Report of Operations, 2d Armored Division," Annex 8; J. Smith to Col Kingman, 18 Sep 41, GHQ La. 1st and 2d Maneuvers Armd Forces; AT Officer, 2d Div, to AT Dir, GHQ Dir HQ, 22 Sep 41, GHQ La. 1st and 2d Maneuvers AT; J. Smith to Col Kingman, 18 Sep 41, GHQ La. 1st and 2d Maneuvers AT. All in RG 337 57D, NA.

46. [Maj] McNair to Col Kingman, 18 Sep 41, GHQ La. 1st and 2d Maneuvers AT; FO 19, 2d Armd Div; Telephone msg, Col Goodman to G–3 Dir Office, GHQ La. 1st and 2d Maneuvers Armd Forces. All in RG 337 57D, NA.

47. [Maj] McNair to Col Kingman, 18 Sep 41; "Checklist on Antitank Groups." Both in GHQ La. 1st and 2d Maneuvers AT, RG 337 57D, NA.

48. Ibid.

49. AT Officer, 36th Div, to AT Dir, GHQ Dir HQ, 21 Sep 41, GHQ La. 1st and 2d Maneuvers AT, RG 337 57D, NA.

50. Telephone msg, Col Goodman to G–3, Dir Office, 18 Sep 41; Telephone msg, Col Blakeney to G–3, Dir Office, 18 Sep 41. Both in GHQ La. 1st and 2d Maneuvers Armd Forces, RG 337 57D, NA.

51. Sawbridge, Comments with Respect to 1st AT Group, 20 Sep 41; D. C. McNair to Col Kingman, AT Action in 1st Phase. Both in GHQ La. 1st and 2d Maneuvers AT, RG 337 57D, NA.

52. Tank Losses, 18 Sep 41, GHQ La. 1st and 2d Maneuvers Armd Forces, RG 337 57D, NA.

53. TWX, Krueger to Dir HQ, 18 Sep 41; D. C. McNair to Lt Col Kingman, 18 Sep 41. Both in GHQ La. 1st and 2d Maneuvers AT, RG 337 57D, NA.

54. Msg, Col E. A. Smith, 18 Sep 41, GHQ La. 1st and 2d Maneuvers Armd Forces, RG 337 57D, NA.

55. Umpire Rpt, 1st Armd Div, 18 Sep 41, Matter Reference Revision of Umpire Manual; AT, 37th Div, to G–3, GHQ Dir HQ, GHQ La. 1st and 2d. Maneuvers AT. Both in. RG 337 57D, NA.

56. Lt Col A. F. Kingman to G–3 Dir, 17 Sep 41, GHQ La. 1st and 2d Maneuvers Armd Forces; Telephone msg, Col Wahl to G–3, Dir Office, GHQ La. 1st and 2d Maneuvers, Armd Forces; Rpt on 38th Div AT Activities, 26 Sep 41, GHQ La. 1st and 2d Maneuvers AT. All in RG 337 57D, NA.

57. Umpire Rpt, 1st Armd Div, Matter Reference Revision of Umpire Manual; 1st Armd Div Umpire to Col Kingman, 19 Sep 41, GHQ La. 1st and 2d Maneuvers Armd Forces; Telephone msg, Maj Nott to G–3, Dir Office, 18 Sep 41, GHQ La. 1st and 2d Maneuvers Armd Forces; AT Officer, 31st Div, to AT Officer, IV Corps, GHQ La. 1st and 2d Maneuvers AT. All in RG 337 57D, NA.

58. Umpire, 1st Armd Div, to Chief Umpire, Second Army, 20 Sep 41, sub: Violations of Umpire Rules, Matter Reference Revision of Umpire Manual, RG 337 57D, NA.

59. Ibid.

60. AT Officer, 31st Div, to AT Officer, IV Corps, GHQ La. 1st and 2d Maneuvers AT, RG 337 57D, NA.

61. Radio Order to Col Waltz, 18 Sep 41; Radio Orders to Ward, 18 Sep 41. Both in GHQ La. 1st and 2d Maneuvers Armd Forces, RG 337 57D, NA.

62. Telephone msg, Col Goodman, 18 Sep 41; Telephone msg, Col Ford to G–3, Dir Office, 18 Sep 41. Both in GHQ La. 1st and 2d Maneuvers Armd Forces, RG 337 57D, NA.

63. FO 20, VII Corps, 18 Sep 41, "Maneuver Report, VII Army Corps"; Rpt of Activities, 33d Div AT Bn and Cos, 22 Sep 41, GHQ La. 1st and 2d Maneuver AT. Both in RG 337 57D, NA.

64. G–3 Rpt 25, VII Corps, 18 Sep 41, "Maneuver Report, VII Army Corps"; Action Participated In By 27th Div AT Bn, 21 Sep 41, GHQ La. 1st and 2d Maneuvers AT. Both in RG 337 57D, NA.

65. G–2 Rpt 26, VII Corps, 19 Sep 41, "Maneuver Report, VII Army Corps"; "Report of Operations, 2d Armored Division," Annex 8; AT Officer, 1st Cavalry Div, to GHQ Dir HQ, 21 Sep 41, GHQ La. 1st and 2d Maneuvers AT. All in RG 337 57D, NA.

66. Operations Directive 5, Second Army, 18 Sep 41; G–2 Rpt 26, VII Corps, 19 Sep 41. Both in "Maneuver Report, VII Army Corps," RG 337 57D, NA.

67. Msg, Lt Col J. A. Smith, 19 Sep 41, GHQ La. 1st and 2d Maneuvers Armd Forces; Telephone msg, Col Blakeney to G–3, Dir Office, 19 Sep 41, GHQ La. 1st and 2d Maneuvers Armd Forces; Telephone msg, Col Goodman to G–3, Dir Office, 19 Sep 41, GHQ La. 1st and 2d Maneuvers Armd Forces; Disposition of 1st, 2d, and 3d AT Groups at Termination of Maneuver, GHQ La. 1st and 2d Maneuvers AT; "Report of Operations, 2d Armored Division," Annex 8. All in RG 337 57D, NA.

68. Telephone msg, Col Kingman to G–3, Dir Office, 19 Sep 41, GHQ La. 1st and 2d Maneuvers Armd Forces; AT Officer, 1st Cavalry Div, to GHQ Dir HQ, 21 Sep 41, GHQ La. 1st and 2d Maneuvers AT. Both in RG 337 57D, NA.

69. Garrett Underhill, "Louisiana Hayride," *Field Artillery Journal*, Dec 41, pp. 907–13.

70. "Report of Operations, 2d Armored Division," Annex 8; Col William Grimes, General Observations, 20 Sep 41, Matter Reference Revision of Umpire Manual; AT Officer, 1st Cav Div, to GHQ Dir HQ, 21 Sep 41, GHQ La. 1st and 2d Maneuvers AT. All in RG 337 57D, NA.

71. Umpire Rpt, 1st Armd Div, 19 Sep 41, Matter Reference Revision of Umpire Manual; G–3 Rpts, I Armd Corps, 19 Sep 41, GHQ La. 1st and 2d Maneuvers Armd Forces. Both in RG 337 57D, NA.

72. Umpire, 1st Armd Div, to Chief Umpire, Second Army, 20 Sep 41, sub: Violations of Umpire Rules, Matter Reference Revision of Umpire Manual, RG 337 57D, NA.

73. FO 21, VII Corps, 19 Sep 41, "Maneuver Report, VII Army Corps," RG 337 57D, NA.

74. Ibid.

75. "Second and Third Army Maneuvers, 1941," MHI Reference Collection, p. 10.

76. "Big Maneuvers Test U.S. Army," *Life*, 6 Oct 41, pp. 33–43; G–3 Rpt 19, VII Corps, 19 Sep 41, "Maneuver Report, VII Army Corps," RG 337 57D, NA.

77. "General McNair's Comments," *Army and Navy Journal*, 4 Oct 41, pp. 136–37.

78. "Comments on First Phase Second Army vs. Third Army Maneuvers," 22 Sep 41, CGSC Library, pp. 5–6.

79. "Comments on First Phase Second Army vs. Third Army Maneuvers," 22 Sep 41, CGSC Library, pp. 2–6. "General McNair's Comments," *Army and Navy Journal*, 4 Oct 41, pp. 136–37.

80. "General McNair's Comments," *Army and Navy Journal*, 4 Oct 41, pp. 136–37.

81. Ibid.

82. Ibid.

83. AT Div Bns; Consolidated Rpt, 43 AT Units; Action Participated in by 27th Div AT Bn; 45th Div Officer to AT Dir, GHQ Dir HQ, 21 Sep 41. All in GHQ La. 1st and 2d Maneuvers AT, RG 337 57D, NA.

84. [AT] Group 1, AT Umpire Rpt, 18 Sep 41, GHQ La. 1st and 2d Maneuvers AT, RG 337 57D, NA.

85. I Armd Corps Umpire to Col Kingman, 20 Sep 41, sub: Tactical Observations, Second Army–Third Army Maneuvers Period 14–19 Sep 41, Matter Reference Revision of Umpire Manual, RG 337 57D, NA.

86. "Report on Second and Third Army Maneuvers, 1941," CGSC Library, p. 19.

87. Ibid.; "Check List for Armored Division," GHQ La. 1st and 2d Maneuvers Armd Forces, RG 337 57D, NA.

CHAPTER 6

Louisiana Phase 2
The Battle for Shreveport

All great battles are named sooner or later. This one should be called the Battle of Bridges. If there is any one lesson which stands out above all others, it is the decisive influence of destroyed bridges.

Lt. Gen. Lesley J. McNair [1]

The conclusion of the first Louisiana maneuver brought only a brief respite to the weary troops of the Second and Third Armies, for General Headquarters had already set in motion the preliminaries of Phase 2. The second maneuver was to be entirely distinct from the first, involving new missions for the opposing commanders and the reconstitution of the Red and Blue armies. General Headquarters detached I Armored Corps headquarters and the 2d Armored Division from Second Army and attached them to the Blue side. In return, Blue Third Army gave up two of the three antitank groups, the 1st and 2d, as well as the parachute company from the 502d Parachute Battalion that had fought with Third Army in Phase 1.[2] As a result, Third Army would outnumber Second Army four corps to one, eleven divisions to seven, and 219,346 men to 123,451, a ratio of nearly 1.8 to 1.[3] Only in the air were Red and Blue equal, each air task force still comprising approximately three hundred combat aircraft.

This disproportion in strength was deliberately conceived. In the first maneuver, the GHQ directors had pitted a large, slow force against a smaller, more mobile one to see whether mobility could offset inferior numbers in a head-on encounter battle. Both the Red and Blue commanders had been given orders to conduct offensive operations. But in the second maneuver, the directors wished to experiment with the ability of an even smaller force to conduct purely defensive operations against an attacker that was superior in virtually every way. Accordingly, General Headquarters deprived Second Army of much of its offensive capability but gave the Red force the simpler, defensive mission.

On 18 September, while the first maneuver was still under way, GHQ director's headquarters sent General Lear a preliminary directive for Phase 2 assigning Second Army the mission of defending Shreveport from the Blue forces based near Lafayette. The directive gave Second Army a zone of about one hundred miles south of Shreveport in which to conduct its defensive operations.[4] To oppose the massive Blue force, Lear opted for a strategy of delay and withdrawal in which the Red army would avoid battle, yielding its territory to buy time "until favorable opportunity is offered to pass to the counteroffensive." [5] He designated a series of five concentric delaying positions, ten to fifteen miles apart, ranging out from Shreveport to a distance of sixty miles. *(Map 3)* Lear's plan called for Second Army to retreat methodically from one to the next, with four divisions on the line and three in reserve, never allowing the advancing Blue army a chance to bring its superior strength to bear. The most comprehensive program of (simulated) demolitions since the Civil War would help keep the Blue invaders at arms' length. Lear's orders specified that "in no case will intact bridges be allowed to fall into the hands of the enemy." [6] Bridges and culverts on every route, both primary and secondary, were to be denied to the enemy.[7]

General Lear may have hoped that by retreating and impeding Third Army's advance he could avoid battle altogether, for none of the plans emanating from his headquarters explained what Second Army was to do if a major battle became either desirable or necessary. The most powerful of his three reserve divisions, the 1st Armored Division, would play no role in projected Red operations until such time as the Second Army reached the final delaying position near Shreveport. This division formulated four tentative plans for counterattacking the Blue invaders.[8] Having demonstrated armor's ability to conduct effective counterattacks in Phase 1, the armored soldiers were eager to prove their worth again. The 1st Armored Division's tentative counterattack plans carried this admonition: "This is the last attack of the maneuver and it is expected that every unit and man will get over, under, or around any obstacle in the way and attain the objective." [9]

Undoubtedly, 1st Armored Division's greatest obstacle to redeeming its honor was General Lear's reluctance to commit his army to battle. Hours before the maneuver began, he decided to yield the first and intermediate delaying positions on the first and

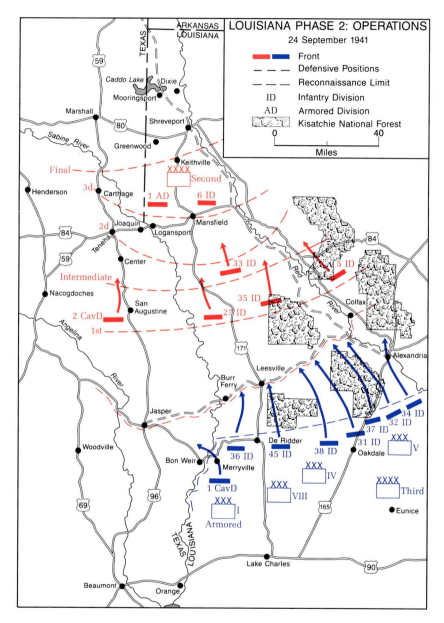

LOUISIANA PHASE 2: OPERATIONS
24 September 1941

Front
Defensive Positions
Reconnaissance Limit
ID   Infantry Division
AD   Armored Division
Kisatchie National Forest

0   40
Miles

ARKANSAS
LOUISIANA

TEXAS

59

Caddo Lake   Dixie
Mooringsport

Marshall   80

Sabine River

Shreveport

Greenwood

Keithville
XXXX
Second

Final

3d   Carthage

Henderson

1 AD   6 ID

2d   Joaquin

84   Tenaha   Logansport
Mansfield

59   Center

Intermediate   33 ID

Nacogdoches

2 CavD   San Augustine   35 ID
1st   27 ID

Angelina River

5 ID

Red River

Colfax

171

Leesville   Alexandria

Burr Ferry

Jasper

34 ID
32 ID
37 ID
31 ID   XXX   V
De Ridder   Oakdale

Woodville

36 ID   45 ID   38 ID

Bon Weir
Merryville   XXX   IV

1 CavD   XXX   VIII   XXXX   Third

96   XXX   I   165   Eunice
Armored

69

TEXAS
LOUISIANA

Lake Charles   90

Beaumont   Orange

MAP 3

second nights of the exercise, irrespective of Blue progress. Lear made his decision without benefit of consultation with his G–2 (intelligence officer), who happened to believe that the first delaying position would be safe from any coordinated Blue attack until the third day of the maneuver.[10] As had been the case in Phase 1, General Lear would rely more upon his own detailed planning than on combat intelligence.

General Krueger's Third Army developed a simpler, more flexible plan of operations that greatly resembled its offensive of the first maneuver. Given the task of capturing Shreveport and destroying the Red forces,[11] Krueger ordered a three-corps advance northward between the Red and Sabine Rivers, from the Blue assembly area centered on Eunice directly toward Shreveport.[12] Krueger hoped to fix the Red army with his frontline infantry divisions and then strike with his powerful army reserve, which consisted primarily of I Armored Corps, less the 1st Armored Division. In place of the 1st Armored, I Armored Corps acquired the 2d Infantry Division and enough trucks to make it a provisional motorized division. As its other division the corps retained General Patton's 2d Armored. This experimental corps organization was largely the brainchild of the corps commander, General Scott, who hoped to use the motorized infantry to seize jump-off positions for the armored division to attack through, and to consolidate captured territory.[13] But at the start of the maneuver, I Armored Corps would be in bivouac, where it was to remain until the opportunity for decisive action presented itself.

By midnight of 21 September both armies were within their assembly areas for the upcoming maneuver, separated by a no man's land twenty to thirty miles wide. General Headquarters restricted the Red army to an area north of the line Jasper-Leesville-Colfax and sequestered the Blue troops south of Bon Weir and De Ridder.[14] At the insistence of Army Chief of Staff Marshall, the redisposition of the two armies included complete logistical changes of base. Although he rarely interfered in planning the GHQ maneuvers, General Marshall abruptly overrode the staff officers who objected that the change of base was unnecessary, difficult, and expensive. He pointed out that armies would have to change their bases in a real war, so they would have to do so in Louisiana.[15]

Supply points were repositioned by 23 September, when General Headquarters issued final orders to the Red and Blue commanders. Each was warned that war was imminent, they were reminded of their respective missions, and they were informed that H-hour was set for the following day. "All restrictions on movements and reconnaissance," the orders read, "[are] removed effective 12:00 Noon, 24 September, after which you are authorized [to] take any action consistent with your mission." [16] The GHQ directive to Second Army reinforced General Lear's inclination to avoid battle by promising him that mythical reinforcements would be forthcoming on 30 September, the day after the maneuver was to end.[17] This meant that if the Second Army could simply stave off destruction and keep the invaders out of Shreveport until the end of the exercise, its mission would be fulfilled and the war would, in theory, continue on more equal terms whether or not Second Army had won any battles.

As H-hour drew near, a powerful hurricane threatened to ruin the maneuver before it began. Winds and rain grounded aircraft, flattened camps, and soaked the troops on their way to the restraining lines. Fortunately for the Army, the 100 mile per hour winds that battered Houston that day missed the maneuver area, but poor weather persisted for much of the exercise.[18]

Despite the weather, operations began as scheduled at noon on 24 September. Third Army swarmed north across the restraining line toward Shreveport and the Red enemy. General Krueger sent the 1st Cavalry Division (reinforced) across the Sabine River into Texas to cover his west flank, and on the east ordered the 34th Division over the Red River at Alexandria.[19] In the main battle zone between the rivers, VIII Corps, IV Corps, and V Corps pushed their cavalry reconnaissance regiments and a total of seven square infantry divisions forward: VIII Corps' 36th and 45th Divisions advanced towards Leesville, IV Corps marched the 38th and 31st Divisions onto the southern slopes of Peason Ridge, and V Corps occupied Alexandria and advanced north along the Red River with the 37th and 32d Divisions. The 43d Division and I Armored Corps (2d Division, 2d Armored Division) constituted the Blue reserve.[20]

Later that afternoon, when the Blue troops had crossed no man's land and reached the Red restraining line, instead of finding the main enemy force, they encountered the first of more than 900 demolitions that would frustrate them throughout the maneuver.[21] The Second Army's engineers blew every bridge on the north-south railroads leading toward Shreveport, making it impossible for Third Army to advance its railheads behind the troops and necessitating instead a truck convoy supply system.[22] Red engineers destroyed the Red River bridges in V Corps' path, thus isolating the east bank, and even floated down the Sabine River in suicide squads to blow the bridges at Burr Ferry and Merryville behind the Blue cavalry that had crossed into Texas. Moreover, virtually every bridge and culvert in the main battle zone between the rivers was posted as de-

A Blue machine gun section advances on the enemy in Louisiana.
(Field Artillery Journal.)

stroyed, slowing Third Army's advance to a crawl and causing traffic
jams that persisted throughout the maneuver.[23]

To make the Third Army's advance as difficult as possible, Second Army covered certain key demolitions with special delay task
forces. These units possessed heavy firepower to give the impression of great strength and sufficient transport to avoid being caught
by superior forces. The delay task forces, about six in number, were
essentially motorized battalion combat teams consisting of two rifle
companies reinforced by a heavy weapons company (mortars and
machine guns), a battery of medium artillery, and some antitank
guns.[24] With the aid of Red cavalry detachments, the delay task
forces repeatedly interrupted the attempts of Blue engineers to repair demolitions, forced the Blue troops to deploy for battle, and
then slipped away before they could be pinned down.

In spite of the mud, demolitions, long-range interdiction artillery, and Red task forces, Third Army succeeded in advancing
about twenty miles by nightfall of the first day. Major Blue forces
reached the vicinity of the Second Army's limiting line, but the
main Red body was still thirty miles away and was even then in the
process of withdrawing another fifteen. Under cover of darkness,

General Lear pulled his frontline troops back from the first to the intermediate delay position: the 2d Cavalry Division, protecting the Texas flank; VII Corps' 27th and 35th Divisions in the main battle zone; and the 5th Division, east of the Red River. The 33d Division, in VII Corps reserve, and the 1st and 2d Antitank Groups, in army reserve, withdrew to the second delaying position. Even farther to the rear, the 1st Armored Division and the 6th Division remained in the vicinity of the third delaying position.[25] As they retreated, the Red troops laid more demolitions to frustrate the advance of the Blue army. In the main battle zone, VII Corps engineers set the charges which divisional engineers detonated once all friendly troops had passed.[26] At dawn on 25 September, forty-five miles of muddy roads and hundreds of new demolitions separated the Red and Blue main forces.

The Second Army barely paused on the intermediate delaying position, even though the Blue army was miles away. General Lear's plan called for a withdrawal from the intermediate delaying position on the night of 25–26 September, and around noon on the 25th Second Army issued orders for the front line divisions to occupy the second delaying position while the 33d Division and antitank groups withdrew to the third delaying position.[27] Lear's reluctance to come to grips with the Blue invaders apparently began to evoke some displeasure at GHQ director's headquarters, for General McNair informed Lear that his mythical reinforcements would not be forthcoming on 30 September after all, telling him, in other words, to fight with what he had. Undoubtedly, part of McNair's distress was due to General Marshall's arriving in the maneuver area on 25 September only to find very little of interest going on.[28]

Despite McNair's admonitions, Lear persisted in avoiding battle, trusting instead in demolitions, rain, and delay task forces. Indeed, although the maneuver was tactically uninspired, Lear's plan of operations was succeeding. The Blue forces quickly discovered that repairing a demolition is much more difficult than executing it; moreover, Third Army's engineer units were undermanned, underequipped, and generally unprepared to cope with the scale of demolitions employed by the Red forces. Throughout 25 September the Blue engineers struggled to open routes while traffic backed up behind them, inviting punishing raids from the 2d Air Task Force.[29] By midnight Third Army's main body was still south of the first delaying position, which the Second Army had abandoned the day before.

During the night of 25–26 September, Second Army continued its retreat to the second delaying position and began preparations for a withdrawal to the third on the following night. Early on 26

September, however, as the Red forces settled into the second delaying position, Second Army's G–2 argued that the Red forces should stand where they were for one day before yielding any more ground.[30] Faced with pressure from the director's headquarters and from his own staff, General Lear finally yielded and ordered the Second Army to remain in place until the evening of 27 September.[31] Ironically, for once Lear would have been better served by adhering to his plans, because General Krueger had just committed the Blue armored reserves. With Second Army standing motionless for a day, Third Army gained an ideal opportunity to catch its elusive foe.

On 25 September, General Krueger had ordered a frontal attack by I Armored Corps against the western sector of the Red VII Corps line. That afternoon, the 2d Division (motorized) moved out of bivouac with orders to secure positions north of Leesville through which the 2d Armored Division was to attack the following morning.[32] Before these orders could be executed, however, Second Army had already begun its withdrawal to the second delaying position, some twenty-five miles removed from the scene of the projected attack. In desperation of ever bringing the Red army to battle, General Krueger abandoned the conventional frontal attack and embraced a daring armored operation that would break the maneuver out of its tactical doldrums, if nothing else.

Third Army's new plan, which General Clark of GHQ later credited to Third Army Chief of Staff Eisenhower, consisted of a wide, two-pronged envelopment of the Red west flank.[33] Covered by the 1st Cavalry Division, which was already west of the Sabine, I Armored Corps was to cross into Texas by two columns and sweep north toward Shreveport. One column, consisting primarily of the 2d Armored Division's 41st Infantry Regiment (minus one battalion) and elements of the 82d Reconnaissance Battalion, plus artillery and other wheeled elements of the division, would make a wide circuit through Texas, actually leaving the maneuver area before turning in and attacking Shreveport from the west. The division's 2d Armored Brigade, followed by the 2d Infantry Division (motorized), was to make an inner envelopment that would lead to a recrossing of the Sabine River in the vicinity of Logansport for the purpose of cutting the Red VII Corps' communications with Shreveport.[34] (Map 4)

Blue commanders and staffs hurriedly completed the new plan and issued orders at 1730 on 25 September, by which time the 2d Division (motorized) had already moved out in accordance with the now defunct frontal assault. Quickly diverted, the motorized infantry columns turned away from Leesville and led I Armored

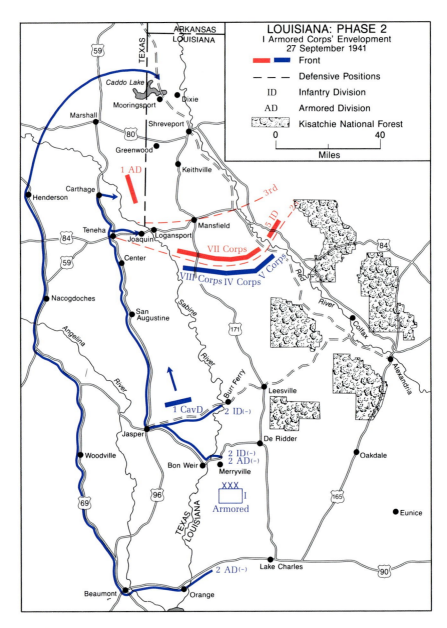

MAP 4

Corps' inner column westward to the Sabine River. At Merryville and Burr Ferry the infantry seized bridgeheads while pontons were laid to replace the highway bridges destroyed by Red forces a day earlier. The Merryville bridge opened around midnight, allowing the tanks of the 2d Armored Brigade to cross around 0200 on 26 September, pass through the infantry bridgeheads, and strike off toward Jasper, Texas. The 2d Division (motorized) then mounted trucks and followed the tanks, except for one regimental combat team that crossed farther north at Burr Ferry.[35]

Sixty miles downstream, 2d Armored Division's ebullient commander, General Patton, led the outer, wheeled, column across the highway bridge at Orange, Texas, about the same time. Delayed only by some demolished bridges (and one bridge that actually collapsed), the outer column raced through Beaumont, Texas, turned north, and by noon on 26 September was near Woodville, approximately seventy miles from its crossing point.[36] The advance nearly stalled at the rain-swollen Angelina River south of Nacogdoches, where the vital highway bridge was posted as destroyed. However, since rising water had covered the simulated charges and since no signs of simulated fuses or other preparations were visible, an umpire accompanying the Blue column conveniently declared the bridge to be improperly demolished and allowed the armored column to cross.[37] That evening Patton brushed aside some elements of the Red 2d Cavalry Division and 4th Cavalry Regiment (the only Second Army units west of the Sabine River) and continued his relentless advance, not pausing for rest until after midnight. Twenty-four hours of virtually continuous driving had brought the outer column to Henderson, nearly two hundred miles from the Sabine River bridge at Orange.[38]

The inner column also made impressive gains on 26 September but could have made more were it not for a breakdown of radio communications with 2d Armored Division headquarters that left the column increasingly under the direct control of General Scott, I Armored Corps commander. Covered to the east by the 1st Cavalry Division and followed by the regimental combat teams of 2d Division (motorized), the 2d Armored Brigade passed through Jasper by noon, overcame minor Red resistance in the vicinity of San Augustine, and stood poised to attack the important crossroads town of Center in force. Reconnaissance elements had already reached the town, but the Blue armored regiments waited on the road for five hours before receiving from 2d Armored Division the go-ahead for an assault on Center, by which time it was too late in the day to mount the attack.[39] However, General Lear's deci-

The 78th Field Artillery Battalion, 2d Armored Division, on maneuvers. *(Field Artillery Journal.)*

sion to hold the Second Army along the second delaying position until the next evening would grant the Blue columns an extra day to turn the Red flank.

Second Army's ill-advised stand on the second delaying position did not stem from ignorance of the Blue armored envelopment. Throughout the Louisiana maneuvers both Krueger and Lear recognized the possibilities of an end run through Texas, in part because Patton's 2d Armored Division had conducted just such an operation during the Third Army exercises that preceded the GHQ maneuvers.[40] General Lear had kept the threat alive during Phase I when he ordered Magruder's 1st Armored Division to conduct a feint towards Teneha, Texas, on the second day of the maneuvers.[41] So when Red aerial reconnaissance spotted I Armored Corps' columns snaking westward toward the Sabine River on the evening of 25 September, the likelihood of an armored sweep through Texas was obvious. Second Army intelligence correctly deduced that the 2d Armored Division and elements of the 2d Division (motorized) joined the Blue cavalry on the west bank of the Sabine that night, and throughout 26 September Red cavalry and air reconnaissance maintained contact with the armored

columns as they drove deep into Texas.[42] As early as 1300 that afternoon, the G–2 officer from VII Corps warned that "Blue can
employ his armored force on the west flank," with a coordinated
attack possibly coming as early as the morning of 27 September.[43]
But for the failure of 2d Armored Brigade's communications, the
Red intelligence estimate may well have been borne out by events.

In spite of prompt and accurate intelligence, Second Army responded indifferently to the Blue armored envelopment. The Red
2d Cavalry Division and 4th Cavalry Regiment faced the armored
columns alone throughout 26, September, aided only by the 2d Air
Task Force, which flew ninety-two sorties against I Armored Corps
on the day.[44] The situation was ready made for aggressive antitank
operations by Second Army's two mobile antitank groups, but General Lear chose instead to keep both units in reserve, where they
could provide passive defense for Shreveport proper. The 1st Antitank Group moved to Keithville, just south of the city, while the 2d
remained in the vicinity of Mansfield. To cover the western approaches of Shreveport General Lear ordered one reinforced rifle
company, detached from the 6th Division, to occupy Greenwood,
and sent the 1st Armored Division's 6th Infantry Regiment to
cover the Sabine River upstream of Logansport.[45] Aside from this
passive mission assigned to its infantry regiment, 1st Armored Division's sole activity on 26 September was to plan possible attacks
against either the Blue armored column closing from the west or
the main Blue force advancing from the south.[46] But Second Army
gave no orders to execute either operation.

One other Red unit had the potential to strike a telling blow
against the Blue columns that stood poised to take Second Army in
flank—Company A of the 502d Parachute Battalion. Had General
Lear sent the parachutists against a key bridge or road junction
along I Armored Corps' lengthening communication lines, he
might seriously have embarrassed the armored envelopment. Instead, on 26 September he squandered the airborne force on a
raid against Eunice, Louisiana, 100 miles behind Third Army's
main body. The parachutists conducted a well-executed drop and
moved out to capture General Krueger's headquarters, only to dis-
cover that Krueger had moved to Oakdale the day before. The Red
parachutists succeeded in destroying some bridges and fuel dumps
before being rounded up by Blue rear-echelon troops, but otherwise the operation hindered Third Army not at all.[47]

In the absence of any effective countermeasures, on 27 September the Blue I Armored Corps wheeled in on Second Army's western
flank. The inner column, led by the 2d Armored Brigade, captured

Center and Carthage early in the day and then turned toward the
Sabine River. The 2d Division (motorized) passed its regimental combat teams through the tank columns and took the lead in the drive
toward the Sabine fords at Deadwood and Joaquin, near Logansport.
But when the Blue infantry reached the river, they found that rising
floodwaters covered the fords and made the way into Second Army's
rear impassable. Pontons were hurriedly brought up, but a full day
would pass before the bridges could be built and a sizable force
crossed over the Sabine.[48] General Lear's only response to the presence of Blue armor and infantry on the Sabine was to move the 2d
Antitank Group to De Berry, near the potential crossing sites.[49]

To the north, I Armored Corps' outer column closed in on the
enemy without interference from nature. Although the master
plan called for General Patton to attack Shreveport from the west
astride the Marshall-Shreveport highway, he chose not to launch a
frontal attack against the Red forces stationed at Greenwood, especially after they were reinforced by a battalion of the 1st Antitank
Group.[50] Instead, he led his column even farther north in a march
that took it around Caddo Lake and behind Shreveport's defenses.
About noon a Red reconnaissance plane spotted the column advancing on Shreveport from the north and erroneously reported
that Patton's regimental-size force comprised half of the 2d Armored Division.[51] Second Army hurriedly dispatched the 6th Division's antitank battalion into the path of the Blue advance and
later reinforced it with the 1st Antitank Group (less one battalion at
Greenwood).[52] Infantry and reconnaissance elements of the Red antitank units met the Blue column fifteen miles north of Shreveport
and halted it before the gun batteries could be brought to bear. The
day ended with Patton's forces and the Red defenders facing each
other along the line Dixie-Mooringsport. For reasons unknown,
however, Second Army withdrew the much-traveled but unfought
1st Antitank Group that night, sending it to Greenwood, where
there was no Blue threat, and leaving the 6th Antitank Battalion to
face Patton's raiding force alone.[53]

While the I Armored Corps' columns completed their envelopment on 27 September, the rest of Third Army continued its frus-
trating frontal advance between the Sabine and Red Rivers. Demolitions, Red task forces, and the Second Army's air forces were the
only enemies the Blue invaders encountered. The dogged pursuit finally paid off that evening when aggressive Blue reconnaissance
forces pushed aside the Red delaying units and caught up with Second Army's main body as it prepared to evacuate the second delaying position.[54] Second Army's one day of immobility not only al-

A 2d Armored Division half-track ditched during the Louisiana maneuvers. *(Armor magazine.)*

lowed the Blue armored corps to envelop the west flank, it also spelled an end to uncontested Red withdrawals. Throughout the night of 27–28 September, Blue forces pressured the Second Army's frontline divisions during their withdrawal to the third delaying position, prompting General Lear to order the 5th Division (unmolested, east of the Red River) to send its artillery in reinforcement of VII Corps.[55]

On the morning of 28 September, Third Army finally brought the Second Army to bay. When the Red VII Corps tried to pull the 27th Division out of the line and replace it with the 33d Division from corps reserve, advancing Blue troops detected the passage of lines and succeeded in forcing a gap in the Red position. The 36th and 45th Divisions of the Blue VIII Corps drove a bulge into the VII Corps line and captured part of Mansfield, the keystone of the third delaying position. In the ensuing battle for control of the city, major Red and Blue forces came to grips for the first time during the maneuver.[56]

With the bulk of the Third Army pinning Second Army along its front, I Armored Corps continued its attempt to roll up the Red west flank. At Joaquin, a regiment of the 2d Division (motorized) plus elements of the 1st Cavalry Division ferried across the Sabine at the ponton site and prepared a bridgehead for the imminent crossing of the 67th Armored Regiment of the 2d Armored Brigade. Several miles upstream at Deadwood, other elements of the 2d Division crossed by ferry and footbridge while engineers constructed an approach road and a ponton bridge for the 66th and 68th Armored Regiments.[57]

Second Army's response to the crossing of the Sabine along its western flank was piecemeal and ineffective. Under orders from army headquarters, the 81st Reconnaissance Battalion of the 1st Armored Division launched a series of uncoordinated attacks against the Blue bridgeheads and suffered almost 100 percent casualties in an operation that could profitably have been assigned to the entire division.[58] The 1st and 2d Antitank Groups, which remained in the vicinity, were ordered aimlessly about but never fired their guns at the Blue crossing forces.[59]

North of Shreveport, General Patton took advantage of the Second Army's growing embarrassment and attacked vigorously, despite the small size of his immediate command. His 41st Infantry Regiment brushed aside the Red 6th Antitank Battalion, pressed south to Shreveport proper, and established a foothold on the western outskirts of the city. Meanwhile, Company B, 82d Reconnaissance Battalion, ferried the Red River north of the city, swung around Shreveport to the east, and drove unopposed into Barksdale airfield, main base of the 2d Air Task Force. Before the audacious Blue raiders could be rounded up, they succeeded in capturing the airfield operations office, prompting umpires to order the base out of action for the day. To counter Patton, General Lear fragmented the 1st Armored Division even further, sending the 69th Armored Regiment off to protect the northern approaches to the city.[60]

At 1655, with the climactic battle of the exercise under way, GHQ director's headquarters abruptly terminated the second Louisiana maneuver. Although Second Army faced Blue invaders on three fronts, the battle was far from being decided. General Patton's force, virtually isolated from the rest of the Third Army at the end of a 300-mile supply line, held at best a tenuous position on Shreveport's outskirts. (He had sustained his column only by purchasing fuel from commercial dealers along the march route.)[61] At the Sabine River bridgeheads, the Blue armored regiments had not yet crossed in force when the maneuver ended, although several units that failed to receive the recall did cross later that evening.[62] The rest of Third Army was still some twenty-five miles from

Shreveport when General Headquarters terminated the maneuver; moreover, Second Army had the final delaying position to fall back on and the better part of three uncommitted reserve divisions with which to defend the city.

Although partisans of the armor school have since implied that I Armored Corps placed the Red army in an untenable position and thus forced the maneuver's termination, General McNair himself stated that "the war was halted, not by the tactical situation, but by the calendar." The troops of the Second and Third Armies had responded to his satisfaction in both maneuvers, and he believed that a prompt conclusion of the exercise was desirable.[63] Perhaps he also felt that yet another day of operations would not have brought the battle for Shreveport to a decision, whereas continuing the maneuver would have necessitated street fighting in Mansfield and Shreveport on Monday morning, 29 September.

In any event, the 100,000 citizens of Shreveport did not question General McNair's decision to end the battle. They broke out red decorations in honor of the army that had defended them, raised chants of "We're for Lear," and rang church bells to celebrate the deliverance of their city from the Blue invaders.[64] The second maneuver may have been disappointing and its termination premature, but, in conjunction with the first maneuver, it had provided the Army with an abundance of lessons to absorb and interpret.

Notes

1. Comments by Lt. Gen. L. J. McNair, 2d Phase, GHQ-Directed Maneuvers, AG 353 (6–16–45) Sec 1–C, RG 407, Army AG Decimal File 1940–45, NA.

2. Operations Directive 6, Second Army, 20 Sep 41, "Maneuver Report, VII Army Corps," RG 337 57D, HQ AGF, GHQ GS G–3, Subject File 1940–Mar 9, 1942, NA.

3. Memo, L.D.B., 25 Sep 41, Training Div File 1st Phase Critique, RG 337 57D, NA.

4. Lt Gen L. J. McNair to CG, Second Army, 18 Sep 41, 1st and 2d Maneuvers (GHQ) La., RG 337 57D, NA.

5. FO 22, VII Corps, 22 Sep 41, 1st and 2d Maneuvers (GHQ) La., RG 337 57D, NA.

6. Ibid.

7. "Maneuver Report, VII Army Corps," App 3, RG 337 57D, NA.

8. Plans for employment of 1st Armd Div, 2d phase, 24 Sep 41, GHQ La. 1st and 2d Maneuvers Armd Forces, RG 337 57D, NA.

9. Ibid.

10. FO 24, VII Corps, 24 Sep 41, 1st and 2d Maneuvers (GHQ) La., RG 337 57D, NA; "Report on Second and Third Army Maneuvers, 1941," CGSC Library, pp. 9–10.

11. Lt Gen L. J. McNair to CG, Third Army, 18 Sep 41, 1st and 2d Maneuvers (GHQ) La., RG 337 57D, NA.

12. Plan of Third Army, 1st and 2d Maneuvers (GHQ) La., RG 337 57D, NA.

13. Houston, *Hell on Wheels*, p. 80.

14. Roadmap of Louisiana, boundaries and limits drawn in, Maneuvers, First Army, 1941, RG 337 57D, NA.

15. Pogue, *Marshall*, p. 89.

16. GHQ Dir HQ to CG, Second Army, 23 Sep 41; GHQ Dir HQ to CG, Third Army, 23 Sep 41. Both in 1st and 2d Maneuvers (GHQ) La., RG 337 57D, NA.

17. GHQ Dir HQ to CG, Second Army, 23 Sep 41, 1st and 2d Maneuvers (GHQ) La., RG 337 57D, NA.

18. "Storm Increases War Game Risks," *New York Times*, 25 Sep 41; "Hurricane Hits Houston in Twist," *New York Times*, 25 Sep 41.

19. Comments by Brig Gen M. W. Clark, 2d Phase, GHQ-Directed Maneuvers, AG 353 (6–16–45) Sec 1–C, RG 407, NA.

20. Ibid.

21. Ibid.; Comments by Lt Gen L. J. McNair, 2d Phase, GHQ-Directed Maneuvers, AG 353 (6–16–45) Sec l–C, RG 407, NA.

22. Msg, Col Carruthers, Umpire Group, HQ Second Army, 24 Sep 41, GHQ La. 1st and 2d Maneuvers Armd Forces, RG 337 57D, NA; Comments by Brig Gen M. W. Clark, 2d Phase, GHQ-Directed Maneuvers, AG 353 (6–16–45) Sec 1–C, RG 407, NA.

23. Sawbridge to Col Kingman, 24 Sep 41, GHQ La. 1st and 2d Maneuvers AT, RG 337 57D, NA; Comments by Brig Gen M. W. Clark, 2d Phase, GHQ-Directed Maneuvers, AG 353 (6–16–45) Sec 1–C, RG 407, NA.

24. G–3 Rpt 21, VII Corps, 25 Sep 41, "Maneuver Report, VII Army Corps"; FO 22, VII Corps, 22 Sep 41, 1st and 2d Maneuvers (GHQ) La. Both in RG 337 57D, NA.

25. G–3 Rpt 21, VII Corps, 25 Sep 41, "Maneuver Report, VII Army Corps"; AT Groups Attached to Second Army, GHQ La. 1st and 2d Maneuvers AT. Both in RG 337 57D, NA.

26. G–3 Rpt 24, VII Corps, 26 Sep 41, "Maneuver Report, VII Army Corps," RG 337 57D, NA.

27. FO 26, VII Corps, 25 Sep 41, "Maneuver Report, VII Army Corps"; Narrative of Actions, GHQ AT Groups Attached to Second Army, GHQ La. 1st and 2d Maneuvers AT. Both in RG 337 57D, NA.

28. McNair, Director, to CG, Second Army, 25 Sep 41, Maneuvers, First Army, 1941, RG 337 57D, NA. "War Games Over, Blues Near Goal," *New York Times,* 29 Sep 41.

29. Blanche D. Coll, Jean E. Keith, and Herbert H. Rosenthal, *The Corps of Engineers: Troops and Equipment,* U.S. Army in World War II (Washington, D.C.: U.S. Army Center of Military History, Government Printing Office, 1958), p. 130; G–2 Rpt 31, VII Corps, 26 Sep 41, "Maneuver Report, VII Army Corps," RG 337 57D, NA; Jno. A. Smith to Col Kingman, 25 Sep 41, GHQ La. 1st and 2d Maneuvers Armd Forces, RG 337 57D, NA.

30. "Report on Second and Third Army Maneuvers, 1941," CGSC Library, p. 10.

31. FO 26, VII Corps, 27 Sep 41, "Maneuver Report, VII Army Corps," RG 337 57D, NA.

32. "Report of Operations, 2d Armored Division," Annex 9, RG 337 57D, NA.

33. Mark Wayne Clark, *Calculated Risk* (New York: Harper and Bros., 1950), p. 16.

34. Telephone msg, Col Blakeney to G–3 Dir Office, 25 Sep 41; Summary of Orders of CG, I Armd Corps, for Operations 25–26 Sep 41. Both in GHQ La. 1st and 2d Maneuvers Armd Forces, RG 337 57D, NA.

35. Checklist for Armd Divs, 2d Armd Div Phase II; Summary of Orders of CG, I Armd Corps, for Operations 25–26 Sep 41; Telephone msg, Col Kingman to G–3 Dir Office, 26 Sep 41. All in GHQ La. 1st and 2d Maneuvers Armd Forces, RG 337 57D, NA. "Report of Operations, 2d Armored Division," Annex 9, RG 337 57D, NA.

36. Telephone msg, Col E. A. Smith to G–3, Dir HQ, 26 Sep 41, GHQ La. 1st and 2d Maneuvers Armd Forces, RG 337 57D, NA.

37. Statement of Maj Theodore A. Seely, Chief Umpire, 41st Inf Regt; "Message No. 1," 24 Sep 41. Both in GHQ La. 1st and 2d Maneuvers Armd Forces, RG 337 57D, NA. Telephone msg, Col Kingman to G–3 Dir Office, 26 Sep 41, GHQ La. 1st and 2d Maneuvers AT, RG 337 57D, NA.

38. "Report of Operations, 2d Armored Division," Annex 9, RG 337 57D, NA.

39. Summary of Orders of CG, I Armd Corps, for Operations, 25–26 Sep 41; Checklist for Armd Divs, 2d Armd Div Phase II; Col E. A. Smith to Lt Col Kingman, 26 Sep 41; Telephone msg, Col E. A. Smith to G–3 Dir Office, 27 Sep 41. All in GHQ La. 1st and 2d Maneuvers Armd Forces, RG 337 57D, NA. "Report of Operations, 2d Armored Division," Annex 9, RG 337 57D, NA; Comments by Brig Gen M. W. Clark, 2d Phase, GHQ-Directed Maneuvers, AG 353 (6–16–45) Sec 1–C, RG 407, NA.

40. Houston, *Hell on Wheels,* pp. 79–80.

41. Umpire Rpt, 1st Armd Div, 15–16 Sep 41, Matter Reference Revision of Umpire Manual, RG 337 57D, NA.

42. G–2 Rpt 32, VII Corps, 26 Sep 41; G–2 Rpt 33, VII Corps, 27 Sep 41. Both in "Maneuver Report, VII Army Corps," RG 337 57D, NA.

43. G–2 Rpt 32, VII Corps, 26 Sep 41; "Maneuver Report, VII Army Corps," RG 337 57D, NA.

44. "Forces in 'Battle' Near Shreveport," *New York Times,* 28 Sep 41.

45. Operations Directive 8, Second Army, 26 Sep 41, 1st and 2d Maneuvers (GHQ) La.; Narrative of Actions, GHQ AT Groups Attached to Second Army, GHQ La. 1st and 2d Maneuvers AT. Both in RG 337 57D, NA.

46. Operations Directive 8, Second Army, 26 Sep 41, 1st and 2d Maneuvers (GHQ) La.; G–3 Rpt 25, VII Corps, 27 Sep 41, and G–2 Rpt 33, VII Corps, 27 Sep 41, "Maneuver Report, VII Army Corps." All in RG 337 57D, NA.

47. Comments by Brig Gen M. W. Clark, 2d Phase, GHQ-Directed Maneuvers, AG 353 (6–16–45) Sec 1–C, RG 407, NA; "Report on Second and Third Army Maneuvers, 1941," CGSC Library, p. 22.

48. G–2 Rpt 34, VII Corps, 27 Sep 41, "Maneuver Report, VII Army Corps"; Summary of Orders issued by CG, I Armd Corps, for Operations 27 Sep 41, GHQ La. 1st and 2d Maneuvers Armd Forces. Both in RG 337 57D, NA. Comments by Brig Gen M. W. Clark, 2d Phase, GHQ-Directed Maneuvers, AG 353 (6–16–45) Sec 1–C, RG 407, NA.

49. Narrative of Actions, GHQ AT Groups Attached to Second Army, GHQ La. 1st and 2d Maneuvers AT, RG 337 57D, NA.

50. Ibid.; Summary of Orders Issued by CG, I Armd Corps, for Operations 27 Sep 41; Telephone msg, Col E. A. Smith to G–3 Dir Office, 27 Sep 41. All in GHQ La. 1st and 2d Maneuvers Armd Forces, RG 337 57D, NA.

51. Rpt on 2d Phase, 1 and 2 AT Groups, GHQ La. 1st and 2d Maneuvers AT, RG 337 57D, NA.

52. Action of AT Units 6th Div, GHQ La. 1st and 2d Maneuvers AT, RG 337 57D, NA.

53. Narrative of Actions, GHQ AT Groups Attached to Second Army, GHQ La. 1st and 2d Maneuvers AT; "Report of Operations, 2d Armored Division," Annex 9. Both in RG 337 57D, NA.

54. Maj Maurice J. Fitzgerald to AT Dir, GHQ Dir HQ, 29 Sep 41, GHQ La. 1st and 2d Maneuvers AT; G–2 Rpt 34, VII Corps, 27 Sep 41, and G–2 Rpt 35, VII Corps, 28 Sep 41; "Maneuver Report, VII Army Corps." All in RG 337 57D, NA.

55. FO 26, VII Corps, 27 Sep 41, "Maneuver Report, VII Army Corps," RG 337 57D, NA.

56. Smith, "AGF Study No. 17," p. 21.

57. Sketch of 2d Armd Div dispositions on 28 Sep 41; Telephone msg, Col E. A. Smith to G–3 Dir Office, 28 Sep 41. Both in GHQ La. 1st and 2d Maneuvers Armd Forces, RG 337 57D, NA. "Report of Operations, 2d Armored Division," Annex 9, RG 337 57D, NA; Rpt on AT Activity, 9 Oct 41, GHQ La. 1st and 2d Maneuvers AT, RG 337 57D, NA.

58. AT Action, 29 Sep 41, GHQ La. 1st and 2d Maneuvers AT, RG 337 57D, NA.

59. Narrative of Actions, GHQ AT Groups Attached to Second Army, GHQ La. 1st and 2d Maneuvers AT; G–3 Rpt 8, VII Corps, 28 Sep 41, "Maneuver Report, VII Army Corps." Both in RG 337 57D, NA.

60. Action of AT Units, 6th Div, GHQ La. 1st and 2d Maneuvers AT; Telephone msg, Col E. A. Smith to G–3, Dir Office, 28 Sep 41, GHQ La. 1st and 2d Maneuvers Armd Forces; Rpt on 2d Phase, GHQ Maneuvers, 29 Sep 41, GHQ La. 1st and 2d Maneuvers Armd Forces; "Report of Operations, 2d Armored Division," Annex 9. All in RG 337 57D, NA.

61. Houston, *Hell on Wheels*, p. 88.

62. "Report of Operations, 2d Armored Division," Annex 9, RG 337 57D, NA.

63. Comments by Lt Gen L. J. McNair, 2d Phase, GHQ-Directed Maneuvers, AG 353 (6–16–45) Sec 1–C, RG 407, NA.

64. "Battle of Shreveport," *Time*, 6 Oct 41, pp. 42–44; Newspaper clippings, GHQ-Directed Army Maneuvers, Maneuver Memo, RG 337 57, HQ AGF, GHQ, NA.

CHAPTER 7

October Interlude

The Army was quick to act upon the experiences gained in Louisiana. General McNair's critique of the second maneuver indicated that there had been fewer faults than in the first but that most deficiencies were repeated. "Nor was it to be expected otherwise," he said, "for faults are not remedied overnight."[1] Within the month General Headquarters devised a program of training intended to remedy the problems uncovered in the GHQ maneuvers. But even before remedial training went into effect, the Army moved to rectify deficient leadership. General McNair blamed inadequate troop training on the lack of discipline, which he in turn attributed to poor officer leadership. "A commander who cannot develop proper discipline must be replaced," he warned. "I feel emphatically that leadership and command can and must be improved— and I refer to no particular echelon."[2] With the close of the Louisiana maneuvers, rumors circulated to the effect that the Army intended to replace fully 30 percent of its commanding officers.

While not denying that wide-ranging officer "reclassifications" were imminent, Secretary of War Henry L. Stimson asked reporters to tone down their references to "purging" the officer corps: "If you write a lot of stories about purging officers, that is not good for the morale either of officers or men."[3] General McNair added his own qualified disclaimer at the Phase 2 critique: "So far as I know, no drastic purge of weak leaders is contemplated, although the issue undoubtedly has been clarified in many cases by performance during these maneuvers."[4]

An officer purge of sorts did, however, occur in the interval between the Louisiana and Carolinas maneuvers. On 29 September, one day after the second Louisiana exercise ended, General Marshall wrote to the commanding generals of each field army urging them to reexamine officer fitness in their commands.[5] And on 7 October General McNair sent Marshall a list of all division commanders in the Army, with a brief recommendation on the fitness of each to retain his command.[6] At about the same time, the removal board (or plucking board, as it was known to the press) began secret deliberations in Washington, D.C., to pass judgment on Regular officers who had been recommended for retirement by their superiors. With these developments the Army's housecleaning got under way, and although the purge affected hundreds of Regular, National Guard, and Reserve officers, the casualty rate amounted to less than 1 percent of the total officer corps.[7]

The higher ranks were not exempt from scrutiny. Many of the Army's corps and division commanders were men of considerable talent and administrative proficiency whose age and lack of experience in handling troops limited their effectiveness. General Marshall made it clear that these caretakers would give way to younger officers once the latter had acquired experience in staff positions and lower-level commands.[8]

Marshall believed that the caretakers should remain in place until their units had completed maneuvers but that afterwards they could be replaced with a minimum of disruption. Although winning or losing maneuvers should have had little to do with the replacement of caretakers, all three of the Second Army's National Guard division commanders were eventually struck down. The first casualty was Maj. Gen. Ralph E. Truman of Missouri, whose 35th Division spent most of the Louisiana maneuvers in a reserve role. General Lear, the army commander, reassigned the 61-year-old Truman to an administrative post immediately after the maneuvers, and within a week General McNair had secured his replacement, 53-year-old Maj. Gen. William H. Simpson, a Regular Army officer. Four months later, Truman retired from federal duty altogether.[9]

The next Second Army general to depart, Maj. Gen. William N. Haskell of the New York National Guard, did not wait to be relieved. Although his long-suffering 27th Division had performed creditably in Louisiana, Haskell at age sixty-three was already one year over the age-in-grade limit for division commanders. His military capabilities were not of the highest order, and McNair felt that Haskell "should go for more than age."[10] On 29 September, the day after the Louisiana maneuvers ended, Haskell voluntarily announced his retirement, effective 1 November. His replacement as commander was Brig. Gen. Ralph N. Pennell of the Regular Army.[11] At age fifty-nine, Pennell would himself give way to a younger man within the year.

The third of the Guard commanders in the Second Army, Maj. Gen. Samuel T. Lawton of the Illinois National Guard, was rated as "dubious" on McNair's list of generals even though his 33d Division had committed no conspicuous blunders in Louisiana. Lawton actually retained command for another seven months, but the search for his replacement began in October.[12]

In the Third Army, where three of the eight National Guard divisions were already commanded by Regulars, the purge of the caretakers centered on IV Corps, which was scheduled to face First Army in the November Carolinas maneuvers. Maj. Gen. Jay L. Benedict, the corps commander, gave way to Maj. Gen. Oscar W. Griswold in mid-October. Griswold elevated the 31st Division's commander, Maj. Gen. John C. Persons, to the post of assistant corps commander. The 43d Division, which like the 31st would accompany the corps to the Carolinas, had not been conspicuous in Louisiana. Maj. Gen. Morris Payne of the Connecticut National Guard turned the division over to Maj. Gen. John H. Hester, Regular Army, on 8 October and retired from federal service on 31 October.[13]

Reassignments and removals after the maneuvers extended to officers of all ranks, not just commanding generals. Here again, National Guard divisions just returned from Louisiana seemed to bear the brunt of the purge. Maj. Gen. Robert S. Beightler of Ohio, one of the few Guard commanders to win a favorable rating from General McNair, announced the removal of 119 officers from the 37th Division soon after the Louisiana maneuvers. The 38th Division, commanded by Maj. Gen. Daniel Sultan, Regular Army, established its own reclassification board to cleanse the rolls of over-age and incompetent officers.[14]

The ruthless removal of so many Guard officers, many of whom had nurtured their units through long, difficult times, touched off an outcry from Guardsmen and civilians who viewed the purge as a War Department plot to eliminate Guard officers altogether in favor of Regulars. The October purge, together with pre-maneuvers removals, left only twelve of the eighteen Guard divisions under Guard commanders and also resulted in the infiltration of more Regulars into the lower ranks. Even though General Marshall went to great lengths to secure promotions from within Guard units and ordered that extraordinary care be taken to choose outstanding Regulars when no Guardsmen were eligible, the suspicion grew nonetheless that the Army operated from ulterior motives.[15] The loudest, but not the most justified, outcry came from Senator Bennett Champ Clark of Missouri when he learned of General Truman's reassignment. (The general's cousin happened to be the junior senator from Missouri, Harry S. Truman.) Clark accused General Lear of making General Truman the scapegoat for Lear's own tactical blunders in Louisiana and publicly asserted that it was Lear who should retire from the Army.[16]

Clark could have pointed out that the only division in Lear's army to suffer a conspicuous and total reverse was the 6th, a Regular (but raw) unit under a Regular commander, Maj. Gen. Clarence S. Ridley. In the first phase at Louisiana, the 6th Division was roughly handled in its unsuccessful defense of Natchitoches and had to be taken out of the line. During Phase 2 the division never left army reserve, except for one rifle company and the division antitank battalion. Perhaps because the division was filled with virtually untrained recruits, General Ridley escaped censure and even earned a mildly favorable comment from General McNair: "apparently coming along well; hardly at his peak yet."[17]

The painful process of purging the officer corps carried with it the more pleasant task of identifying young officers of demonstrated ability. Among those considered for higher command in October, but not elevated at that time, was Brig. Gen. Ira T. Wyche, who had commanded the 1st Antitank Group in Louisiana. Another was the Third Army chief of staff, Dwight D. Eisenhower, who received his brigadier general's star just as the maneuvers ended.[18]

While the Army wrestled with leadership issues in the wake of the Louisiana maneuvers, it also reassessed its force structuring and tactical doctrines. In general, and particularly among the traditional arms, the maneuvers confirmed the soundness of existing practice. Infantry observers reconfirmed their satisfaction with the triangular division and their preference for the triangular over the square division.[19] Marshall and McNair discussed various methods of "triangularizing" the National Guard divisions, such as splitting some into two, detaching excess troops for overseas duty, or simply leaving each division with an extra regimental combat team. Although the War Department publicly denied any intention of restructuring the Guard divisions, Marshall and McNair agreed that the conversion "should proceed as expeditiously as is practicable."[20]

Within the Cavalry branch there was also satisfaction with the maneuvers experience and with the use of the mixed horse portee–mechanized cavalry regiment as a corps reconnaissance element. An observer from the Command and General Staff School reported that the mixed regiment functioned best when the horse squadron provided a base of fire while the mechanized squadron served as the maneuver force.[21] But another officer, Capt. (later General) Bruce Palmer, Jr., who actually served with the 6th Cavalry Regiment in Louisiana, found that regimental headquarters tended to assume direct control of the mechanized squadron and ignore the horse elements.[22] In any event, the chief of the Cavalry chose to perceive the Louisiana experience as a reprieve for his branch from threatened extinction.[23]

Even field artillerymen spoke well of the maneuvers. In previous field exercises, the lack of an artillery umpiring system had prevented that arm from playing much of a role in battle. But in the Louisiana maneuvers special artillery umpires had at least attempted to impose realistic effects from artillery fire. Out of some 2,600 fires executed in the Louisiana exercises, umpires marked 95 percent of the areas where shells would have fallen.[24] Even though higher commanders had often tended to disperse their artillery, and unit umpires on the receiving end frequently overlooked artillery casualties, the artillerymen still felt that in Louisiana they had been part of the game and had performed to satisfaction.[25]

Ground umpires in Louisiana found losses from air attack even easier to ignore than those from artillery fire, but the Army Air Forces' first maneuver in conjunction with ground forces was considered a success nonetheless. On the first of his two visits to the maneuvers, General Marshall gained the impression that the 2d Air Task Force was acting less as an air support unit than as an independent air force, but General Lear, Second Army's commander, felt otherwise. The press quoted him as saying, "I got everything I asked for from the aviation." [26] General McNair assured Marshall that there was "not the slightest suggestion of an independent air force" and that air support of ground operations had been "surprisingly effective." [27] The air officers who agreed that Louisiana had been a success included General Arnold, the chief of the Army Air Forces. He reported that the air support command concept (on which the air task forces had been patterned) was sound, although details remained to be worked out.[28] To the air service, Louisiana validated the principle of concentrating aviation under one air commander, both because it prevented ground officers from misusing combat aviation and because it provided a flexibility and economy of force not possible if air units were tied down to specific corps and divisions.[29]

In addition to warming the Army Air Forces to the idea of ground support, the maneuvers helped persuade reluctant ground officers that air support had much to offer to the ground battle. Even if umpires neglected to impose the proper casualties for air attacks, commanders could not help but notice the attack aircraft swooping back and forth along their columns. To bring the lesson home with live ammunition, General McNair had arranged a bombing demonstration at Barksdale airfield prior to the second Louisiana maneuver. Forty-five aircraft, including heavy bombers,

medium bombers, dive bombers, and strafing fighter aircraft, demolished a target area that included both wood targets and obsolete armored vehicles before a crowd of 4,000 officers.[30] By the
time the Louisiana maneuvers ended, air officers reported an increasing tendency on the part of ground officers to utilize aviation
to the fullest.[31]

This is not to say that the Louisiana maneuvers ushered in a
golden era of air-ground understanding. Air officers were most interested in close support missions (later termed interdiction) of
their own choosing within a broad mission set by the ground commander, and they continued to shy away from direct support of
frontline forces. Problems uncovered in earlier tests reappeared in
Louisiana and, although they were detected anew, continued to
defy solution. The fundamental roadblock to effective direct air
support in Louisiana was the time-consuming practice of channel-
ing ground requests through air task force headquarters. In the 2d
Air Task Force, an average time of over one hour and twenty minutes elapsed between initiation of a request and the arrival of support aircraft at the target.[32] The request process was awkward but
had the advantage of allowing the air task force to devote a majority of sorties to the interdiction missions that it considered to be
most remunerative and kept aircraft away from dangerous frontline ground fire because all but the most vital direct-support requests were screened out.

In those cases where direct-support requests won approval from
the air task force, supporting aircraft arrived at the target area with
no means of talking to the ground unit being supported, or even of
communicating with the corps air support demand unit that had
forwarded the request. Airmen found that ground-based radio sets
were "completely unsatisfactory"[33] and that the radios in some aircraft were little better.[34] Ground units had no prescribed method of
revealing their positions to friendly aircraft or of directing planes
towards the intended target. Unfortunately, the maneuvers produced few suggestions on how such problems could be solved.[35]
The absence of communication between air and ground at the
front, in conjunction with limited fuel capacities in aircraft, fear of
hostile aviation, and Army Air Forces reticence, precluded the possibility of keeping planes airborne over the battlefield where they
could have responded immediately to ground requests.[36]

In spite of all these unsolved problems, the air support experiment in Louisiana had been an unprecedented success. The
Army's first test of large-scale armored operations there, however,
had not. Unfavorable terrain, inclement weather, and underuti-

lization by higher headquarters hobbled the armored forces. Such factors were beyond the Armored Force's control, but armor officers recognized that a serious internal problem had also contributed to the disappointments in Louisiana—the baffling inability of the armored divisions to bring their enormous power to bear on the battlefield. As General Patton described the problem to the officers of 2d Armored Division, "We still fail to use every weapon every time. . . . Each time we fight with only one weapon when we could use several weapons, we are not winning a battle, we are making fools of ourselves." [37] Patton was not alone in his analysis of armor's problems, for the most common criticism of armored operations in Louisiana to appear in GHQ director's headquarters reports was armor's failure to combine tank operations with supporting infantry and artillery action. [38]

General Devers, the new head of the Armored Force, attributed part of the problem to undertrained officers and poor staff work, but a great deal of the difficulty seemed to reside in the armored division's table of organization. [39] In Louisiana, the armored division had operated as if it were a collection of single-arm regiments rather than a combined-arms team. With the exception of the division commander himself, there existed no command link joining the armored brigade with the infantry regiment or the reconnaissance battalion. Since the armored brigade was the division's major striking force, the division commander tended either to turn the bulk of the division over to his armored brigade commander, as Patton did in Phase 2, or demote the brigade commander to control of one regimental column, as both Patton and Magruder did in the first phase. In the latter case, the tank regiments, infantry regiments, and reconnaissance battalion all went about their separate missions with nobody below the division commander possessed of the authority to coordinate their activities.

This organizational defect translated into bad tactics in Louisiana. Since regimental commanders had no direct tie-in with reconnaissance elements, armored columns repeatedly ran head-on into prepared enemy defenses without the knowledge of enemy dispositions that would have allowed the tanks to maneuver around and attack from the rear, as recommended by armored doctrine. With only a two-battalion infantry regiment in the division, and that often unavailable, tank commanders found themselves attacking positions that would have fallen easily to foot soldiers. Lacking a clear command link between tank and infantry elements, foot troops were not always employed even when they were available. As a result, a few defenders could stop entire armored columns in their tracks by tying down the leading tanks with a few antitank guns, secure in the knowledge that neither infantry, artillery, nor flanking action from another column was likely to be brought to bear against them.

A new divisional organization already under study would replace the single-arm regiments with combined-arms teams, but the Armored Force needed more immediate help if the mistakes of Louisiana were not to be repeated in the Carolinas maneuvers. On 8 November, General Scott, I Armored Corps commander, sent to his division commanders a memo outlining the tactical mistakes committed in Louisiana and presenting new methods of offensive operations designed to avoid them. Rather than sending armored columns blindly down the road with tanks leading, in future maneuvers the division commanders were to keep their tank elements in concealed bivouacks while infantry and reconnaissance screens swept the zone of advance up to a specified phase line. Only when reconnaissance had secured routes free of defenses and demolitions would the tanks make their advance to the phase line, where they would enter a new bivouac while the reconnaissance elements swept the next zone.[40]

Under this procedure, reinforced reconnaissance forces, and not tank elements, would be the first to encounter the enemy. Scott ordered his division commanders to allow each column some discretion in choosing its route of advance so that columns could attack weak spots in the enemy's line, as developed by reconnaissance, rather than batter head-on against prepared defenses. Furthermore, the divisions were to take more care in tailoring the composition of their columns to reflect the type of enemy opposition expected so that the appropriate elements would not be stuck at the rear of a column when their presence was required in front. Scott specifically ordered that tanks should not be committed to the attack until the other arms had provided proper support, "utilizing all available means" to facilitate the armored thrust.[41]

The aim of Scott's reforms for the Carolinas maneuvers was to bring all of the armored division's elements into play so that armor could conduct the type of decisive operations denied it in Louisiana. As he reminded Patton and Magruder, "The mission of armored units should be to advance rapidly to critical locations in rear of the hostile front lines from which they can act to disrupt the enemy system of supply, communication, and command, and to assist in his complete destruction. In this advance, the attack and destruction of forward elements are merely incidental."[42]

General Scott based his reform measures on observations of antitank practices in Louisiana, confident that no major alteration in antitank doctrine would occur before the Carolinas maneuvers. He was not mistaken, for there was no rethinking of antitank doctrine in light of the Louisiana experience. The perceived antitank victory over armor in Louisiana, and the absence of an antitank branch to initiate reforms, contributed to complacency. General McNair could have been the instigator of reform, but he remained convinced that mobile, aggressive antitank warfare, as embodied in the three GHQ antitank groups, constituted the appropriate antidote to blitzkrieg operations.

The source of McNair's confidence is not clear, for the Louisiana maneuvers revealed that virtually nobody but McNair believed in or practiced the aggressive antitank concept. General McNair's own son, who served a GHQ director's headquarters liaison officer at the maneuvers, noted as much in his written report: "I still have seen no indication of offensive action for the three [antitank] groups. I am afraid that the commanders of the groups and the higher commanders (corps and division) are not convinced that they can be employed in this manner." [43] Another liaison officer, Lt. Col. Ben M. Sawbridge, who accompanied the antitank groups in Louisiana, was even more outspoken:

> . . . offensive action of guns alone against armored forces would be possible only in rare instances and then only in the event of a criminal blunder on the part of the hostile armored force commander. Offensive action against armored elements by an AT Gp. will be possible only if the AT Gp. is provided with forces of a nature adequate to break thru security screens and hold off infantry elements while the guns get in their work. So we come back to a task force and I believe that such a force is necessary if the spirit of the GHQ directive as to offensive action is to be carried out.

In place of the existing group of three antitank battalions, Sawbridge proposed a task force which would include infantry, engineers, motorized reconnaissance elements, light tanks, and self-propelled antitank cannon. This organization, he felt, could operate as a viable offensive unit. [44]

The higher commanders in Louisiana, not understanding or believing McNair's antitank doctrine, had relied on their provisional divisional antitank battalions for defense against armored attacks and got good service from them. Not knowing what, then, to do with the mobile antitank groups, the commanding generals simply left them in reserve. During Phase 1 in Louisiana, General Krueger's Third Army controlled all three groups throughout the five-day maneuver, three days of which saw extensive hostile armored activity. Yet Krueger succeeded in engaging but one of the groups, the 1st, at the battle for Mount Carmel on 18 September, in what was a passive, defensive antitank effort. In Phase 2 Krueger had the 3d Antitank Group; lacking an army mission for the group, he attached it to VIII Corps, which in turn attached it to 45th Division. This division broke up the group into battalions for static missions. Throughout the maneuver the 3d Antitank Group was forced to draw its supplies from a railhead over 100 miles distant because none of its host units knew how it fit into their system of supply.[45]

General Lear of the Second Army, who acquired the 1st and 2d Antitank Groups in Phase 2 did no better with them. As if mesmerized by I Armored Corps' envelopment of his west flank, Lear continually shifted the groups about, but not once did they fire their guns at enemy armor. The 1st Group occupied 6 positions and traveled a total of 122 miles; the 2d manned 5 positions and logged 110 fruitless miles.[46]

But to judge by subsequent events, one might believe that the antitank groups had dominated the Louisiana maneuvers, for the McNair antitank philosophy was rapidly becoming an article of faith in the Army. In October, an Army demonstration staged at Fort Belvoir, Virginia, for a group of dignitaries that included Vice President Henry A. Wallace, Secretary of War Stimson, several congressmen, and a party of foreign military attaches concluded with a small-scale rehearsed battle in which every type of unit—ground, air, and airborne—took part. Of all the possible scenarios to follow, the Army chose mobile antitank weapons to deliver the decisive blow that destroyed the enemy and won the day.[47] McNair's antitank philosophy enjoyed its first vindication, but a script had been necessary to ensure satisfactory results.

Among those not infected by antitank enthusiasm were the officers of the Armored Force, who still resented the facility with which antitank guns had been allowed to dispatch tanks in the maneuvers. The Armored Force chief, General Devers, went public with doubts about the entire antitank concept in a speech to a group of civilian industry representatives. He stated categorically that the only defense against tanks was to have more tanks.[48] But Devers could do little to stem the growth of an antitank doctrine that enjoyed the support of both Marshall and McNair. When the preparations for the Carolinas maneuvers began, the three antitank groups traveled to the new maneuver area and joined with the First Army. They were augmented with additional equipment, especially radios and scout cars, and underwent additional training, but otherwise their composition and tactical doctrine were essentially unchanged.[49]

Lt. Gen. Hugh A. Drum, commander of the First Army, was delighted to obtain the antitank groups. Drum, no advocate of armored warfare, believed wholeheartedly in the antitank concept. The Army's senior field commander, this 62-year-old general had achieved his greatest fame in 1918, when, as First Army chief of staff, he planned the AEF's maiden offensive against the St. Mihiel salient. Drum never discarded the World War I mentality and even in 1941 preferred slow, methodical infantry-artillery operations to the bold cut and thrust of the blitzkrieg. He was one of the few generals to advocate the retention of square divisions, on the grounds that the triangular division lacked staying power in sustained combat.[50] Drum had no intention of letting armor dominate the Carolinas exercises: his determination to make the antitank concept work was exceeded only by his determination to win the maneuvers.

To stop I Armored Corps' two armored divisions, which would go to his opponent, General Drum counted on the 4,321 guns of First Army capable of antitank action, 764 of which were organized into six regimental-size antitank units.[51] Three of these latter were the Louisiana veteran antitank groups provided by the Army, which Drum redesignated GHQ–X, Y, and Z. Built around three antitank battalions each (except GHQ–X, which had two), the groups also included an infantry company apiece plus other supporting and reconnaissance troops.[52] In addition, Drum created three similar units of his own, which he called TA (for tank attacker) 1, 2, and 3. TA–1 included the provisional 93d Tank Destroyer Battalion, which was equipped with the first makeshift self-propelled antitank guns—75-mm. field pieces mounted on the beds of standard M3 halftracks. TA–1 also boasted a motorized infantry battalion, a conventional antitank company, and a company of light tanks. (Chart 6) TA–2 consisted of three antitank battalions and a tank company. TA–3 was solely an artillery force.[53]

The mission assigned to TA–3 was the semifixed defense of rear-area installations, but General Drum gave TA–1 and TA–2 a mission that paraphrased McNair's antitank philosophy: "The action of the detachment[s] will always be offensive, moving to meet hostile threats and to destroy hostile forces before they can have decisive effect on the Army's operations."[54]

General Drum's antitank preparations received an unexpected assist a few days before the maneuvers began when General McNair issued a maneuver memorandum that granted infantry troops the capability of knocking out tanks by hitting them with simulated hand grenades in the form of small bags of flour. General Scott protested immediately that the new rule was grossly unrealistic: "If hand grenades would destroy tanks we would quit building them." He warned McNair that more fights between

CHART 6—TANK ATTACKER DETACHMENT 1, CAROLINAS MANEUVERS, 1941

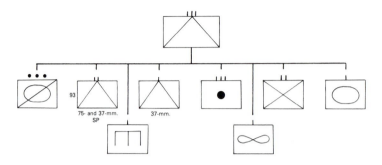

tankers and infantry would result, and that in any event the new rule contradicted the *Umpire Manual,* which stated explicitly that all infantry within 100 yards of a hostile tank were neutralized and unable to take action of any kind.[55] General Scott's protests were futile, and the flour bag rule stood, much to the disgust of the armored soldiers and to the benefit of General Drum. With flour bags, and with the six special antitank units (which, in contrast to Krueger and Lear, he was determined to utilize), Drum could reasonably hope to negate the enemy's two armored divisions and then crush him decisively with the straightforward, carefully orchestrated infantry-artillery battle that Drum knew best.

For a general who thought so little of mechanization and mobile warfare (he even broke up and cannibalized First Army's cavalry regiments), General Drum was surprisingly mindful of the possibilities of air operations.[56] While an instructor at Fort Leavenworth in 1923 he had written a treatise on dive bombing,[57] and ten years later he chaired a board that recommended making the air service an autonomous branch of the Army.[58] In the first Carolinas maneuver, First Army's air arm, the 1st Air Support Command, would consist of the 6th Pursuit Wing (six Army squadrons reinforced by one Marine squadron) and the 3d Bombardment Group (three squadrons of light bombers plus one Navy dive-bomber squadron).[59] The 1st Air Support Command, however, lacked the medium bombers necessary to conduct the full range of air operations.[60]

Drum was also alive to the potential of airborne troops, which would be represented in the Carolinas by the 502d Parachute Battalion under GHQ control. General Headquarters would provide each side in turn with the use of the battalion; so, in preparation for those times when the parachutists would be under enemy colors, General Drum created a special antiairborne task force to protect the First Army's rear areas. Designated AB–1, the force included a cavalry platoon, elements of an infantry regiment, and a field artillery battalion. AB–1's mission was to move rapidly to the scene of a hostile airborne assault and destroy the parachute force on the ground.[61]

General Drum's opponent in the Carolinas maneuvers, Maj. Gen. Oscar W. Griswold, commanded a radically different force and held an attitude toward warfare diametrically opposed to that of General Drum. Griswold's IV Corps, an army in all but name, numbered 100,000 to First Army's 195,000. Whereas Drum's First Army consisted of three corps, five square and three triangular divisions, plus one antiairborne and six antitank units, Griswold commanded only two square divisions, the I Armored Corps with its two armored divisions, and a division unique in the Army—the 4th Motorized Division. The 4th was designed specifically for large-scale armored operations and had trained in conjunction with the 2d Armored Division at Fort Benning earlier that year. It possessed two fully motorized infantry regiments, a mechanized regiment, and enough trucks to move the entire division without shuttling. Although the motorized division could not remedy the shortage of infantry in the armored divisions, it could, as the 2d Division had done in Louisiana, fix the enemy for armored attacks, exploit advantages won by the armored divisions, and, most importantly, consolidate gains, thus freeing the armored forces to continue their attack into the enemy's rear.[62] Before he took command of IV Corps, General Griswold had led the 4th Motorized Division, so although he was new to high command, he boasted no little experience as commander of a mobile force.

Even more so than the first phase in Louisiana, then, the Carolinas maneuvers would be a test of mechanized mobility against numerical superiority. General Griswold's IV Corps represented the greatest collection of mechanized units in Army history, and to augment its mobility even further, the General Staff instituted an experimental reorganization of IV Corps' two cavalry regiments, the 107th and the 6th, both of which were veterans of Louisiana. The 107th traded its mechanized squadron for the 6th's horse-portee squadron, making it all horse and the 6th all mechanized. The reorganization elicited a protest from General Herr, the Cavalry branch chief, who claimed that the men and animals of the horse squadrons involved were unfit for such an experiment. The matter found its way to the desk of General Marshall, who assumed that Herr was more upset about not being consulted in the matter than he was about the reorganization itself, whereupon he dismissed Herr's objections.[63]

Aside from its greater mobility, IV Corps' only advantage over the First Army would be in the air. Griswold's air arm, the 3d Air Support Command, consisted of the 2d Pursuit Wing (one Marine and six Army pursuit squadrons) and the 10th Bombardment Wing (one Navy and seven Army bomb squadrons), which together with noncombat planes totaled 366 aircraft to 1st Air Support Command's 320.[64] To speed up the reaction time for ground requests, 3d Air Support Command designated one of its three bombardment groups as the combat air support unit. This group assumed all of the direct frontline support functions and handled requests without referring to command headquarters, thus eliminating one link in the communications chain and freeing the rest of the command for other operations.[65]

In one intangible but potentially decisive area General Drum possessed an advantage that, together with First Army's numbers, compensated for IV Corps' superior air power and mobility—command experience. Griswold was seven years younger than Drum and had been a major general only since July, whereas Drum's lieutenant generalcy, and his command of First Army, dated from 1939. Griswold took over IV Corps just one month before the Carolinas maneuvers began. He had to learn the art of high command and assemble his force at the same time. He admitted his handicap freely: "My experience has been limited in the field of high command and I really feel like a gawky high school boy who suddenly finds himself on a college campus."[66] By contrast, Drum's command was a familiar one, leaving nothing to distract him from his maneuvers preparations.

Throughout September and October, the two forces gathered in the maneuver area. First Army's units arrived first, after conducting record-setting motor convoy movements, and on 6 October First Army embarked upon preliminary corps and army training. Division-versus-division and corps-versus-corps exercises continued into November. The IV Corps, with two of the three divisions it had employed in Louisiana, traveled to the maneuver area, where it was joined by the 4th Motorized Division for preliminary training exercises. On 2 November, I Armored Corps arrived with the 1st and 2d Armored Divisions for the final corps and army exercises.[67]

On 9 November General McNair established director's headquarters in Monroe, North Carolina, and prepared to receive the dignitaries who came to observe the exercises. The secretary of war, three senators, twenty-two members of the House of Representatives, and foreign attaches from Britain, Canada, the Soviet Union, and Latin America accepted invitations.[68] With the cast of characters fully assembled, First Army and IV Corps concluded their preliminary maneuvers, and GHQ director's headquarters made it known that the Carolinas army-versus-army maneuvers would begin on 16 November.[69]

Meanwhile, during the interlude between the Louisiana and Carolinas maneuvers, the Army's preparation for war took on an urgency it had not known since the dark summer of 1940. In Russia, the rains and mud of autumn had already begun to slow the German drive on Moscow, but the world nonetheless expected any day to hear that the city had fallen. A militant government gained power in Tokyo, threatening the United States in the Pacific, and in the Atlantic U-boats had just claimed their latest American victim, the U.S. Navy destroyer *Reuben James*. Congress was debating the repeal of neutrality and considered arming American merchant ships in the Atlantic. According to a Gallup poll released in early October, American voters of every geographic section and of both parties supported President Roosevelt's order for U.S. warships to shoot German U-boats on sight.[70] When the Carolinas maneuvers began, war seemed not only likely but, to many, inevitable. Even so, no American could know that the Carolinas maneuvers would be the Army's last peacetime training exercise.

Notes

1. Comments by Lt Gen L. J. McNair, 2d Phase, GHQ-Directed Maneuvers, AG 353 (6–16–45) Sec 1–C, RG 407, Army AG Decimal File 1940–45, NA.

2. Ibid.

3. "The Ax Falls," *Time*, 20 Oct 41, pp. 35–36; "Nation Requires Army Big As Now," *New York Times*, 2 Oct 41.

4. Comments by Lt Gen L. J. McNair, 2d Phase, GHQ-Directed Maneuvers, AG 353 (6–16–45) Sec 1–C, RG 407, NA.

5. Watson, *Chief of Staff*, p. 243.

6. Memo, CofS GHQ for Gen Marshall, 7 Oct 41, sub: High Commanders, Box 76, Folder 31, Corresp, GCM Library.

7. Watson, *Chief of Staff*, pp. 243–46.

8. Marshall, *Papers 2*, pp. 631–32 (Marshall to Maj Gen Walter K. Wilson, 7 Oct 41), p. 562n.

9. "General Lear Accused," *New York Times*, 16 Oct 41; U.S. National Guard Bureau, *Official National Guard Register* (Washington, D.C.: Government Printing Office, 1943), p. 1183; Memo, CofS GHQ for Gen Marshall, 10 Oct 41, sub: High Commanders, Box 76, Folder 31, Corresp, GCM Library.

10. Memo, CofS GHQ for Gen Marshall, 7 Oct 41, sub: High Commanders, Box 76, Folder 31, Corresp, GCM Library.

11. "Gen. Pennell Made Head of 27th," *New York Times*, 6 Nov 41.

12. Memo, CofS GHQ for Gen Marshall, 7 Oct 41, sub: High Commanders, Box 76, Folder 31, Corresp, GCM Library.

13. Ibid.; "Operations of Age Rule Starts Reshaping of Army Divisions," *New York Times*, 11 Oct 41; *National Guard Register* (1943), p. 911.

14. "Cross Sections of Army Life and Training," *New York Times*, 4 Oct 41.

15. Watson, *Chief of Staff*, p. 260; Memo, ACofS for AG, 22 Sep 41, Microfilm Reel 14, Item 484, GCM Library.

16. "General Lear Accused," *New York Times*, 16 Oct 41.

17. Memo, CofS GHQ for Gen Marshall, 7 Oct 41, sub: High Commanders, Box 76, Folder 31, Corresp, GCM Library.

18. Ibid.

19. Conclusions, G–3, "Maneuver Report, VII Army Corps," RG 337 57D, HQ AGF, GHQ GS G–3, Subject File 1940–Mar 9, 1942, NA.

20. "McNair Praises Antitank Work," *New York Times*, 25 Nov 41; Conference in Office of CofS, 7 Oct 41, Microfilm Reel 287, Item 4327, GCM Library; Memo, CofS for ACofS G–3, 6 Oct 41, Box 65, Folder 54, Directives, G–3 1941–42, GCM Library.

21. "Report on Second and Third Army Maneuvers, 1941," CGSC Library, p. 18.

22. Bruce Palmer, Jr., Oral History, pp. 26–27, MHI Research Collection.

23. Herr and Wallace, *Cavalry*, p. 251.

24. "Artillery Fire Marking During Second-Third Army Maneuvers," *Field Artillery Journal*, Nov 41, pp. 900–901; Memo, Chief of Field Artillery for CofS, 6 Oct 41, 354.2 Rpts, 1941, RG 337 57, HQ AGF, GHQ, NA.

25. Ibid.

26. "War Games Over, Blues Near Goal," *New York Times*, 29 Sep 41; Marshall to Gen Lesley J. McNair, 20 Sep 41, Box 76, Folder 31, Corresp, GCM Library.

27. Memo, Lt Gen L. J. McNair for Gen Marshall, 24 Sep 41, Box 76, Folder 31, Corresp, GCM Library.

28. Memo, Maj Gen H. H. Arnold for CofS, 8 Oct 41, RG 337 57, NA.

29. "Report on 2d Air Task Force Participation in Louisiana Maneuvers," Sec II, pp. 2–3, 353/2 Air Forces, RG 337 57, NA.

30. "Bombers Thrill War Games Troops," *New York Times*, 23 Sep 41; "Object Lesson," *Time*, 6 Oct 41, p. 48.

31. "Reports on Employment of Aviation in Close Support of Ground Troops [3d ATF]," 30 Sep 41, p. 3, 353/28 Air Ground, RG 337 57, NA.

32. "Report on 2d Air Task Force Participation in Louisiana Maneuvers," Sec II, pp. 22–23, 353/2 Air Forces, RG 337 57, NA.

33. "Reports on Employment of Aviation in Close Support of Ground Troops [3d ATF]," 30 Sep 41, p. 2, 353/28 Air Ground, RG 337 57, NA.

34. "Report on 2d Air Task Force Participation in Louisiana Maneuvers," Sec II, p. 38, 353/2 Air Forces, RG 337 57, NA.

35. "Final Report on Employment of Aviation in Close Support of Ground Troops," 9 Jan 42, p. 2, 353/28 Air Ground, RG 337 57, NA.

36. "Report on 2d Air Task Force Participation in Louisiana Maneuvers," Sec II, p. 29, 353/2 Air Forces, RG 337 57, NA.

37. Martin Blumenson, ed., *The Patton Papers 1940–1945* (Boston: Houghton Mifflin, 1974), p. 43.

38. See rpts in GHQ La. 1st and 2d Maneuvers Armd Forces, RG 337 57D, NA.

39. Houston, *Hell on Wheels*, p. 88.

40. Maj Gen C. L. Scott to CG, 1st Armd Div, 8 Nov 41; Unsigned note, 24 Nov 41. Both in Training Memoranda, Performance of AT, RG 337 57D, NA.

41. Maj Gen C. L. Scott to CG, 1st Armd Div, 8 Nov 41, Training Memoranda, Performance of AT, RG 337 57D, NA.

42. Ibid.

43. Checklist on AT Units, 3d AT Group, 2d Phase, GHQ La. 1st and 2d Maneuvers AT, RG 337 57D, NA.

44. Rpt on 2d Phase, 1st and 2d AT Groups, GHQ La. 1st and 2d Maneuvers AT, RG 337 57D, NA.

45. Data on Movements 1st AT Group, 2d Phase; Data on Movements 2d AT Group, 2d Phase; Rpt on 2d Phase, 3d AT Group. All in GHQ La. 1st and 2d Maneuvers AT, RG 337 57D, NA.

46. Ibid.

47. "Panzers Crushed in an Army Show," *New York Times*, 3 Oct 41.

48. "Answer to Tanks Held More Tanks," *New York Times*, 21 Oct 41.

49. Brig Gen M. W. Clark to CG, Third Army, 25 Sep 41, Tab 27, Current Maneuver File, RG 337 57D, NA.

50. "First Army Maneuvers 1940, Final Report," RG 337 57D, NA; Jean R. Moenk, *A History of Large Scale Army Maneuvers in the United States* (Ft. Monroe, Va.: HQ, USCAC, 1969), p. 25.

51. Critique by Lt Gen L. J. McNair, 1st Phase, "General Clark's Personal Copy, First Army vs. IV Corps Maneuvers, November 15–30, 1941," (hereafter cited as "Clark's Copy"), RG 337 57D, NA.

52. Maneuver Memo 49, First Army, 31 Oct 41, "First Army Maneuvers 1941, Final Report," RG 337 57D, NA.

53. Ibid.

54. Ibid.

55. Maj Gen C. L. Scott to Lt Gen L. J. McNair, 12 Nov 41, Training Div File 1st Phase Critique, RG 337 57D, NA.

56. Memo, Lt Col W. B. Augur for G–3, 22 Nov 41, Training Div File 1st Phase Critique, RG 337 57D, NA.

57. "General Drum," *Life,* 16 Jun 41, pp. 84–96.

58. Russell F. Weigley, *History of the United States Army* (New York: Macmillan, 1967), p. 413.

59. Aviation in GHQ-Directed Maneuvers, 17 Nov 41, Training Div File 1st Phase Critique; Ltr of Instructions 1, GHQ, 14 Oct 41, "First Army Maneuvers 1941, Final Report." Both in RG 337 57D, NA.

60. Comments by Lt Gen H. A. Drum [Phase I critique], "Clark's Copy," RG 337 57D, NA.

61. Maneuver Memo 49, First Army, 31 Oct 41, "First Army Maneuvers 1941, Final Report," RG 337 57D, NA.

62. "The New Motorized Division," *Field Artillery Journal,* Oct 41, pp. 715–23; "Infantry of Future?" *Newsweek,* 17 Nov 41, pp. 39–40.

63. Memo, CofS for ACofS G–3, 8 Oct 41, Box 65, Folder 38, Directives Deputy CofS, 10–12/41, GCM Library.

64. Aviation in GHQ-Directed Maneuvers, 17 Nov 41, Training Div File 1st Phase Critique; Lt Gen L. J. McNair to CG, IV Army Corps, 14 Oct 41, "Clark's Copy." Both in RG 337 57D, NA.

65. "Final Report on Employment of Aviation in Close Support of Ground Troops," 9 Jan 42, p. 3, 353/28 Air Ground, RG 337 57, NA.

66. Critique on 1st Phase, GHQ Carolinas Maneuvers, Gen Griswold, "Clark's Copy," RG 337 57D, NA.

67. "Drum Says Force America's Need," *New York Times,* 4 Oct 41; "A Halt for Action by U.S. Motorcycle Troops," *New York Times,* 3 Nov 41.

68. See 353 5–15–41, Sec 1–A, RG 407, NA.

69. Ltr of Instructions 1, GHQ, 14 Oct 41, "First Army Maneuvers 1941, Final Report," RG 337 57D, NA.

70. "62% Favor Shoot-At-Sight Policy," *New York Times,* 3 Oct 41.

CHAPTER 8

Carolinas Phase 1
The Battle of the Pee Dee River

GHQ director's headquarters crafted the first Carolinas maneuver so as to produce a head-on encounter battle between two very different military forces. Drum's First Army, representing the Blue nation, was a traditional infantry-oriented force with a traditionally minded commander. General Headquarters instructed Drum to assemble his army of three corps, eight infantry divisions, and six regimental-size antitank groups in an area centered on Hoffman, North Carolina, twenty miles east of the Pee Dee River. Seventy-five miles and two rivers to the west, Griswold assembled his reinforced IV Corps, the Red army, on the west bank of the Catawba-Wateree River. Griswold's command included two infantry divisions, one motorized division, and the two armored divisions of I Armored Corps.[1]

General McNair, acting once more as maneuvers director, gave both armies offensive missions designed to produce a collision in the region between the Catawba and Pee Dee Rivers. He instructed Drum to cross the Pee Dee River (the designated international boundary between the Red and Blue states), advance westward into Red territory, and prevent the Red army from crossing the Catawba River in force.[2] To Griswold, McNair gave the mission of crossing the Catawba, marching east to the Pee Dee, and preventing a Blue invasion of the Red nation.[3]

Two days before the maneuver began, General Headquarters issued final orders to the army commanders elaborating on earlier instructions and refining the manner in which the initial encounter between the two forces would occur. To give IV Corps an opportunity to exploit its mobility and initiate combat before the larger Blue army could cross in overwhelming force, the new orders gave Griswold permission to begin crossing the Catawba River at 0630 on 16 November, one hour before the First Army was authorized to cross the Pee Dee. On the other hand, General Headquarters prohibited all air-ground attacks until 0800, thus affording the First Army a thirty-minute grace period in which to initiate river-crossing operations before the superior Red air force would be allowed to interfere.[4]

Not surprisingly, the two commanders planned for very different battles. In First Army Field Order No. 1, issued on 14 November, General Drum outlined in great detail the methodical, conventional manner in which he intended to crush the Red opponent. First Army would cross the Pee Dee on a seventy-mile front, three corps abreast, with cavalry reconnaissance units in the lead, followed by special brigade-size crossing detachments. While the crossing detachments established corps bridgeheads, engineers were to begin building ponton bridges in the expectation that the highway spans over the Pee Dee would come under concentrated Red air attack. Engineers were also instructed to blow every bridge over the Pee Dee and its tributaries for hundreds of miles on either side of the maneuver area to forestall any wide flanking operations by the Red armor.[5]

Once his army had successfully negotiated the river barrier, Drum's field order called for a methodical general advance within prearranged zones to a first objective line roughly halfway between the Pee Dee and Monroe, North Carolina, and then to a second objective line running through Monroe itself. Drum's intention was to neutralize the Red armor with First Army's six special antitank units and thus gain freedom for his eight infantry divisions to grapple with and grind down IV Corps' two. From the outset, special efforts would be made to turn IV Corps' north flank and envelop the Red army with overwhelming strength.[6] In sum, Field Order No. 1 constituted a throwback to the art of war as practiced in 1918. (Map 5)

General Drum's determination to win the maneuver at all costs was evident not only in the great detail with which he planned his battle but also in the infractions of GHQ rules that First Army committed even before the maneuver began. According to the original GHQ directive, First Army was to be within its concentration area, ten to fifteen miles east of the Pee Dee, by dark on 15 November. First Army was permitted to conduct reconnaissance up to the river.[7] Drum, however, positioned his brigade-size crossing forces directly on the riverbank and then endeavored to conceal this infraction from General Headquarters. When GHQ discovered these troops outside the concentration area, General McNair ordered them back. McNair also discovered that some of First Army's signal troops had taken the farsighted but illegal precaution of laying telephone lines across the Pee Dee for use during and after the crossings. One of the illegal circuits actually ran into a private home and tied into the Wadesboro telephone exchange.[8]

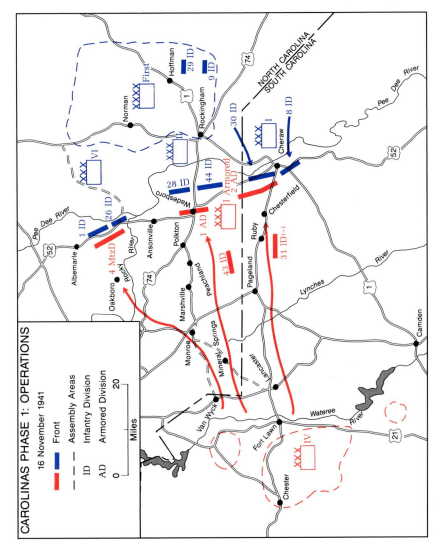

CAROLINAS PHASE 1: OPERATIONS

16 November 1941

Front

Assembly Areas

ID   Infantry Division

AD   Armored Division

0   20

Miles

MAP 5

Given First Army's preponderance of strength (195,000 men to IV Corps' 100,000), it is curious that General Drum should have felt compelled to violate GHQ instructions so flagrantly. Realistically, of the two commanding generals, Griswold would have been much more justified in breaking the rules. With only two infantry divisions to the enemy's eight, Griswold would be almost entirely dependent on the mobility and firepower of the two Red armored divisions and one motorized division. As Griswold saw it, IV Corps' only chance to prevail would be to force the Blue army off balance at the outset and keep it off balance, retaining the initiative with speed of maneuver and use of interior lines, and avoiding a positional wrestling match with the slower but larger foe.[9]

To establish the climate of mobile warfare, Griswold planned to open the battle by crossing the Catawba with his three mobile divisions abreast and then sending them on a race to the Pee Dee frontier to contain the Blue bridgeheads as quickly as possible. Following more slowly, IV Corps' two infantry divisions were to secure the vital road center of Monroe and then take over the containment of the Blue bridgeheads from the mobile divisions, freeing the latter to concentrate and attack decisively in any direction.[10] Griswold's air arm, the 3d Air Support Command, was to keep the Blue bridgeheads from building up faster than the Red forces containing them. Griswold directed his air commander, Col. Asa N. Duncan, to exploit the Red superiority in medium bombers by destroying the Pee Dee bridges and keeping them destroyed.[11]

This contest between the swift and the strong commenced at 0630 on 16 November. The IV Corps began crossing the Catawba River with the 4th Motorized Division on the north flank, the 1st Armored in the center, and the 2d Armored on the southern wing. Given an hour's head start, Red reconnaissance units raced to within a few miles of the Pee Dee before encountering Blue crossing forces. One element of the 82d Reconnaissance Battalion, 2d Armored Division, actually worked its way across the river into Blue territory, where it had the good fortune to stumble upon General Drum himself, who was inspecting the First Army crossing operations. The armored soldiers succeeded in capturing the general but soon released him. According to some accounts, Drum managed to talk his captors into releasing him; according to others, umpires ordered his release on the grounds that the reconnaissance party would be unable to remove the general to the west bank.[12]

Aside from his temporary incarceration, General Drum's river crossing proceeded according to plan. In the thirty-minute grace period between H-hour and the release of ground attack aircraft, all three First Army corps successfully moved their reconnaissance elements to the west bank.[13] Promptly at 0800, however, the Red 3d Air Support Command launched the first of twenty-three raids against the Pee Dee bridges. Flying in at low level and accepting the resultant heavy casualties (sixty-six Red aircraft ruled out for the day),[14] the Red bombers struck all six spans and put them off limits for two to four hours. Aircraft returned throughout the day to keep the spans closed.[15]

Undaunted by the loss of its highway bridges, the First Army proceeded to move its crossing detachments to the west bank in assault boats, improvised ferries, footbridges, and, later in the day, two ponton bridges. The crossing of VI Corps on the northern wing was the most successful. The VI Corps, commanded by Maj. Gen. Karl Truesdell, passed elements of the 26th Division and GHQ–Y (Drum's designation for the 2d Antitank Group) to the west bank of the Pee Dee in the vicinity of Norman, North Carolina. These Blue invaders pushed back elements of the Red 4th Motorized Division and established a secure bridgehead by nightfall, prompting General Drum to release the 1st Division from army reserve for use by VI Corps. Drum also moved TA–1 (one of First Army's three home-grown antitank groups) to the VI Corps zone on the east bank.[16]

To the south of VI Corps, Maj. Gen. Lloyd R. Fredendall's II Corps made less headway. The northern of the corps' two divisions, the 28th, crossed without incident. The 44th Division in the south of the corps zone, unaware that the crossings were unopposed, fired off an artillery preparation before crossing, wasting considerable ammunition and delaying operations by ten precious minutes.[17] When the barrage subsided, the corps reconnaissance units in 44th Division's zone raced across the highway bridge toward Wadesboro but advanced less than ten miles before encountering and recoiling from elements of the 81st Reconnaissance Battalion, 1st Armored Division.[18] The buildup of Red armored strength in its front prevented II Corps from greatly extending its bridgehead for the rest of the day.

Red armored forces also contained the bridgehead of First Army's southern wing. The I Corps, commanded by Maj. Gen. Charles F. Thompson, passed elements of the 30th and 8th Divisions, reinforced by GHQ–Z, to the west bank in the vicinity of Cheraw. The 30th Division's lead elements pressed only five miles inland before being attacked and driven back by tanks of the 2d Armored Division.[19] General Drum rushed TA–2 to the east bank of the Pee Dee across from Cheraw in case the Red tanks should break through to the bridge.[20]

Although Red forces had contained two corps bridgeheads out of three by the afternoon of 16 November, IV Corps' mobile units were in no position to concentrate for a decisive stroke. In the sixty-mile dash from the Catawba to the Pee Dee they had lost their coherence and arrived at the battle zone in fragments, making it impossible for the Red commanders to launch coordinated attacks against the slowly growing Blue bridgeheads. Nor could the mobile divisions withdraw and regroup, for IV Corps' two infantry divisions were still far to the rear. By utilizing all three mobile divisions to develop and contain the enemy crossings, General Griswold left himself with no unengaged units to effect a concentration of force. Instead, the motorized and armored divisions were tied down in piecemeal defensive operations along sixty miles of front for the remainder of the day.

By the next morning IV Corps' two infantry divisions had come up to assist in the chore of containing the bridgeheads. The 43d Division attached itself to the 1st Armored Division in the center of the Red line, and the 62d Brigade Combat Team from the 31st Division came under the control of the 2d Armored Division in the south. (The remainder of the 31st entered IV Corps reserve.) [21] Under cover of darkness, however, the First Army had taken advantage of the freedom from aerial intervention and crossed the remaining combat elements of all three corps to the west bank, with the exception of some field artillery units. Daybreak on 17 November revealed six complete Blue divisions west of the Pee Dee—VI Corps' 1st and 26th in the north, II Corps' 28th and 44th in the center, and I Corps' 30th and 8th in the south.[22] Each corps also controlled one of the GHQ antitank groups, and First Army still held reserves consisting of the three tank attacker units and two more divisions, the 9th and 29th, on the east bank. With daylight the Red 3d Air Support Command resumed its bridge attacks, but strong Blue forces on both banks reduced bombing efficiency and increased Red losses from antiaircraft fire; umpires ruled out 115 Red aircraft for the day.[23]

The river obstacle behind him, General Drum ordered his Blue army to proceed with the general offensive beginning at 0630. The attack quickly bore fruit on the northern wing, where General Truesdell's VI Corps advanced two divisions abreast against the 4th Motorized Division and the 6th Cavalry Regiment. By late afternoon the Blue 1st and 26th Divisions had pivoted toward the south, bending the Red line back at right angles and linking up with the Blue II Corps to the southeast. Reinforcing success, General Drum sent the 29th Division to VI Corps later in the day but instructed

Truesdell not to commit it to the line without permission from First Army.[24] Prompt commitment of the 29th might have broken the Red line entirely, for the overmatched 4th Motorized was fighting a battle it was ill prepared to wage—a stubborn but fragile delaying action. By nightfall the 4th had retreated across the Rocky River and thus gained a brief reprieve behind that obstacle.[25]

The 4th Motorized Division's lonely stand enabled General Griswold to concentrate forces in the center and south, where solid Red counterattacks jarred the Blue invaders and restricted their progress. When II Corps, in the center of the Blue line, pushed columns toward Wadesboro, they collided with strong elements of General Magruder's 1st Armored Division and the attached 43d Infantry Division. Red tanks overran one column of the Blue 44th Division east of Wadesboro and drove the survivors back toward the river.[26] To the north of town, the Blue 191st Tank Battalion encountered the 13th Armored Regiment of the 1st Armored Division and lost nine tanks in the engagement. Hours later, the 13th was still on hand when the 191st Battalion spearheaded another attack with the result that sixteen more Blue tanks were ruled out in tank-versus-tank combat.[27]

Farther south, it was the reinforced Red 2d Armored Division that forestalled the Blue advance. Bolstered by the 62d Brigade and the 107th Cavalry Regiment, General Patton's tanks repeatedly but unsuccessfully assaulted the town of Cheraw throughout most of the morning. Patton's tankers first launched a series of regimental-size attacks that broke up against positional antitank defenses in what must have seemed like a replay of the battle of Mount Carmel. The Blue defenders, GHQ–Z and the 30th Division, blocked every road into Cheraw with antitank positions and held the town itself in strength. Around noon Patton finally pulled his forces back and organized a coordinated attack, using every available tank and full artillery support. About 1500 a force of twelve medium tanks assaulted Cheraw from the north along the Wadesboro-Cheraw highway to fix the Blue defenses. The tanks were halted by twelve antitank guns, but meanwhile another force of thirty-three tanks and twelve scout cars slipped around the antitank position and, traveling overland, reached Cheraw at a spot where only three antitank guns were deployed. The Red tanks overran the Blue defenses and roared into town.[28]

Pandemonium broke out in Cheraw with the sudden arrival of Red armor. While the Red force battled with twenty-four antitank and antiaircraft guns in the city streets, tank and antitank umpires argued over who controlled the town. Finally a major from GHQ di-

rector's headquarters rushed to the scene and declared that the victory belonged to the Red tanks. He instructed the Blue defenders of
Cheraw, which included Maj. Gen. Henry Russell's 30th Division
command post, to evacuate the town, only to find that the bridges
across the Pee Dee River had been destroyed. Another intervention
from General Headquarters was required before the bridges were
reopened and the vanquished Blue defenders withdrawn.[29]

The 2d Armored Division's costly victory at Cheraw (176 tanks
were ruled out) broke the Blue line and isolated the bulk of the
30th and 8th Divisions from the rest of First Army. But no sooner
had General Patton claimed his prize than he was ordered to relin-
quish it, for General Griswold had decided that the time had come
to concentrate his armored divisions and bring their mobility into
play. The 1st and 2d Armored having stabilized the Red line and
blunted the Blue offensive in the center and the south, Griswold
ordered Patton to turn his sector over to the 62d Brigade and retire after dark toward Pageland for redeployment in the north. Magruder's 1st Armored gave its frontage to the 43d Division and
moved to assembly positions near Marshville.[30]

With the presence of the First Army west of the Pee Dee established, General Griswold turned to a strategy of interior lines to
preserve IV Corps' position. The Blue II and I Corps had been
stunned into virtual immobility on 17 November. Griswold hoped
that the armored divisions could deal similarly with VI Corps in the
north before the other two Blue corps recovered. The imper-
turbable General Drum, however, refused to cooperate. He had his
center and southern corps moving again at dawn on 18 November.
With no armored division to interfere, II Corps pressed its 28th Division into Polkton and the 44th through Wadesboro against stubborn resistance from the Red 43d Division. In the south, I Corps
threw the Red 62d Brigade out of Cheraw at dawn, and elements of
the 30th Division marched into Chesterfield that afternoon. The
restored Blue line resembled a gigantic 7 with the base at Chesterfield and the tip at Fairview, near Charlotte.[31]

The northern front was relatively stable on 18 November,
largely due to the efforts of the 1st Armored Division. Early that
morning the Blue 1st and 26th Divisions had renewed their punish-
ment of the overmatched 4th Motorized, driving the Red division
back from the Rocky River and threatening the defenders with envelopment.[32] At 0700 General Magruder received orders to take his
division from the assembly area near Marshville and attack the Blue
VI Corps in flank and rear.[33] Magruder hastily organized the 1st Armored into three columns and led them north to the attack.

Two of the three columns struck the Blue VI Corps head-on and ground to a halt. One, comprising the 13th Armored Regiment, ran into the 26th Antitank Battalion near Oakboro, where it was stopped and eventually surrounded. The second, led by the division's 6th Infantry Regiment, stalled at the Rocky River when the infantrymen tried to storm the bridge without dismounting from their halftracks. But Magruder's third column, consisting of the 1st Armored Regiment, found the western anchor of VI Corps' line and passed by cleanly. At nightfall, the regiment was deep in the Blue rear near Albemarle, where it bivouacked for the night without having lost a single tank.[34] (Map 6)

The division's reserve unit, the 69th Armored Regiment, followed the 1st Armored Regiment to Albemarle that night but found that the flank route was already closing. Without infantry to keep the roads free from Blue patrols, the Red tanks had no secure communication line to IV Corps. Furthermore, the division was so dispersed by nightfall, and radio communications so inadequate, that General Magruder found it impossible to coordinate his scattered units.[35]

General Drum leapt at the opportunity to turn his prize antitank forces loose upon the distressed 1st Armored Division. When he learned of the 1st's attack, he released TA–1 to VI Corps control and sent it west of the Pee Dee. After dark, TA–1 and VI Corps' GHQ–Y attempted to coordinate an attack against the 1st Armored Regiment's bivouac near Albemarle. En route to the rendezvous, however, GHQ–Y stumbled upon a company-size detachment of the armored division's 81st Reconnaissance Battalion encamped near Oakboro. The Blue antitank group encircled that bivouac instead and, finding the outposts asleep, sent a 60-man raiding party charging in the camp. Umpires ruled out one-third of the 160 men, 8 tanks, and 9 halftracks of the reconnaissance company, but GHQ–Y missed the rendezvous with TA–1 at Albemarle.[36]

The 1st Armored Regiment prepared to leave the Albemarle bivouac about 0630 on 19 November with orders to strike south toward Ansonville and Wadesboro. At the same moment the commander of TA–1, Col. John T. Kennedy, tired of waiting for GHQ–Y and decided to attack the armored camp alone. The two forces collided in a desperate battle that cost the 1st Armored approximately fifty tanks, not to mention numerous real casualties resulting from acid-smoke bottles and flour-bag grenades reinforced with rocks.[37] Despite its total lack of infantry, the 1st Armored Regiment fought its way through TA–1 and drove thirty miles directly across the VI Corps rear to the town of Ansonville. When the 1st Armored Division headquarters and the 69th Armored Regiment tried to follow

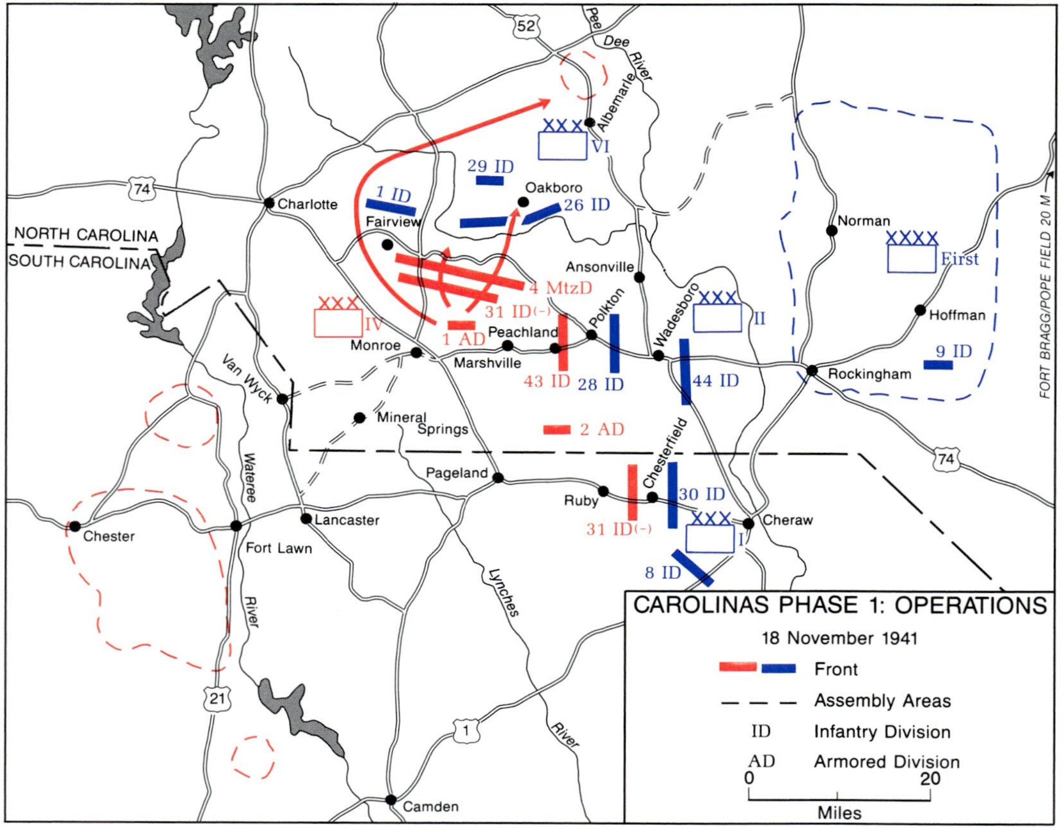
CAROLINAS PHASE 1: OPERATIONS
18 November 1941
Front
Assembly Areas
ID Infantry Division
AD Armored Division
0
20
Miles
NORTH CAROLINA
SOUTH CAROLINA
Charlotte
Fairview
Oakboro
Albemarle
Pee Dee River
Ansonville
Wadesboro
Polkton
Peachland
Marshville
Monroe
Van Wyck
Mineral Springs
Pageland
Ruby
Chesterfield
Cheraw
Lancaster
Fort Lawn
Chester
Camden
Norman
Hoffman
Rockingham
Wateree River
Lynches River
FORT BRAGG/POPE FIELD 20 M
74
52
21
1
1 ID
29 ID
26 ID
VI
4 MtzD
31 ID(-)
1 AD
IV
43 ID
28 ID
44 ID
II
2 AD
30 ID
31 ID(-)
I
8 ID
First
9 ID

MAP 6

the 1st Armored Regiment, they ran into a thoroughly aroused antitank defense that included not only TA–1, but GHQ–Y and elements of the 29th Division as well. Also devoid of infantry, the 69th lost nineteen tanks and was driven well north of Albemarle and cut off from all friendly forces.[38]

The third tank regiment of the 1st Armored Division, the 13th, tried to fight its way east from Oakboro to link up with the 1st Armored Regiment for a thrust on Wadesboro, but the Blue troops encircling it were too stubborn. When darkness halted its struggles, the 13th had lost eighty-four tanks and was still six miles from its rendezvous.[39]

General McNair understated the case when he said that the affairs of 19 November left the 1st Armored Division in "a very unfavorable position."[40] The GHQ observer attached to the division, Lt. Col. Robert W. Hasbrouck (wartime commander of the 7th Armored Division), commented, "I should say that Div. commander had lost control of his division on Wednesday 19 November."[41]

The IV Corps' hopes for transforming the 1st Armored Division's predicament into a victory on 19 November rode on the success of a 2d Armored Division–4th Motorized Division thrust toward Wadesboro that was designed to pierce the Blue center and rescue Magruder's scattered armored elements.[42] The 4th, on the left of the attack, made some initial progress, but the 2d Armored, supporting it to the south, ran into an impervious antitank defense in the Ruby-Chesterfield area. After wasting most of the day in piecemeal attacks against their old foe GHQ–Z, which Drum quickly reinforced with TA–2, the 2d Armored Division pulled out of the battle and swung farther north to attack closer to the 4th.[43] The new attack went in about 1445 and met with some success (scattered Red units apparently reached Wadesboro), but darkness halted the battle with the 2d Armored Division still twenty miles from the 1st.[44] Meanwhile, the First Army continued to grind forward, with VI Corps advancing two to five miles despite the hostile armored elements in its rear, and II Corps' 28th Division reaching Peachland, only fifteen miles from Monroe.[45]

Curiously, the quietest of the three Blue corps on 19 November was I Corps on the southern end of the line. The I Corps troops made little progress, even after the 2d Armored Division withdrew from their sector, leaving only weak cavalry forces to hold the Red line.[46] Despite I Corps' timidity, General Griswold realized that a determined Blue thrust against his southern flank could easily envelop it, just as VI Corps had turned the Red north wing. Consequently, when darkness fell IV Corps instructed the 2d Armored Division to break off the Wadesboro operations and return to the bivouac area near Pageland, where it would be available to shore up the southern end of the line.[47]

The most spectacular Red operation of the day had even less impact on the battle than the attack of the mobile divisions and, in fact, took place more than fifty miles to the east. At 0818 fourteen Red dive bombers, seventeen horizontal bombers, and forty-six pursuit planes attacked the 1st Air Support Command air base at Pope Field, on the grounds of Fort Bragg. Moments later 394 soldiers, 36 officers, and 9 umpires of the 502d Parachute Battalion jumped from 36 transports in a perfectly planned and executed surprise attack. The parachutists had orders to secure the field in preparation for the landing of another 400 men of an airborne (i.e., air-transported) infantry battalion on loan from the 2d Division. Although the Blue defenders were surprised, Pope Field had planned for just such a contingency, and soon the base was swarming with 600 to 700 defenders who theoretically eliminated the Red parachutists. Even though the parachutists failed to secure the field, GHQ officials decided to allow the airborne battalion to make its landing for the sake of the training experience it would afford and for the elucidation of assorted high-ranking observers who had collected for the show. The parachute-airborne attack made no contribution to the Red cause except for closing Pope Field to Blue aircraft for a few hours.[48]

The Reds could have used some help of a more practical nature, for by nightfall on 19 November IV Corps was in deep trouble. The 1st Armored Division was still marooned behind an advancing enemy, despite the best efforts of Griswold's two most powerful remaining formations to relieve it. General Griswold felt unable to commit the 2d Armored Division to a more prolonged relief attempt for fear that once he committed the 2d elsewhere, Blue would crush IV Corps' south flank. No reserves remained to the Red commander, whereas Drum's First Army boasted two uncommitted divisions. Adding to Griswold's burden was the knowledge that the 3d Air Support Command had been theoretically destroyed that day: umpires assessed the loss of 314 Red aircraft, 254 to antiaircraft fire, out of a possible 366.[49] Staff work at Red headquarters degenerated as the crisis deepened. The IV Corps did not issue its orders for 20 November until 2300 on the 19th, too late for subordinate units to do their own reconnaissance and staff work effectively.[50]

On 20 November, the disintegration of the Red force accelerated. The day opened inauspiciously for IV Corps with the destruction of one of the 1st Armored Division's marooned regiments. At 0615 the 69th Armored Regiment and division headquarters, bivouacked

Antiaircraft sound-detection and searchlight equipment on maneuvers. *(Courtesy of the Dwight D. Eisenhower Library.)*

north of Albemarle, were preparing to launch another breakout attempt toward the south when Blue antitank forces closed in for the kill. TA–1 led the attack, three battalion combat teams abreast, with GHQ–Y supporting on the left. When the Red tanks tried to fight their way through, they found every route blocked, and soon the entire armored encampment was surrounded. The Blue troops wheeled their antitank guns right up to the camp perimeter. The 69th had no infantry with which to interfere. Then TA–1's 93d Tank Destroyer Battalion drove its experimental self-propelled weapons (75-mm. guns mounted on halftracks) directly into the Red bivouac. The 69th Armored Regiment disintegrated completely. General Magruder abandoned the decimated force and flew out in a liaison plane to rejoin the remnants of his division around Ansonville. As an officer with TA–1 later remarked, "It was something new to armored forces to be opposed by troops which would carry the fight to them." [51]

When General Magruder arrived at Ansonville, he found the 1st Armored Regiment there subsisting on captured gasoline and supplies and preparing to mount another attack toward Wadesboro for an anticipated linkup with Patton's 2d Armored Division. The futility of the operation quickly became apparent. Instead, I Armored Corps ordered Magruder to bring the 1st and 13th Armored Regiments directly toward Red lines.[52] Magruder complied, and by the time darkness fell, the surviving remnants of the 1st Armored

Division had reached the area of Marshville, whence they had launched their attack three days earlier. But Marshville was already in Blue hands, and the division was still well behind enemy lines.[53]

By any reasonable standard the 1st Armored Division should have ceased to exist. Its losses on 20 November totaled 141 tanks, making its cumulative tank loss for the maneuver 471, well in excess of the division's authorized strength.[54] Only the maneuver rule-book, which returned destroyed and captured equipment to service every midnight, kept it in the field at all.

That same day, the 2d Armored and 4th Motorized Divisions launched another attack from the Pageland area toward Wadesboro in an attempt to relieve some of the pressure on the 1st Armored, but their efforts led only to further disaster. The 4th's attack carried it head-on into the advancing II Corps Blue troops, who quickly swarmed around the motorized division's flanks. The 8th Infantry Regiment, leading the 4th's advance, was cut off and surrounded by the Blue 44th Division four miles northwest of Chesterfield. The crippled 4th was obliged to retreat, abandoning its encircled regiment.[55]

Blue troops harassed the 4th Motorized Division with impunity, for the 2d Armored Division's hastily planned attack, scheduled for 0900, was more than five hours late getting started. The division launched its attack about 1430 in so tentative a manner that GHQ–X, immediately in front of the thrust, reported that the Reds were engaged in only minor patrolling.[56] Nonetheless, First Army reacted vigorously to the presence of Red armor. The I Corps immediately closed in on the 2d Armored from the south with GHQ–Z and TA–2; and TA–1, flushed with its victory over the 69th Armored Regiment near Albemarle, menaced the 2d from the north.[57] General Griswold immediately called off the attack, even though the 2d Armored Division had barely contacted the enemy.[58] He could not afford to sacrifice one armored division in a gamble to rescue the other, especially after the mauling of the 4th Motorized.

In effect, all three of IV Corps' powerful mobile divisions fell out of action on 20 November, leaving only two infantry divisions and three cavalry regiments to face the Blue onslaught. This was exactly the scenario General Drum had envisioned. With the Red motorized and armored divisions neutralized, Drum urged his First Army to close in on the Red defenders. In the south, I Corps advanced steadily toward Pageland and established a foothold on the Pageland-Monroe highlands.[59] Drum's center corps, II Corps, encircled the 4th Motorized Division's stranded 8th Regiment with the troops of 44th Division, contained the 1st Armored Division remnants near Marshville with the 28th Division, and still managed to push troops to within a few miles of Monroe.[60]

General Truesdell's VI Corps, now able to ignore the enemy armor behind its lines, scored decisive gains in the north. Drum finally released the 29th Division for the advance toward Monroe, giving Truesdell a three-division front—the 29th, 1st, and 26th—to bully the Red 31st Division, which had one brigade detached. As VI Corps' drive to the south converged with II Corps' westward advance, the 26th Division was pinched out, so Truesdell passed it behind the other two divisions and recommitted it on the right of 29th Division. The VI Corps now completely outflanked the Red defenders, who began retreating so precipitously that the 29th Division mounted its leading elements in trucks to pursue. At 1700 the 1st Division cut the Monroe-Wadesboro highway on the eastern outskirts of Monroe.[61]

While the disasters of 20 November unfolded, General Griswold decided to pull his beleaguered forces back into a new V-shaped defensive line with its apex at Monroe and its flanks refused toward the Catawba River. In the south, the 62d Brigade succeeded in disengaging from the slow-moving I Corps and withdrawing to the new line, but in the north aggressive VI Corps troops followed the 31st Division right into the new positions.[62] Griswold placed the crippled 4th Motorized Division in corps reserve at Mineral Springs to recuperate, and his staff worked to develop a 2d Armored Division attack for the next day that would relieve the pressure on the new IV Corps front. The plan, completed at midnight, essentially called for a repeat of the division's attack toward the northeast, with the aim of diverting II Corps' advance. Griswold also ordered the 1st Armored Division remnants to strike toward the northwest from their bivouac near Marshville in an attempt to deflect the onrushing VI Corps.[63]

It was unusual that the maneuver even continued into 21 November. Although General Headquarters had set no time limit for the maneuver, the 21st marked its sixth day, whereas the Louisiana maneuvers had each lasted five days. Continuing the maneuver would allow only three full days to redeploy before the Phase 2 exercise, as compared to four days between phases in Louisiana. Perhaps General McNair allowed the maneuver to continue in order to give IV Corps a final opportunity to stabilize its front and end the exercise on a more positive note. In any event, McNair was to terminate the maneuver promptly when IV Corps failed to reverse its fortunes.

General Drum's First Army opened 21 November with a coordinated attack at dawn in which all three corps scored gains and advanced vigorously. The converging VI and II Corps pinched out the 1st Division, which Drum diverted to the task of mopping up the assorted Red units stranded behind First Army's lines. By 0830 Blue troops were swarming into Monroe.[64]

The hastily organized Red armored counterattacks could do little to offset the loss of Monroe. Nonetheless, the 2d Armored Division attacked toward Peachland at 0800, while the 1st struck out against the 26th Division's advance into Monroe. The two armored forces had just engaged the enemy, and were already attracting the inevitable antitank and infantry opposition, when General McNair decided that nothing they could do would alter the fate of IV Corps. At 0840 GHQ director's headquarters terminated the maneuver.[65]

General Drum and his First Army had won the most decisive victory of any GHQ maneuver so far. The IV Corps ended the battle of the Pee Dee River pinned into a pocket fifteen miles across with its back to the Catawba River and its front line broken at Monroe. Moreover, the battle had proceeded exactly as Drum had planned. Equally satisfying to the Blue general was the thoroughness with which First Army had neutralized the enemy armored force: the 1st Armored Division had been virtually eliminated as an effective unit, and the two Red armored divisions together had suffered the staggering total of 844 tanks ruled out, 82 more than their combined tables of organization called for.[66] Admittedly, many tanks were destroyed by questionable means. One hundred thirteen Red tanks fell victim to the nearly useless .50-caliber antitank machine gun and another 47 to the highly unrealistic flour-bag grenade.[67]

General McNair was not entirely pleased with the Blue performance despite General Drum's masterful handling of First Army and the magnitude of his victory. In a confidential critique, McNair reproved Drum for First Army's violation of concentration-area instructions before the maneuver.[68] McNair was also aware that Blue troops had utilized ration trucks, immune from capture under GHQ rules, to conduct informal reconnaissance excursions deep into Red lines. One such truck apprehended by GHQ observers was found to contain one can of coffee, one box of sandwiches, and a half-dozen men.[69]

McNair also criticized Drum's conduct of the battle. He admonished First Army for displaying insufficient aggressiveness and stated that Drum should have reinforced the decisive VI Corps front more promptly and with more strength. He also questioned the degree to which Drum's headquarters had planned the minute details of the battle before it had even begun: "Initial field orders of the First Army were too long, contained contingent matter more suitable to a [subordinate] commander's planning, and were reminiscent of the technique used in World War I."[70] Much the same could be said for Drum's entire approach to the maneuver.

Even though IV Corps had suffered the most thorough maneuvers defeat to date, General Griswold and his command had not disgraced themselves. Facing overwhelming numerical odds, IV Corps had never been able to disengage its mobile forces for decisive blows without thinning its lines to the breaking point. McNair suggested that Griswold could have used motorized infantry and reconnaissance elements to contain the Blue bridgeheads on the first day, leaving the armored divisions free for decisive maneuver. But he offered no suggestion as to how the operations of subsequent days could have been improved, except to point out that such attacks as IV Corps launched were conducted in piecemeal fashion.[71]

General McNair stated publicly that the maneuver was ". . . the most complete and informing armored action ever seen in the United States. . . ."[72] But for armor the major import of the maneuver was to reemphasize the crying need for more infantry within the armored division and better cooperation between infantry and armored divisions. McNair remarked that, given adequate infantry support, 1st Armored Division's outflanking of the Blue north wing might have been decisive.[73] Seconding McNair's observations, General Griswold commented upon the scarcity of infantry in IV Corps as a whole,[74] as did GHQ observers who repeatedly noted that the paucity of infantry within the armored division cost the tankers dearly.[75]

GHQ observers also asserted that antitank units were still getting too much credit for the armored force's difficulties. Undeniably, the antitank groups performed better than they had in Louisiana, but, as the observer attached to the 2d Armored Division, Maj. Branner P. Purdue, pointed out, "It is believed success of AT units due to piecemeal [armored] attacks . . . rather than to AT units' effectiveness."[76] General McNair, however, was pleased with the antitank performance. At the general critique following the maneuver, the text of which was made public, he drew specific attention to the fact that 983 tanks from both sides had been ruled out of action in the course of the battle, with guns accounting for 90 percent. McNair did, however, acknowledge that such tank losses may well have been unrealistically high.[77]

The armored units themselves took consolation in the delays they imposed on Blue operations and in the damage they did to enemy units. General Scott, I Armored Corps commander, exaggerated considerably when he claimed that the Red mechanized forces had captured ten times as many prisoners and equipment as had the entire Blue army, but he spoke for the armored force when he remarked, "Maybe we haven't won the war, but we sure punished hell out of them." [78]

The Armored Force, and the Army as a whole, was beginning to learn that the tank was not an irresistible offensive weapon and that a small army could not expect to overwhelm an alert, determined, numerically superior foe merely because the inferior force possessed armored units. But the armored troops and the Red IV Corps would have one final opportunity to redeem themselves in the second maneuver a few days hence, when they would be assigned a defensive mission more in keeping with their relative strength. Meanwhile, the weary troops of both Red and Blue forces rested, enjoyed a belated Thanksgiving dinner, and moved to new concentration areas.

Notes

1. "First Army Maneuvers 1941, Final Report," Sec V; Slide 5, First Army N.C. Maneuvers 1941. Both in RG 337 57D, HQ AGF, GHQ General Staff G–3, Subject File 1940–Mar 9, 1942, NA.

2. Ltr of Instructions 1, GHQ, 14 Oct 41, "First Army Maneuvers 1941, Final Report," RG 337 57D, NA.

3. Lt Gen L. J. McNair to CG, IV Army Corps, 4 Oct 41, "Clark's Copy," RG 337 57D, NA.

4. Brig Gen Mark W. Clark, Deputy Director, Critique of 1st Phase, GHQ-Directed Maneuvers (hereafter cited as Critique of 1st Phase . . . Clark), "Clark's Copy," RG 337 57D, NA.

5. FO 1, HQ First Army, 14 Nov 41, "First Army Maneuvers 1941, Final Report," RG 337 57D, NA.

6. Ibid.

7. Lt Gen L. J. McNair to CG, First Army, 22 Dec 41, "Clark's Copy," RG 337 57D, NA.

8. Ibid.; Maj Emil Lenzer to Signal Officer, GHQ, 14 Nov 41, Training Div File 1st Phase Critique, RG 337 57D, NA.

9. HQ IV Army Corps, Critique of 1st Phase, "Clark's Copy," RG 337 57D, NA.

10. Critique by Lt Gen L. J. McNair, 1st Phase, GHQ-Directed Maneuvers, Carolina Area; McNair to Lt Col H. McD. Monroe, 16 Nov 41. Both in "Clark's Copy," RG 337 57D, NA. Slide 7, First Army N.C. Maneuvers 1941, RG 337 57D, NA.

11. Critique of Carolina Maneuvers by Lt Gen D. C. Emmons, "Clark's Copy," RG 337 57D, NA.

12. Telephone msg, Col Ennis to G–3, Dir Office, 7 Nov 41, Training Div File 1st Phase Critique, RG 337 57D, NA; Houston, *Hell on Wheels,* p. 98.

13. "First Army Maneuvers 1941, Final Report," 16 Nov 41, RG 337 57D, NA.

14. Aircraft Losses for 16 Nov, Training Div File 1st Phase Critique, RG 337 57D, NA.

15. Critique by Lt Gen L. J. McNair, 1st Phase, GHQ-Directed Maneuvers, Carolina Area; Critique of 1st Phase . . . Clark. Both in "Clark's Copy," RG 337 57D, NA.

16. "First Army Maneuvers 1941, Final Report," 16 Nov 41; Slide 7, First Army N.C. Maneuvers 1941; Critique of 1st Phase . . . Clark, "Clark's Copy." All in RG 337 57D, NA.

17. Memo, Lt Col Peter P. Rhodes for Gen Clark, 17 Nov 41, Training Div File 1st Phase Critique, RG 337 57D, NA.

18. Notes, Maj Learcy, 16 Nov 41, Performance of AT, RG 337 57D, NA.

19. Director's Rpt, Col John B. Thompson, 16 Nov 41, Performance of AT; Comments on First Phase, First Army vs. IV Corps, 22 Nov 41, Comments by Lt Gen McNair. Both in RG 337 57D, NA.

20. FO 2, HQ First Army, 16 Nov 41, "First Army Maneuvers 1941, Final Report," RG 337 57D, NA.

21. Critique of 1st Phase . . . Clark, "Clark's Copy," RG 337 57D, NA.

22. "First Army Maneuvers 1941, Final Report," 17 Nov 41; Communique, G–3, "Clark's Copy," RG 337 57D, NA.

23. McNair to Lt Col H. McD. Monroe, 17 Nov 41, "Clark's Copy"; Aircraft Losses for 17 Nov, Training Div File 1st Phase Critique. Both in RG 337 57D, NA.

24. FO 3, HQ First Army, 17 Nov 41, "First Army Maneuvers 1941, Final Report," RG 337 57D, NA.

25. Communique, G–3, "Clark's Copy," RG 337 57D, NA.

26. Rpt submitted by Hasbrouck, 17 and 18 Nov 41, Performance of AT, RG 337 57D, NA.

27. Ibid.

28. Critique of 1st Phase . . . Clark, "Clark's Copy"; Lt Gen L. J. McNair to CG, 1st Army, 22 Dec 41, "Clark's Copy"; Maj B. P. Purdue to Col Kingman, 18 Nov 41, Performance of AT; Rpt on Armd Operations (unsigned), Performance of AT; Memo (unsigned) for Dir, GHQ Maneuvers, Final Rpt, 21 Nov 41, Performance of AT. All in RG 337 57D, NA.

29. Memo, Maj B. P. Purdue for Deputy Dir, 18 Nov 41; Memo, Col John B. Thompson for Dir, 17 Nov 41. Both in Training Div File 1st Phase Critique, RG 337 57D, NA.

30. Losses 1st Phase, Tank Losses Nov 41; Critique of 1st Phase . . . Clark, "Clark's Copy." Both in RG 337 57D, NA.

31. "First Army Maneuvers 1941, Final Report," 18 Nov 41; McNair to Lt Col H. McD. Monroe, 18 Nov 41, "Clark's Copy." Both in RG 337 57D, NA.

32. Ibid.

33. Rpt by Lt Col R. W. Hasbrouck, 18 Nov 41, Performance of AT, RG 337 57D, NA.

34. Ibid.; Comments on 1st Phase, 1st Army vs. IV Corps, 22 Nov 41, Comments Lt Gen L. J. McNair; Notes (unsigned) TA–1,18–19 Nov 41, Performance of AT; Rpt of Tank Losses, 1st Armd Div, 18 Nov 41, Tank Losses Nov 41. All in RG 337 57D, NA.

35. Lt Col R. Hasbrouck, Matters To Be Covered [in critique], Performance of AT, RG 337 57D, NA; "Blue Pincers Aim to Hem Red Army," *New York Times*, 21 Nov 41.

36. Lt Paul E. Bailey to Chief Umpire, First Army HQ, Misc Papers in connection with revision of Umpire Manual; Notes (unsigned), 18–19 Nov 41, Performance of AT. Both in RG 337 57D, NA.

37. Critique of 1st Phase . . . Clark, "Clark's Copy"; Rpt of Tank Losses, 1st Armd Div, 19 Nov 41, Tank Losses Nov 41; Memo, Lt Col John B. Lentz for Gen Clark, 20 Nov 41; Training Div File 1st Phase Critique. All in RG 337 57D, NA.

38. "First Army Maneuvers 1941, Final Report," 19 Nov 41; McNair to Lt Col H. McD. Monroe, 20 Nov 41, "Clark's Copy"; Rpt of Tank Losses, 1st Armd Div, 19 Nov 41, Tank Losses Nov 41. All in RG 337 57D, NA.

39. McNair to Lt Col H. McD. Monroe, 19 Nov 41, "Clark's Copy"; Rpt of Tank Losses, 1st Armd Div, 19 Nov 41, Tank Losses Nov 41. Both in RG 337 57D, NA.

40. McNair to Lt Col H. McD. Monroe, 19 Nov 41;"Clark's Copy," RG 337 57D, NA.

41. R. W. Hasbrouck, 1st Armd Div Operations, Performance of AT, RG 337 57D, NA.

42. McNair to Lt Col H. McD. Monroe, 19 Nov 41, "Clark's Copy," RG 337 57D, NA.

43. Map of Operations, GHQ–Z, 19 Nov 41; Map of Operations, TA–2, 19 Nov 41; John B. Thompson, Asst Dir Rpt, 19 Nov 41. All in Performance of AT, RG 337 57D, NA.

44. Critique of 1st Phase . . . Clark, "Clark's Copy"; "First Army Maneuvers 1941, Final Report," 19 Nov 41. Both in RG 337 57D, NA.

45. Ibid.

46. Lt Gen L. J. NcNair to CG, First Army, 22 Dec 41, "Clark's Copy," RG 337 57D, NA.

47. Critique of 1st Phase . . . Clark; HQ IV Army Corps, Critique on 1st Phase. Both in "Clark's Copy," RG 337 57D, NA.

48. McNair to Lt Col H. McD. Monroe, 19 Nov 41, "Clark's Copy"; Critique of 1st Phase . . . Clark, "Clark's Copy"; Telephone msg, Col Williams to G–3, Dir Office, 19 Nov 41, Training Div File 1st Phase Critique; Memo, Col R. C. Candee for Dir, 20 Nov 41, Training Div File 1st Phase Critique; Memo, Lt Col Lowell Rooks for Gen Clark, 19 Nov 41, Training Div File 1st Phase Critique. All in RG 337 57D, NA.

49. Aircraft Losses for 19 Nov 41; Aviation in GHQ-Directed Maneuvers, 17 Nov 41. Both in Training Div File 1st Phase Critique, RG 337 57D, NA.

50. Col John B. Thompson, Rpt, 20 Nov 41, Performance of AT, RG 337 57D, NA.

51. Stuart Lewis, "Tank Attackers in Action," *Field Artillery Journal*, May 42, pp. 348–52; "First Army Maneuvers 1941, Final Report," 20 Nov 41, RG 337 57D, NA; Notes (unsigned) TA–1, GHQ–Y, 20 Nov 41, Performance of AT, RG 337 57D, NA; Learcy, Rpt on AT Units, Performance of AT, RG 337 57D, NA.

52. Memo, R. W. Hasbrouck for Armd Forces Dir, 20 Nov 41, Performance of AT, RG 337 57D, NA.

53. Critique of 1st Phase . . . Clark, "Clark's Copy"; Lt Gen L. J. McNair to Sec War, 21 Nov 41, Training Div File 1st Phase Critique. Both in RG 337 57D, NA.

54. Losses 1st Phase, Tank Losses Nov 41, RG 337 57D, NA.

55. McNair to Lt Col H. McD. Monroe, 21 Nov 41; Critique of 1st Phase . . . Clark. Both in "Clark's Copy," RG 337 57D, NA.

56. Map of Operations, GHQ–Z, Performance of AT; Map of Operations, TA–2, Performance of AT; Col John B. Thompson, Rpt, 20 Nov 41, Performance of AT; Critique of 1st Phase . . . Clark, "Clark's Copy." All in RG 337 57D, NA.

57. Critique of 1st Phase . . . Clark, "Clark's Copy," RG 337 57D, NA.

58. Col John B. Thompson, Rpt, 20 Nov 41, Performance of AT; Losses 1st Phase, Tank Losses Nov 41. Both in RG 337 57D, NA.

59. "First Army Maneuvers 1941, Final Report," 20 Nov 41, RG 337 57D, NA.

60. McNair to Lt Col H. McD. Monroe, 21 Nov 41, "Clark's Copy," RG 337 57D, NA.

61. FO 5, HQ First Army, 19 Nov 41, "First Army Maneuvers 1941, Final Report"; Critique of 1st Phase . . . Clark, "Clark's Copy." Both in RG 337 57D, NA.

62. McNair to Lt Col H. McD. Monroe, 20 and 21 Nov 41; Critique of 1st Phase . . . Clark. Both in "Clark's Copy," RG 337 57D, NA.

63. McNair to Lt Col H. McD. Monroe, 21 Nov 41, "Clark's Copy"; Col John B. Thompson, Asst Dir Rpt, 21 Nov 41, Performance of AT. Both in RG 337 57D, NA.

64. "First Army Maneuvers 1941, Final Report," 21 Nov 41; McNair to Lt Col H. McD. Monroe, 21 Nov 41, "Clark's Copy"; Critique of 1st Phase . . . Clark, "Clark's Copy." All in RG 337 57D, NA.

65. Critique of 1st Phase . . . Clark, "Clark's Copy," RG 337 57D, NA.

66. Rpt of Tank Losses 16–21 Nov 41, Tank Losses Nov 41, RG 337 57D, NA.

67. Ibid.

68. Lt Gen L. J. McNair to CG, First Army, 22 Dec 41, "Clark's Copy," RG 337 57D, NA.

69. Memo, Col Wm. C. Chase for G–3 Dir, GHQ Dir HQ, 23 Nov 41, Training Div File 2d Phase Critique, RG 337 57D, NA.

70. Lt Gen L. J. McNair to CG, First Army, 22 Dec 41, "Clark's Copy," RG 337 57D, NA.

71. Lt Gen L. J. McNair to CG, IV Army Corps, 7 Jan 42, "Clark's Copy," RG 337 57D, NA.

72. "McNair Praises Antitank Work," *New York Times*, 25 Nov 41.

73. Lt Gen L. J. McNair to CG, IV Army Corps, 7 Jan 42, "Clark's Copy," RG 337 57D, NA.

74. HQ IV Army Corps, Critique of 1st Phase, "Clark's Copy," RG 337 57D, NA.

75. See Rpts on Performance of AT, RG 337 57D, NA.

76. Matters To Be Covered In Critique, Maj B. P. Purdue, Performance of Antitank, RG 337 57D, NA.

77. Critique of 1st Phase . . . Clark, "Clark's Copy," RG 337 57D, NA.

78. "Blue Pincers Aim to Hem Red Army," *New York Times,* 21 Nov 41.

CHAPTER 9

Carolinas Phase 2
The Battle for Camden

General Headquarters created an entirely new strategic scenario for the second Carolinas maneuver. A new east-west international boundary, the Monroe-Wadsville highway, separated the Blue nation to the north from its southern Red neighbor. Instead of giving offensive missions to both armies as in Phase 1, GHQ, as in the second Louisiana maneuver, placed the smaller force on the defensive. General Griswold, commander of the Red IV Corps, received the following instructions from director's headquarters even before the first maneuver was over: "Strong Blue forces of all arms are advancing south through Greensboro and Winston-Salem. Movement appears to be increasing in intensity. As yet, no violations of the frontier have been reported. You will immediately move your army corps and attached troops . . . and organize and defend a bridgehead covering the crossing of the Wateree River at Camden."[1] With the conclusion of Phase 1, Griswold complied, moving his force into a GHQ-designated concentration area, north of Camden, between the Catawba-Wateree and the Pee Dee Rivers.[2]

General Drum, while given an offensive mission for First Army, was unaware that his opponent's assignment was the defense of Camden. "Strong Red forces of all arms, advancing from the southwest, are reported to be crossing the Wateree River near Camden," his orders read. "Your army, with attached troops . . . will be concentrated at once . . . for a later advance to destroy any hostile forces east of the line Catawba River–Wateree River."[3] General Headquarters reinforced First Army at the expense of IV Corps in preparation for Phase 2. The 17th Bombardment Group (two squadrons) left the Red 3d Air Support Command and joined First Army's 1st Air Support Command, thus roughly equalizing the two air arms. General Headquarters also attached the 502d Parachute Battalion to Drum's command.[4]

The assembly area assigned to the Blue army was an awkward one. The VI Corps' area lay west of the Pee Dee River, near the international boundary, but II and I Corps were required to assemble east of the water barrier. General Drum attempted to compensate for First Army's unfavorable initial dispositions by once again violating his instructions, this time even more blatantly than he had in the first maneuver. Instead of holding his forces approximately five to ten miles from the boundary, as ordered, Drum assembled I Corps directly on the frontier east of the Pee Dee. On the west bank, he ordered VI Corps to move out of its legal assembly areas to positions nearer the boundary several hours before the maneuver started. General Headquarters detected these infractions, but, according to General McNair, "Correction of this violation was not ordered because of the hardship which would have been caused to the troops."[5] (Curiously, at the critique following Phase 1 General Drum had stated firmly that soldiers found in violation of maneuver rules should be removed from the exercise, with the exception, one might suppose, of senior lieutenant generals.)[6]

The second Carolinas maneuver began at 0630 on 25 November, under clear, cold skies. In contrast to the assertiveness with which he sought unfair advantages before the maneuver, General Drum's opening moves were marked by caution. He ordered the 1st Air Support Command to cover First Army's flanks by bombing all Pee Dee River bridges from Cheraw south, and he instructed his flank units to erect tank barrier lines east and west to the maneuver area boundaries and beyond.[7] *(Map 7)*

With his flanks thus secured, Drum proceeded to deploy his army into a great crescent-shaped formation, three corps abreast, with the concavity facing the Red army. If the numerically inferior Red forces attempted to advance, or even hold their ground, Drum's crescent would envelop and destroy them. The VI Corps, already west of the Pee Dee, moved its two divisions (the 26th and 29th) southward from their illegal positions near the international boundary to an objective line running east and south from Monroe. Although it met with no opposition, VI Corps halted on that line and went over to the defensive, in compliance with orders from First Army.[8] The II Corps, forming the center of the crescent, crossed the Pee Dee and quickly formed up east of VI Corps. Two of II Corps' divisions, the 28th and 9th, crossed without incident, but on the corps right Brig. Gen. James I. Muir decided that the Pee Dee was too low for his 44th Division to float across on boats as planned. His crossing site being immediately downstream from a hydroelectric plant, Muir ordered the dam operators to raise the

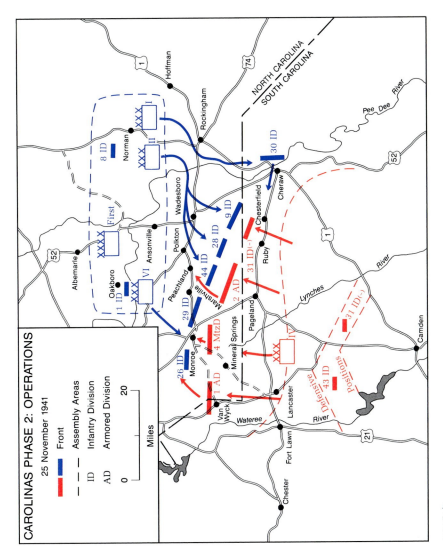

CAROLINAS PHASE 2: OPERATIONS

25 November 1941

Front

Assembly Areas

ID   Infantry Division

AD   Armored Division

Miles

0   20

MAP 7

water level by opening spillways and flooding the channel below. Surprisingly, they complied, and the 44th negotiated the Pee Dee, wasting 65,000 kilowatt-hours worth of water in the process.[9]

The I Corps occupied the southeastern wing of First Army's crescent-shaped initial objective line. Proceeding southward along the east bank of the Pee Dee with its sole division, the 30th, I Corps seized the highway bridge linking Wadesboro and Rockingham, which it turned over to II Corps coming south along the west bank. The I Corps itself remained on the east bank and continued farther south to the vicinity of Cheraw. When ordered to cross the river and seize Cheraw at once, I Corps discovered that friendly aircraft had destroyed the highway and railroad bridges several hours earlier as part of General Drum's flank-protection program.[10] While engineers labored to repair the spans, 30th Division began crossing by assault boat, footbridge, and ferry. The next day First Army engineers supplemented the existing bridges at Cheraw with a ponton bridge that was removed from another site, transported eighty miles, emplaced, and opened to traffic within seventeen hours.[11]

Backing up the three corps that formed the great crescent, General Drum commanded a powerful army reserve. One antiairborne and six antitank units stood behind the lines to counter any Red initiatives. The 1st and 8th Divisions (triangular), both fully motorized by the attachment of three quartermaster truck companies apiece, were available for employment once General Drum ascertained that Red IV Corps had moved into First Army's concave trap.[12]

Red operations on this first day of the maneuver seemed to indicate that IV Corps intended to defend the Monroe-Cheraw line. Within a few hours of the initiation of hostilities, Blue advance elements felt the effects of short, sharp, Red counterattacks, particularly along the northern face of First Army's crescent. General Griswold had organized his three mechanized units, the 4th Motorized and 1st and 2d Armored Divisions, into combined-arms columns, each column including infantry, artillery, and tanks. The 2d Armored Division directed its columns against the VI Corps–II Corps boundary east of Monroe and quickly discovered a gap between the two Blue forces. (Apparently, General Fredendall, II Corps commander, knew of the gap between his right and the VI Corps left, but had done nothing to close it.)[13] An infantry company and eighteen tanks pushed through the gap and reached the international boundary at Peachland before being stopped, encircled, and eliminated.[14]

Although the Peachland incursion was a relatively minor nuisance, VI Corps was soon fighting desperately on its right (western) flank.

The 1st Armored Division launched three columns against the western extremity of the Blue line, two of which broke through minimal opposition and turned VI Corps' flank west of Monroe.[15] The 4th Motorized Division assaulted Monroe itself and by nightfall occupied half of the town. Monroe, which happened to be the site of GHQ director's headquarters, became the scene of a formless, confused brawl. According to a GHQ observer, "They are fighting on the roofs of houses, they are fighting in yards, they have got town jammed up with halftracks firing blanks. They had the fire department out twice on account of smoke pots. It is rather a difficult situation."[16] General Headquarters finally suggested that all umpires in Monroe raise red flags, thus halting the battle and leaving Monroe half Red and half Blue for the night.[17]

The Red threat within and west of Monroe thoroughly rattled General Truesdell's VI Corps. First Army sent GHQ–Z and the 1st Division into the VI Corps zone with the provision that they be committed only with General Drum's permission. Truesdell's staff quickly drew up plans for a retreat to a better defensive line, with 1st Division deployed to meet an attack from the rear. "If Red's mission was to delay the Blue force . . . its operations have accomplished that mission completely so far as VI Corps is concerned," reported the GHQ liaison officer attached to corps headquarters. "If [First] Army directs an offensive mission VI Corps will *not* be mentally oriented."[18]

From General Drum's perspective, the events of 25 November confirmed that the Red army intended to make the Monroe front its primary line of defense. All three of his opponent's mechanized divisions had launched major attacks that had stunned VI and II Corps, whereas I Corps at Cheraw faced only light opposition. Drum issued orders for 26 November accordingly. The VI Corps and II Corps were to stand on the defense at Monroe, while I Corps pushed west from Cheraw, taking the Red army from the rear.[19]

Unknown to General Drum, his Red adversary had no further intention of fighting for Monroe. General Griswold's mechanized units were under orders to deliver spoiling attacks but to avoid becoming tied down in a protracted battle. Meanwhile, well to the south of the Monroe battle, IV Corps' infantry divisions, the 31st and 43d, were preparing two concentric defensive lines, between the Catawba-Wateree and Lynches Rivers, covering Camden. The line of retreat for the Red mechanized units fighting at Monroe did not necessarily run directly from Monroe to Camden, as General Drum assumed. Actually, Griswold contemplated their withdrawal to the west bank of the Catawba, whence they could be reintroduced to the east bank within the Camden defensive position.[20]

In accordance with Griswold's scheme, the 1st and 2d Armored Divisions disengaged most of their columns during the night of 25–26 November and prepared to renew their limited counterattacks at daylight. The 4th Motorized Division and a composite infantry-cavalry brigade known simply as the Task Force took over the 1st Armored Division zone west of Monroe, while the 31st Division assumed part of the 2d Armored Division sector southeast of town and sent troops to oppose I Corps at Cheraw.[21]

Misfortune beset the Red cause during the night. In a now familiar pattern, corps orders reached the armored divisions too late for the division staffs to complete their own preparations for the next day's operations. Furthermore, the 2d Armored Division spent the hours of darkness fending off a persistent II Corps attack and was in no condition to jump off at sunrise.[22] Of greater consequence were two harassing operations that General Drum sent against Camden on the evening of 25 November (even though he was still unaware that the Red army's mission was the defense of that city). The first of these operations involved a successful drop of the 502d Parachute Battalion on the western approaches of Camden's river bridges, closing the spans for the night.[23] In the second operation, a Blue scouting force known as Army Reconnaissance Detachment No. 2 mounted a raid on Red depots in the Camden area and came away with a full copy of the IV Corps maneuver plan, complete with maps and overlays. The reconnaissance detachment promptly rushed the document to Drum's headquarters by motorcycle.[24]

Initially, First Army's operations on 26 November reflected General Drum's mistaken conviction that the decisive battle of the maneuver would be fought on the Monroe front. The VI Corps cleared Monroe of Red troops and then reverted to limited operations. The 30th Division of I Corps pressed due west from Cheraw against stubborn resistance offered by the Red 31st Division. The II Corps contacted I Corps with its left flank, making the Blue crescent continuous.[25]

But at 0900, following an examination of the captured Red plans, General Drum took the unusual step of revoking the daily field order and replacing it with a new one. Drum now knew that the main Red defensive position was not at Monroe and that Camden was really the key to the maneuver. Furthermore, I Corps' westward advance from Cheraw would not cut off the Red mechanized units but would at best only push them west of the Catawba-Wateree, an eventuality that suited the IV Corps plan perfectly.

General Drum's revised field orders reoriented all First Army operations towards Camden. The I Corps had just begun to advance west when Drum reinforced it with the 8th Division and TA–2 from army reserve, and redirected it toward the southwest and Camden.[26] The I Corps, 30th Division, and 8th Division had not distinguished themselves in the first maneuver, and a halfhearted march toward Camden added no luster to their records. Unfavorable terrain and dogged Red resistance slowed the Blue drive considerably.[27]

The II Corps, covering I Corps' right, actually made better progress. The 28th Division captured Chesterfield, cutting direct communications between the Red 31st Division, facing I Corps, and the rest of the Red front.[28] The convergence of I and II Corps pinched out the latter corps' 9th Division, which entered army reserve.[29]

Now aware that the Red mechanized divisions had a potential escape route westward over the Catawba River, General Drum ordered VI Corps to block that retreat by sending the 29th Division southwest from Monroe toward Lancaster. The attack was no sooner under way than it collided head-on with the Red 1st Armored and 4th Motorized Divisions, which were finally mounting the day's long-delayed spoiling attack. Although the 29th's attack came to a halt, the Red force lost thirty-six tanks when the 13th Armored Regiment of the 1st Armored Division launched an assault, without infantry support, that ran into the Blue 29th Antitank Battalion. The 69th Armored Regiment, reinforced with infantry and artillery, was temporarily cut off by GHQ–Y, GHQ–Z, and elements of the 29th Division and lost an additional twenty-eight tanks.[30]

After dark General Griswold again withdrew his mechanized spearheads to reorganize and prepare for subsequent operations. Griswold sent the 43d Division from corps reserve to assume the 2d Armored Division sector in the Pageland area, but through a planning mix-up of tragic proportions, the 1st Armored Division withdrew from the line, leaving only the brigade-size Task Force holding eighteen miles of the extreme west flank between Monroe and the Catawba River.[31]

At 0630 on 27 November, General Truesdell's VI Corps resumed its efforts to cut the Red mechanized forces off from the Catawba. General Drum released TA–1 and the 1st Division to reinforce the blow, which had as its specific objectives the bridges at Van Wyck and Fort Lawn.[32] But when the 1st Division jumped off behind TA–1's mobile antitank screen, it encountered only the overextended Task Force and broke through the Red front with barely a pause. Finding nothing but empty roads before them, the Blue forces drove well beyond their intended objectives, and early in the afternoon seized the town of Lancaster, deep within Red territory.[33] Not only was the Red escape route over the Catawba closed, but TA–1 and the 1st Division stood only thirty miles from Camden, which General Drum now knew to be the key to defeating his Red opponent. Moreover, Drum had a triangular division in army reserve, the 9th, poised to exploit just such an opportunity, whereas General Griswold's IV Corps had every unit in the line, with nothing available to counter the Blue forces at Lancaster. For the moment, General Drum stood on the verge of another smashing maneuvers victory.

The Red mechanized forces saved the day for General Griswold and IV Corps. For two days I Armored Corps had tried in vain to organize a coordinated attack, employing both armored divisions, against the II Corps–VI Corps boundary. At about the same time that the Blue 1st Division entered Lancaster, the two-division armored attack finally came off. The objective was Pageland, which the 1st Armored Division attacked from the west and the 2d from the south. General Patton's 2d Armored Division encountered stiff opposition and eventually diverted most of its strength to meet a series of determined counterattacks.[34] But General Magruder's 1st Armored pierced the Blue lines and sent the 69th Armored Regiment deep into hostile territory. *(Map 8)*

The Red armored attack electrified General Drum's command. The VI Corps committed GHQ–Y to the Pageland fray, II Corps committed GHQ–X, and I Corps loaned TA–2 to help contain the armored penetrations. Moreover, the Pageland assault distracted General Drum from the potentially decisive opportunity afforded by 1st Division's uncontested presence in Lancaster. The 9th Division, in army reserve, went to fend off the 69th Armored Regiment near Peachland rather than reinforcing the 1st Division at Lancaster.[35] Drum's concern with the integrity of the II Corps–VI Corps front even led him to order the suspension of the 1st Division's southward advance. First Army directed the 1st to turn east at Lancaster and attack the Red armored divisions from behind.[36] The division was able to advance only a short distance against mounting opposition before darkness fell and umpires halted the operation. Thus, General Drum lost a golden opportunity to march into Camden and win the maneuver with one bold stroke.

In any event, Drum's concern with preserving the First Army front from armored penetrations was unfounded, for the armored divisions had shot their bolt for the day, and nothing was more certain to encourage their withdrawal than the Blue threat against Camden. In fact, General Griswold reacted to the loss of Lancaster by ordering the entire Red army back toward Camden. At 1545 1st Armored Division broke off the Pageland operation and soon had its regiments on the road to the vicinity of Lancaster, where it and the 4th Motorized converged to hold the door open for IV Corps' re-

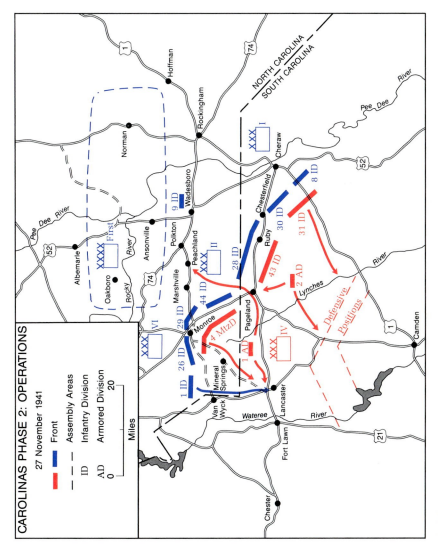

CAROLINAS PHASE 2: OPERATIONS

27 November 1941

Front

Assembly Areas

ID   Infantry Division

AD   Armored Division

0   20

Miles

MAP 8

treat.[37] The 2d Armored Division received orders to proceed to Lancaster as well, but while the division was en route Griswold rerouted it directly to the Camden defensive position, where it anchored the north face of the new IV Corps perimeter.[38] After a stubborn retreat, the 43d and 31st Divisions linked up with the 2d Armored and established the eastern perimeter along the Lynches River.[39]

General Drum did not at first realize that IV Corps had eluded his grasp. On the evening of 27 November he issued an exuberant and misleading message to his troops: "Red forces East of Catawba now definitely encircled by our First Army from Fort Lawn bridge over Catawba to Middendorf on U.S. Number One." [40] The following morning he ordered 1st Division (which had not been reinforced) to resume its eastward push from Lancaster, even though the bulk of IV Corps had long since slipped past that line. Early on 28 November, Maj. Gen. Donald Cubbison, the 1st Division commander, surveyed the Red 1st Armored and 4th Motorized Divisions arrayed against him and quickly abandoned the eastward assault. "The main object of life right now is to hold the town," reported a GHQ observer with the Blue forces in Lancaster.[41] The 1st Division and TA–1 covered the fringes of town with artillery and antitank guns in expectation of a Red mechanized attack. When the assault came at daylight, the Red forces gained footholds in the southern and eastern outskirts of town, but of greater importance was the 1st Division's inability to interfere with the establishment of the Camden defensive perimeter.[42]

It was not until 1000 that General Drum decided to reinforce VI Corps for an attack from Lancaster toward Camden. The 29th Division, which had been pinched out of the II Corps line earlier that day, and the temporarily motorized 9th Division joined the 1st in Lancaster. The assault commenced at 1500 but met with little success. Twenty-four hours earlier the roads to Camden had been open, but on this day powerful Red mechanized forces barred the way.[43]

With the threat from Lancaster blunted, General Griswold proceeded to pull his armored divisions into the Camden defensive perimeter, from which he planned to launch armored counterattacks against the converging Blue forces the next day. The 4th Motorized Division fell back from Lancaster and relieved the 2d Armored on the northern face of the position. Griswold committed a serious blunder, however, when he ordered the armored divisions to detach their infantry, artillery, and reconnaissance elements to help bolster the infantry divisions on the perimeter. To be sure, IV Corps was weak in infantry, but every maneuvers experience to date had demonstrated the impotence of armored forces that lacked the support of other arms. General Scott, I Armored Corps commander,

A 1st Infantry Division motor convoy. *(DA photograph.)*

and the armored division commanders tried in vain to change Griswold's mind.[44] The IV Corps was saved from potential embarrassment on that score when General Headquarters terminated the maneuver at 1620, in the midst of IV Corps' defensive redeployment.[45]

The second Carolinas maneuver, which had lasted only four days, ended without a clear tactical decision. In its final report for the 1941 maneuver season the First Army claimed that when the maneuver was terminated, ". . . Red forces were contained in a pocket from which it would have been difficult to extricate them."[46] The pocket, of course, was a defensive position of IV Corps' own choosing, which covered Camden admirably and from which IV Corps had no desire to be extricated. General McNair confirmed that IV Corps had fulfilled its assignment: "At the termination of the maneuvers Red still retained possession of the area necessary for the accomplishment of its assigned mission."[47]

The IV Corps' primary instruments in accomplishing its mission had been the two armored divisions, which, with the aid of the 4th Motorized Division, forestalled major Blue advances for two days and, when the Blue breakthrough occurred, moved swiftly and effectively to establish a new IV Corps front. The Red armor regained much of the prestige it lost in the first maneuver. In

Phase 2 the 1st and 2d Armored Divisions reported the capture of 4,788 Blue prisoners, the capture or destruction of 2,540 vehicles of all types, and the destruction of 618 antitank guns, all at a cost of 462 tanks ruled out (as compared to 844 in Phase 1).[48]

General McNair's satisfaction with the Carolinas maneuvers was evident in the confidential remarks that he sent to the commanding generals afterwards. ". . . the maneuvers were well-planned and executed in most essentials and indicated intensive and intelligent collective effort toward achievement of training goals." [49] At the general critique on 30 November, McNair addressed the one great question that the GHQ maneuvers were intended to answer:

> The question is asked repeatedly, "Are these troops ready for war?" It is my judgement that, given complete equipment, they certainly could fight effectively. But it is to be added with emphasis that losses would be unduly heavy, and the results of action against an adversary such as the German might not be all that could be desired. In spite of the remarkable progress of the year just past, there must be no idea in anyone's mind that further training is unnecessary.[50]

General McNair had every reason to feel satisfied, for the improvement in training over the preceding year had indeed been extraordinary, especially so because it took place at a time of great expansion and doctrinal modernization. As of 30 November 1941, no further expansion of the Army was contemplated (in fact, President Roosevelt had decided to cut back on ground troops in favor of the Navy and Army Air Forces), and although the maneuvers had uncovered numerous deficiencies, such was to be expected.[51] The post-maneuvers remedial training could be conducted with relative leisure.

Notes

1. Lt Gen L. J. McNair to CG, IV Army Corps, 20 Nov 41, "Clark's Copy," RG 337 57D, HQ AGF, GHQ GS G–3, Subject File 1940–Mar 9, 1942, NA.

2. McNair to Lt Col H. McD. Monroe, 25 Nov 41, "Clark's Copy," RG 337 57D, NA.

3. Lt Gen L. J. McNair to CG, First Army, 20 Nov 41, "Clark's Copy," RG 337 57D, NA.

4. Ibid.

5. Lt Gen L. J. McNair to CG, First Army, 22 Dec 41, "Clark's Copy," RG 337 57D, NA.

6. Comments by Lt Gen H. A. Drum [Phase 1 Critique], "Clark's Copy," RG 337 57D, NA.

7. FO 7, HQ First Army, 23 Nov 41, "First Army Maneuvers 1941, Final Report," Sec V, RG 337 57D, NA.

8. Critique of Second Phase, GHQ-Directed Maneuvers, Carolina Area, by Brig Gen Mark W. Clark, "Clark's Copy"; "First Army Maneuvers 1941, Final Report," Sec V. Both in RG 337 57D, NA.

9. "Let There Be Water," *Time,* 8 Dec 41, p. 66.

10. "First Army Maneuvers 1941, Final Report," Sec V; McNair to Lt Col H. McD. Monroe, 25 Nov 41, "Clark's Copy"; Critique of 2d Phase . . . Clark, "Clark's Copy." All in RG 337 57D, NA.

11. "First Army Maneuvers 1941, Final Report," Sec V, RG 337 57D, NA.

12. FO 7, HQ First Army, 23 Nov 41, "First Army Maneuvers 1941, Final Report," RG 337 57D, NA.

13. Rpt, Liaison Officer with VI Corps, 25 Nov 41, Training Div File 2d Phase Critique, RG 337 57D, NA.

14. Asst Dir Rpt, Lt Col R. W. Hasbrouck, 25 Nov 41, 2d Phase 1 and 2 Armd Divs; G–3 Rpt 21, 2d Armd Div, 26 Nov 41, 2d Phase 1 and 2 Armd Divs. Both in RG 337 57D, NA.

15. Asst Dir Rpt, Lt Col John B. Thompson, 25 Nov 41, 2d Phase 1 and 2 Armd Divs, RG 337 57D, NA.

16. Telephone msg, Lt Col Ennis to G–3 Dir Office, 25 Nov 41, Training Div File 2d Phase Critique, RG 337 57D, NA.

17. Ibid.

18. Rpt, Liaison Officer with VI Corps, 25 Nov 41, Training Div File 2d Phase Critique, RG 337 57D, NA.

19. FO 8, HQ First Army, 25 Nov 41, "First Army Maneuvers 1941, Final Report," RG 337 57D, NA.

20. McNair to Lt Col H. McD. Monroe, 25 Nov 41, "Clark's Copy," RG 337 57D, NA.

21. Ibid.; Critique of 2d Phase . . . Clark, "Clark's Copy." Both in RG 337 57D, NA.

22. G–3 Rpt 22, 2d Armd Div, 26 Nov 41, 2d Phase 1 and 2 Armd Divs, RG 337 57D, NA.

23. Lt Col Lloyd D. Brown for G–3 Dir, 28 Nov 41, Training Div File 2d Phase Critique; Lt Col Clarence M. Tomlinson for Gen Clark, 28 Nov 41, Training Div File 2d Phase Critique; Lt Gen L. J. McNair to CG, IV Army Corps, 7 Jan 42, "Clark's Copy." All in RG 337 57D, NA.

24. "First Army Maneuvers 1941, Final Report," Sec V; Comments, GHQ Maneuvers 2d Phase, by Lt Gen Hugh A. Drum, 30 Nov 41, "Clark's Copy." Both in RG 337 57D, NA.

25. FO 8, HQ First Army, 25 Nov 41, "First Army Maneuvers 1941, Final Report," RG 337 57D, NA.

26. FO 9, HQ First Army, 26 Nov 41, "First Army Maneuvers 1941, Final Report," RG 337 57D, NA.

27. Critique of 2d Phase . . . Clark, "Clark's Copy"; Lt Gen L. J. McNair to CG, First Army, 22 Dec 41, "Clark's Copy." Both in RG 337 57D, NA.

28. G–3 Rpt 22, 2d Armd Div, 26 Nov 41, 2d Phase 1 and 2 Armd Divs, RG 337 57D, NA.

29. FO 9, HQ First Army, 26 Nov 41, "First Army Maneuvers 1941, Final Report," RG 337 57D, NA.

30. Ibid.; Map, Operations GHQ–Y 26 Nov 41, 2d Phase 1 and 2 Armd Divs; Asst Dir Rpt [unsigned], 2d Phase 1 and 2 Armd Divs; Maj B. P. Purdue, Rpt on TA–l, 2d Phase 1 and 2 Armd Divs Tank Losses Nov 41. All in RG 337 57D, NA.

31. Msg from Buchanan [undated], Training Div File 2d Phase Critique; Critique of 2d Phase . . . Clark, "Clark's Copy." Both in RG 337 57D, NA.

32. FO 10, HQ First Army, 26 Nov 41, "First Army Maneuvers 1941, Final Report," RG 337 57D, NA.

33. McNair to Lt Col H. McD. Monroe, 27 Nov 41, "Clark's Copy"; Critique of 2d Phase . . . Clark, "Clark's Copy"; "First Army Maneuvers 1941, Final Report," Sec V. All in RG 337 57D, NA.

34. McNair to Lt Col H. McD. Monroe, 27 Nov 41, "Clark's Copy"; Asst Dir Rpt, Lt Col R. W. Hasbrouck, 27 Nov 41, 2d Phase 1 and 2 Armd Divs; G–3 Rpt, 2d Armd Div, 27 Nov 41, 2d Phase 1 and 2 Armd Divs; Map, Plan of Attack, 2d Armd Div, 27 Nov 41, 2d Phase 1 and 2 Armd Divs. All in RG 337 57D, NA.

35. McNair to Lt Col H. McD. Monroe, 27 Nov 41, "Clark's Copy"; "First Army Maneuvers 1941, Final Report," Sec V. Both in RG 337 57D, NA.

36. McNair to Lt Col H. McD. Monroe, 27 Nov 41, "Clark's Copy," RG 337 57D, NA.

37. Asst Dir Rpt, Col John B. Thompson, 27 Nov 41, 2d Phase 1 and 2 Armd Divs, RG 337 57D, NA.

38. Asst Dir Rpt, Lt Col R. W. Hasbrouck, 27 Nov 41, also 28 Nov 41, 2d Phase 1 and 2 Armd Divs; G–3 Rpt, 2d Armd Div, 28 Nov 41, 2d Phase l and 2 Armd Divs. All in RG 337 57D, NA.

39. McNair to Lt Col H. McD. Monroe, 28 Nov 41, "Clark's Copy," RG 337 57D, NA.

40. Drum to CGs, I, II, and VI Army Corps, 27 Nov 41, "First Army Maneuvers 1941, Final Report," RG 337 57D, NA.

41. Telephone msg, Col Ennis to G–3 Dir Office, 28 Nov 41, Training Div File 2d Phase Critique, RG 337 57D, NA.

42. Critique of 2d Phase . . . Clark, "Clark's Copy"; G–3 Rpt, 2d Armd Div, 28 Nov 41, 2d Phase 1 and 2 Armd Divs. Both in RG 337 57D, NA.

43. McNair to Lt Col H. McD. Monroe, 28 Nov 41, "Clark's Copy"; "First Army Maneuvers 1941, Final Report," Sec V. Both in RG 337 57D, NA.

44. McNair to Lt Col H. McD. Monroe, 28 Nov 41, "Clark's Copy"; Asst Dir Rpt, Col John B. Thompson, 28 Nov 41, 2d Phase 1 and 2 Armd Divs; Asst Dir Rpt, Lt Col R. W. Hasbrouck, 28 Nov 41, 2d Phase 1 and 2 Armd Divs; G–3 Rpt, 2d Armd Div, 28 Nov 41, 2d Phase 1 and 2 Armd Divs. All in RG 337 57D, NA.

45. McNair to Lt Col H. McD. Monroe, 28 Nov 41, "Clark's Copy," RG 337 57D, NA.

46. "First Army Maneuvers 1941, Final Report," Sec V, RG 337 57D, NA.

47. Lt Gen L. J. McNair to CG, IV Army Corps, 7 Jan 42, "Clark's Copy," RG 337 57D, NA.

48. Result of Action, I Armd Corps, Tank Losses Nov 41, Rpt of Tank Losses 16–21 Nov 41, Rpt of Tank Losses 25–28 Nov 41, RG 337 57D, NA.

49. Lt Gen L. J. NcNair to CG, IV Army Corps, 7 Jan 42, "Clark's Copy," RG 337 57D, NA.

50. Critique of 2d Phase GHQ-Directed Maneuvers [McNair], "Clark's Copy," RG 337 57D, NA.

51. Watson, *Chief of Staff,* pp. 362–66.

CHAPTER 10

After the Maneuvers
Defects and Remedies

With the completion of the North Carolina Maneuvers the Army will have entered into a new cycle of development. The past year, in effect, has been one of some turmoil involving the organization of units, federalising of the National Guard, inducting selectees directly into organizations, the establishment of Training Centers and the construction and development of facilities. This has involved the execution of a training program under great difficulties, which is now climaxing with the last of the extensive maneuvers, to be followed by the release of large numbers of officers and men from active service.

General George C. Marshall [1]

On 3 December 1941, three days after the official conclusion of the Carolinas maneuvers, Secretary of War Stimson convened a meeting in Washington, D.C., to discuss their implications. The meeting included Undersecretary Robert P. Patterson and Assistant Secretaries John J. McCloy and Robert A. Lovett. Representing the General Staff were Chief of Staff General Marshall, and his three deputy chiefs, Maj. Gen. William Bryden, Maj. Gen. Richard C. Moore, and Maj. Gen. H. H. Arnold (also commander of the Army Air Forces). General McNair, the GHQ chief of staff, and his operations and training officer, General Clark, represented General Headquarters.

General McNair opened the meeting with a commentary on the accomplishments of the training season just completed. Training had progressed satisfactorily in 1941, he felt, and the leadership of large units had improved noticeably in the course of the maneuvers. The maneuvers, however, had also revealed a disturbing deficiency in the training of individuals and small units. McNair reported favorably on the antitank experiment in the maneuvers and suggested that the Army continue to stress the development of antitank units, weapons, and tactics. He mentioned that armored units had not always been used correctly but said little else about the participation of tanks in the maneuvers, except to note that 760 tanks of the two armored divisions had been stopped by an equal number of mobile antitank guns in the Carolinas maneuvers. He felt that the "outstanding question" settled in the GHQ maneuvers was that the tank could be stopped.[2]

Of the ground elements, McNair spoke unfavorably only of the horse cavalry. He noted that equestrian troops had performed "magnificent" physical feats in the Louisiana maneuvers but that neither there nor in the Carolinas had horse cavalry demonstrated any great advantage over mechanized cavalry. General Marshall observed that whereas the corps reconnaissance regiments (horse-mechanized) had been created with the object of detailing the horse elements to the divisions for close-in reconnaissance, in practice the divisions preferred to organize their own motorized reconnaissance elements, which worked satisfactorily in the maneuvers.[3]

McNair commented briefly on the air-ground aspect of the maneuvers, saying only that air units "had added a great deal of impetus" to the maneuvers and that cooperation between air and ground elements had shown improvement, but that a great deal of work remained to be done in the development of tactics and techniques. General Arnold confirmed that air-ground coordination still needed work. He also observed that air units in the maneuvers had been underutilized, because aircraft had flown an average of only three hours a day, whereas he thought they were capable of flying six.

The War Department officials seemed much more concerned with problems of air support than were the generals. Undersecretary Patterson had sensed a lack of "air awareness" during his visits to the maneuvers, and Assistant Secretary McCloy commented upon instances in which antiaircraft guns failed to fire at aircraft and ground units failed to conceal their vehicles from air observation. The military men agreed with the civilian officials that air-ground communication was poor, but the conference produced no suggestions on how this or any other of the many problems related to ground-support aviation should be rectified.[4]

In fact, the 3 December meeting never progressed to the point of concrete proposals in any area, for the conferees could not be sure what the future held for the Army's ground forces. President Roosevelt's shifting of priorities toward the Navy, the Army Air Forces, and lend-lease forced Marshall to contemplate the discharge of the National Guard divisions beginning in February 1942. In that event, Marshall planned to replace the Guardsmen with new drafts of selectees who would be trained for about a year, whereupon they, too, would be released into the reserves.[5] The object of this plan was the creation of a reserve manpower pool rather than the honing of active-duty combat-ready units. Paradoxically, the Army also had to be prepared for the immediate outbreak of hostilities and a program of major expansion, given the repeal of the neutrality acts in November, the undeclared naval conflict against U-boats in the North Atlantic, and the deteriorating relations with Japan. Thus, little was said on 3 December regarding the future course of ground forces training. Generals McNair and Clark spoke only of a small-unit remedial training program for those units that had participated in the maneuvers.[6]

The inadequacy of small-unit training revealed in the maneuvers was particularly distressing. General McNair, GHQ observers, and even civilian correspondents noted throughout the maneuvers that many small units displayed little proficiency in the skills that they should have mastered during their mobilization training programs.

Put simply, small units behaved as if they did not know how to protect themselves from enemy action or how to bring effective force of their own to bear upon the enemy. Maneuvers troops showed little regard for defensive tactics and did little to avoid hostile fire. Secure in the knowledge that only blanks were being discharged, soldiers would maneuver openly in the face of small-arms fire rather than utilize cover. They often ignored artillery fire and sometimes stood in the open to watch air attacks that would have killed them in real war.[7]

When it came to taking the battle to the enemy, far too many small-unit commanders proved unable to execute basic tactics. They were especially weak in the employment of supporting weapons that had been added to rifle units under General Lynch's recent reforms. Machine guns and mortars were often sited incorrectly, artillery support often went unrequested, and the troops failed to maneuver as coordinated units. Moreover, unit commanders were slow to establish communications with higher headquarters, failed to establish contact with adjacent units, neglected to maintain contact with the enemy by reconnaissance, and compounded their units' deficiencies by issuing unclear or ambiguous orders.[8]

In sum, the new infantry doctrine was not being successfully executed. The remedial training phase discussed at the secretary of war's conference addressed this failure. In fact, General Headquarters had long since drawn up and issued its post-maneuvers training program. On 30 October 1941, before the Carolinas maneuvers had even begun, General McNair sent a directive to the commanding generals of the four field armies and to the chief of the Armored Force outlining a four-month remedial training period to follow the GHQ maneuvers. Like the 1941 training program, remedial training was to be progressive, beginning with the rudiments of basic training and carrying through to the training of regiments, with particular emphasis placed on battalion training. There would be more live firing of weapons, small arms as well as artillery, both on the range and in the field under combat conditions.

Rather than relying on the corps and armies to determine small unit proficiency,[9] General Headquarters drafted three standardized proficiency tests that all small units were required to pass in the course of the remedial training program, one each for the rifle platoon, the artillery battery, and the infantry battalion.[10] The rifle platoon test required the unit to march into combat, deploy into an effective formation, fire its weapons, and capture an objective held by a simulated enemy. GHQ included detailed grading criteria by which the platoon's performance would be judged. Points were awarded for the brevity and clarity of the lieutenant's orders, his skill at utilizing the unit's firepower, and the number of targets hit. With a score of 70 percent or higher the platoon could proceed to company and battalion training. A lower score meant that the unit would repeat platoon training.[11]

The field artillery battery test required the battery to occupy a designated position, prepare it for use, establish defenses, and set up communications with a simulated battalion headquarters. The second part of the test required the battery to register its weapons on a target specified by battalion, deliver a barrage (using live ammunition), and shift fire to another target without repositioning the guns. The battery was graded on the proficiency with which it organized the position, its mastery of the techniques of plotting fires, and its accuracy in laying barrages.[12]

In the battalion test, which was to be administered near the end of the four-month remedial training period, the entire 900-man infantry battalion, supported by artillery, was required to conduct a coordinated assault under battlefield conditions. The test included a night approach march, a live artillery preparation fired over the heads of the troops, and a dawn assault against a simulated enemy position. Grading depended upon the conduct of the approach; the assembly in jump-off positions; the skill with which the battalion commander reconnoitered, planned, and ordered his attack; and the ability of the battalion to execute his orders. The commander's judgment in positioning support weapons and in committing the battalion reserve at an appropriate time were specifically evaluated.

Points were deducted if the battalion failed to maintain appropriate contact with regimental headquarters and with adjacent units.[13]

The post-maneuvers training directive of 30 October, and the attached tests, signaled a significant shift in GHQ training policies. They represented an admission on the part of General Headquarters that large-scale free maneuvers contributed little to the training of small units. General McNair had insisted all along that the GHQ maneuvers were not conducted solely for the benefit of the higher echelons, but by 30 October GHQ tacitly acknowledged that small-unit tactical proficiency did not improve in the course of large-scale maneuvers.[14] In fact, some officers, such as Colonel Collins, VII Corps chief of staff in Louisiana, observed a deterioration in basic skills during army-versus-army maneuvers. He noted that companies and battalions tended to get lost in the "big picture," leading to carelessness and the development of bad habits.[15] The directive of 30 October revealed a new conviction on the part of General Headquarters that whatever the individual and small unit might learn about campaigning in the field during large maneuvers, fundamental skills were better taught in smaller, closely controlled field exercises.

The post-maneuvers training directive also inaugurated a trend toward closer standardization of training throughout the Army. Through 1941, General McNair had issued training guidelines, and GHQ observers had monitored training progress with spot checks, but the actual authority for training small units had been largely delegated to the corps and field armies. Such decentralization proved to be unsatisfactory when small units arrived at the GHQ maneuvers without having mastered the fundamentals of the Mobilization Training Program. Beginning with the 30 October directive, General Headquarters (and its successor in the training role, Army Ground Forces) exercised closer supervision of training. Training directives emanating from GHQ began to cover areas once left to the discretion of the field army commanders, and GHQ observers kept a closer watch on testing procedures.[16]

The motto of the post-maneuvers training period might well have been "back to basics." In 1941 attention had been focused upon the activation of divisions, corps, and armies, and upon the integration of tank, antitank, and air elements into the combat team. By contrast, post-maneuvers training centered upon small infantry-artillery forces. Neither the directive of 30 October nor the 3 December conference dealt with training units larger than the regiment, and no provision was made for the participation of armored elements in the four-month remedial training period. General

McNair specifically recommended that air-ground training be post-poned; hence the reticence of the generals to commit themselves on the air-ground issue at the secretary of war's conference.[17]

The tank, antitank, and air forces returned from the maneuvers preoccupied with their own affairs. One major development of this period was the creation of an antitank quasi-arm. At the 3 December conference, General McNair informed the secretary of war that antitank development should be stressed. This was less a recommendation than a justification of policies well under way. Planning for a major antitank buildup within the Army had begun as early as August, even as the experimental antitank groups prepared for the Louisiana maneuvers. On 18 August, a special planning branch of the War Department's G–3 Section issued recommendations calling for an enormous antitank arm consisting of no fewer than 220 battalions. Based on a projected 55-division Army, this G–3 report suggested that one battalion be allotted to each division (as was already the practice), that 55 battalions be assigned to corps and field army reserves, and that 110 be attached directly to General Headquarters as an antitank reserve for the entire Army.[18]

General Headquarters disagreed with certain aspects of the G–3 proposal, and no action was taken until 7 October. On that date General Marshall held an antitank conference to iron out differences of opinion and to lay the groundwork for the activation of an antitank arm. The participants, who included Generals McNair and Clark, agreed that an antitank force should be established and that it should bear the designation tank destroyer, for psychological reasons. Marshall also authorized the activation of a tank destroyer center to train antitank units, develop tactical doctrines, and test equipment. He directed that plans be drawn up for the organization of sixty-three tank destroyer battalions.[19] The 93d Tank Destroyer Battalion, which fought successfully in the Carolinas maneuvers as part of TA–1, was the prototype for these units.

Armor's failure to dominate the GHQ maneuvers might be interpreted as a validation of the emergent antitank program. General Devers, chief of the Armored Force, was disinclined to give antitank forces much credit. "We were licked by a set of umpires rules," was his assessment of the tank-antitank confrontation.[20] But General Marshall felt justified in proceeding with the tank destroyer project. On 27 November (which was, coincidentally, the same day that TA–1 led the 1st Division to the capture of Lancaster, South Carolina), the War Department issued orders for the activation of the Tank Destroyer Tactical and Firing Center at Fort Meade, Maryland. The center came under the direct control of the War Department General Staff. The War Department also ordered the activation of fifty-three tank destroyer battalions directly responsible to General Headquarters.[21]

The tank destroyer arm became a virtually autonomous force on 3 December, when another War Department order directed that all divisions redesignate their antitank battalions as tank destroyers and surrender them to GHQ control. This surprising move, which ran counter to the General Staff proposal that each division retain its organic antitank battalion, eliminated a valuable component of the infantry division. Antitank battalions had performed well in the maneuvers, particularly in Louisiana, where they accounted for the great majority of tanks ruled out. Now the divisions would possess as organic antitank elements only the antitank companies of each infantry regiment.

One of the first activities of the Tank Destroyer Tactical and Firing Center was to codify doctrine, drawing heavily on British experiences in North Africa as well as on the actions of antitank elements in the GHQ maneuvers.[22] The planners steadfastly adhered to General McNair's dictum that massed tanks represented the primary armor threat and that the proper response was massed antitank fire. Like the antitank groups employed in the maneuvers, tank destroyer battalions were not to serve as frontline units but rather were to form special antitank reserves at the division, corps, field army, and GHQ levels.

Tank destroyer doctrine rested on the two principles of high mobility and high firepower that had characterized the maneuvers antitank groups. High mobility would allow the tank destroyer battalions (combined into groups or brigades if the situation demanded) to rush to the scene of a hostile armored penetration and occupy selected gun positions. Utilizing their superior firepower, the tank destroyers were then to ambush and destroy the enemy tanks. On occasions when friendly forces were on the offensive, the tank destroyers were to seek out enemy tank concentrations, use their mobility to surround the less mobile tanks, and destroy them with gunfire.[23]

This tank destroyer doctrine was unique to the U.S. Army. No other army pooled highly mobile antitank elements into a general antitank reserve. The tank destroyer motto, "Seek, strike, and destroy," and the shoulder patch, a black panther crushing a tank in its jaws, symbolized the aggressive spirit that permeated tank destroyer doctrine.[24]

The Armored Force embarked upon a post-maneuvers reorganization program as well, and although its reforms led to certain innovations, in general it moved closer to the German model rather than toward unique developments in the manner of the tank destroyer force. Since its inception in the summer of 1940, the Armored Force had paralleled German thought and practice in many respects, with the important exception of the *Kampfgruppe* concept. In sharp contrast to the German model, American armored doctrine separated tanks, infantry, and artillery, both organizationally and tactically.

The GHQ maneuvers revealed this to be a serious defect. Throughout the maneuvers, the armored divisions repeatedly encountered situations that demanded the presence of infantry and artillery among the tank elements. In particular, hostile antitank positions that stopped tanks with ease under the maneuver rules would have posed much less of a problem had the other arms been available to every armored column. Accordingly, in the Carolinas maneuvers both armored divisions attempted to organize themselves into balanced *Kampfgruppe*-like columns especially tailored for the operation at hand. The attempt fell short of complete success for several reasons, the most obvious of which was the imbalance of available force—each division had only two infantry battalions to support eight battalions of tanks. Furthermore, reconstituting the columns for each operation was time consuming, a drawback compounded by the late receipt of orders from higher headquarters. "I do not believe the method . . . of reforming C.T.'s [combat teams] is a good idea. Takes too long to regroup them . . . delay is caused by units not having worked together in the same team," reported Col. John B. Thompson, the GHQ observer accompanying the 2d Armored Division in the Carolinas.[25] Brig. Gen. Orlando Ward, commander of the 1st Armored Brigade, suggested to the Army chief of staff, "We should have teams consisting of infantry, artillery, and tanks working together all the time and then if it is necessary to augment one arm or the other it can be done without disruption."[26]

Just such a reform had been under study in the Armored Force for many months, based largely on armor trends among the European belligerents, but Generals Devers and Marshall awaited the end of the GHQ maneuvers before instituting any major changes.[27] On 4 December, Marshall issued a memo to his deputy chief of staff authorizing a restructuring of the armored division: "Gen. Devers brought up to me the tank reorganization. He stated that there was a general unanimity in the matter among the higher ranking officers, and that nothing in the South Carolina maneuvers had caused him to change his views. I agreed to approve the reorganization."[28]

The reorganization, which became official on 1 March 1942, resulted in a leaner, more balanced armored division.[29] To redress the imbalance between tanks and infantry, the division gave up one of its three armored regiments and increased the infantry regiment from two battalions to three. The ratio of tank to infantry battalions, which had been eight to two in the old organization, became six to three in the 1942 division. Eliminated altogether were the anomalous armored brigade headquarters and certain superfluous service elements.[30]

The reorganization also rationalized the armored division's artillery component. In place of the armored brigade's two-battalion artillery regiment and a separate battalion under division headquarters, the 1942 division had three uniform battalions, all under the administrative control of division headquarters.[31] The development of a self-propelled howitzer in 1942 contributed even more to the effectiveness of armored artillery. An experimental model consisting of a 105-mm. howitzer mounted on a medium tank chassis won approval in February after only five days of testing and entered production that summer under the designation M7.[32] The self-propelled gun granted mobility to armored artillery equal to that of the division's tanks and halftrack-borne infantry, thus improving artillery's ability to cooperate with the other arms.

Perhaps the most significant feature of the 1942 armored division was the presence of two new brigade-level headquarters, known as combat commands, that paralleled the function of the German *Kampfgruppen*. Like the *Kampfgruppen*, combat commands were temporary task forces that could include any desired combination of combat elements and could be reconfigured to meet changing tactical requirements. Most importantly, the combat command system facilitated the intimate interaction of infantry, artillery, and tanks at the small-unit level, where it was most needed.[33]

The post-maneuvers armored reorganization signaled the end of the Chaffee era in armored development. Chaffee's vision of tanks and infantry fighting in different places at different times gave way to a doctrine of close cooperation among the elements. One other major feature of the 1942 reorganization that represented a departure from Chaffee was the passing of the light tank from its place of dominance in American armored doctrine. Since the days of the 7th Cavalry Brigade (Mechanized), mobility had counted for more than armor or firepower. Thus the light tank of thirteen tons, mounting machine guns and a 37-mm. gun, had become the mainstay of doctrine as it developed under Chaffee. Light tanks outnumbered mediums two to one under 1940 tables of organization. One can discern a cavalrylike emphasis on mobility in several of the armored operations in the GHQ maneuvers, particularly Patton's envelopment of Shreveport.[34]

But in Europe the light tank had fallen into disfavor by the end of 1941, and in both the Soviet and North African wars, medium tanks of twenty to thirty tons, carrying guns in the 75-mm. range, dominated the battlefield. Even heavier tanks were on the way. The GHQ maneuvers revealed the vulnerability of light tanks to anti-tank fire, even if umpire rules exaggerated the lethality of that fire. These developments persuaded General Devers to draw back from Chaffee's commitment to mobility at the expense of armor and firepower. Consequently, under the 1942 reorganization the number of light tank battalions in the armored division dropped from six to two, and the medium battalions increased from two to four, giving the division a clear preponderance of medium tanks.[35]

Moreover, the medium tank battalions soon were to be equipped with a new weapon to replace their makeshift M3 mediums. Beginning in 1942, American armored divisions received the new M4 Sherman tank that served throughout World War II.

Whereas the post-maneuver trend in the Armored Force was toward closer integration among elements, the Army Air Forces maintained and even enhanced its separation from the ground arms. In the wake of the maneuvers came a widespread outpouring of approval for the air support command concept. Ground officers such as Griswold and Lear joined top air officers Arnold and Emmons in declaring their basic satisfaction with air support as it was practiced in the maneuvers.[36] This post-maneuvers harmony may have been good for relations among the arms, but it only helped conceal the thorny issues that continued to divide the services.

The area that cried the loudest for attention was the one that the Army Air Forces was least inclined to pursue—direct support of frontline troops. In the Carolinas, as in Louisiana, the air commands displayed much more proficiency in interdiction-type operations and devoted the majority of missions to them: of the 167 raids flown by the 1st and 3d Air Support Commands, 99 went against airdromes, railroads, and bridges; 37 against armored and mechanized units (by preference, those detected in their assembly areas behind the lines); and 31 against miscellaneous targets, including enemy frontline troops.[37] The air support commands actively resisted the dissipation of force that small-scale direct-support operations would necessitate and generally made no attempt to attack what they considered to be unremunerative targets.[38]

Air doctrine maintained that air units should not, as a rule, be assigned to missions within friendly artillery range, so no matter how badly the frontline troops might need close-in air support, their requests were likely to be turned down.[39] The air support commands preferred to conduct operations of their own choosing.

On the other hand, ground commanders did not fully appreciate the capabilities and limitations of air power. They could not be trusted to discern the feasible from the impractical, nor did they understand the importance of air missions executed beyond their line of sight. The air support command was a compromise that satisfied neither the airman's desire for centralized autonomy nor the ground soldier's demand for maximum support at the cutting edge of battle.

After the maneuvers the Army Air Forces officially implemented the air support command concept, but with an increased emphasis on the centralization of air assets. In April 1942 the War Department issued *Aviation in Support of Ground Forces: Field Manual 31–35*, which derived in part from experience gained during the GHQ maneuvers. This manual indicated that air support commands would be assigned to each field army but that observation aircraft would be their only permanent, organic aircraft. For combat aircraft the air support command (and thus the field army) would be dependent upon a theater air commander who would attach combat units for ground support purposes. Control of the air support command would be by collaboration between its commander and the field army commander.[40]

Field Manual 31–35 perpetuated the roundabout method of requesting direct support of the front lines, which had worked without great success in the GHQ maneuvers and which virtually guaranteed that there would be no communication between supporting aircraft and the ground unit being supported. A ground unit desiring air support was to pass the request along its own chain of command to the division or corps, where an air liaison officer would pass judgment on it. If the request met with his approval, he would relay it to air support command headquarters, where the request would again be scrutinized. Only after headquarters approved the request would orders go out to an airfield for a unit to take off and execute the mission. Once in the air, the only communication between aircraft and ground units would be through the liaison officer at division or corps headquarters.[41]

The air-ground doctrine which the Army Air Forces took to war had the advantage of keeping air power concentrated in the hands of air officers, who could deploy it economically where it

Laying a pierced steel plank runway: the "Marston mat." *(U.S. Army Corps of Engineers.)*

was needed most. The ground soldier's demands for direct support were not satisfied.

The most innovative aviation-related development to come out of the GHQ maneuvers occurred at the initiative of private industry, against the direct opposition of the Army Air Forces. Early in 1941 the aircraft firms of Piper, Aeronca, and Taylor had approached the Army with an offer to loan eleven light aircraft of the Cub variety, complete with pilots, for testing in the artillery spotting and liaison roles during the 1941 maneuvers season. These planes proved so useful in the summer corps and army maneuvers that the Army rented them, civilian pilots and all, for the GHQ maneuvers. Nicknamed the Grasshopper Squadron, these eleven planes flew an estimated 400,000 miles and performed approximately 3,000 non-combat missions during the 1941 maneuvers season without losing a single plane. Powered by 65-horsepower engines, the Grasshoppers cost about one-tenth as much as a standard observation plane, required less maintenance, and could be flown from virtually any level surface. The success of the Grasshopper Squadron prompted the War Department to order that six to ten such light planes, flown by Army, not Army Air Forces, pilots, be assigned organically to every division for artillery spotting and general liaison. These lowly Grasshoppers were the ancestors of what would become Army aviation in the postwar period.[42]

Of even greater significance to future aerial operations was an experiment conducted near Marston, North Carolina (not far from Hoffman), during the November maneuvers. There the 21st Engineer Regiment (Aviation) constructed a 3,000-foot runway on virgin ground for use by the 1st Air Support Command. The job took eleven days and consumed eighteen railroad carloads of a new product known as pierced steel planking. The Carnegie Illinois Steel Company had developed the planking for the War Department based on reports from the European war that spelled out the need for a readily portable material that could make grass runways usable by modern aircraft. After considerable experimentation in conjunction with the Corps of Engineers, Carnegie developed a steel panel, 10 feet by 15 inches, pierced by 87 holes, that weighed only 66.2 pounds. Such panels could be positioned and interlocked without special tools and could be easily lifted and transported to a new site. The 21st Engineers used 36,000 of these panels to fabricate the airstrip at Marston.

The pierced steel plank, or Marston mat, was later employed in every theater of World War II. It gave Allied air forces the ability to create instant airfields wherever reasonably level ground could be had. By war's end, Army engineers could build a 5,000-foot runway, capable of handling even heavy bombers, in as little as seventy-two hours. When General Arnold inspected the original Marston mat in November 1941, he pronounced it "the year's greatest achievement in aviation." [43]

Aside from the Grasshopper experiment and the Marston mat, there was disappointingly little development of tactical aviation after the GHQ maneuvers. Additional maneuvers or tactical exercises might have pointed up some of the problems inherent to the air support command system, but even if the Army had been interested, it was not to get the opportunity. Nor would there be a maneuvers rematch between a full-fledged tank destroyer force and a reorganized armored division. One week after General McNair delivered the final critique of the Carolinas maneuvers, the nation was at war.

Notes

1. Memo of General Instructions, 17 Oct 41, G–1/15942–74, Microfilm Reel 14, Item 526, GCM Library.

2. Memo for Sec War, Notes on Conference, 4 Dec 41 Microfilm Reel 116, Item 2714, GCM Library.

3. Ibid.

4. Ibid.

5. Watson, *Chief of Staff*, pp. 362–66; Marshall, *Papers 2*, pp. 676–79 (Memo, Robert L. Sherrod for David W. Hulburd, Jr., 15 Nov 41, sub: General Marshall's Conference Today).

6. Memo for Sec War, Notes on Conference, 4 Dec 41, Microfilm Reel 116, Item 2714, GCM Library.

7. "General McNair's Comments," *Army and Navy Journal*, 4 Oct 41, pp. 136–37; Garrett Underhill, "Louisiana Hayride," *Field Artillery Journal*, Dec 41, pp. 907–13; "Lessons From the Maneuvers," *Field Artillery Journal*, Dec 41, pp. 914–17; "Report on Second and Third Army Maneuvers, 1941," CGSC Library; GHQ Dir HQ, "Comments on First Phase—Second Army vs. Third Army Maneuvers," 22 Sep 41, CGSC Library; Comments by Lt Gen L. J. McNair, 2d Phase, GHQ-Directed Maneuvers, AG 353 (6–16–45) Sec 1–C, RG 407, Army AG Decimal File 1940–45, NA; Brig Gen Mark W. Clark, Deputy Dir, Critique of 1st Phase, GHQ-Directed Maneuvers Carolinas, "Clark's Copy," RG 337 57D, HQ AGF, GHQ GS G–3, Subject File 1940–Mar 9, 1942, NA; Critique by Lt Gen L. J. McNair, 1st Phase, GHQ-Directed Maneuvers, Carolina area, "Clark's Copy," RG 337 57D, NA; GHQ Dir HQ, "Comments on 1st Phase— First Army vs. IV Army Corps Maneuvers, 1941," 22 Nov 41, "Clark's Copy," RG 337 57D, NA; Critique of 2d Phase, GHQ-Directed Maneuvers, Carolina Area, by Brig Gen Mark W. Clark, "Clark's Copy," RG 337 57D, NA; Critique of 2d Phase GHQ-Directed Maneuvers [McNair], "Clark's Copy," RG 337 57D, NA; Lt Gen L. J. McNair to CG, First Army, 22 Dec 41, "Clark's Copy," RG 337 57D, NA; Lt Gen L. J. McNair to CG, IV Army Corps, 7 Jan 42, "Clark's Copy," RG 337 57D, NA.

8. Ibid.

9. Wiley and Govan, "AGF Study No. 16," pp. 36–38; Collins, *Lightning Joe*, pp. 104–05.

10. CofS GHQ to All Army Commanders and Chief of the Armd Force, 30 Oct 41, sub: Post-Maneuver Training, (6–16–41)–(6–20–41), 353/652–C (10–30–41), RG 407, NA.

11. Ibid., Encl 1.

12. Ibid., Encl 2.

13. Ibid., Encl 3.

14. "General McNair's Comments," *Army and Navy Journal*, 4 Oct 41, pp. 136–37.

15. Collins, *Lightning Joe*, p. 115.

16. Wiley and Govan, "AGF Study No. 16," p. 115.

17. Kent Roberts Greenfield, "AGF Study No. 35: Army Ground Forces and the Air-Ground Battle Team" (Historical Section, AGF, 1948), p. 9.

18. U.S. Army Tank Destroyer Center, "Tank Destroyer History, Inception through 8 May, 1945," by Historical Officer, Tank Destroyer Center, 1945, One, I, p. 15.

19. Conf in Office of CofS, 7 Oct 41, Microfilm Reel 287, Item 4327, GCM Library.

20. "Second Battle of the Carolinas," *Time*, 8 Dec 41, p. 66.

21. U.S. Army Tank Destroyer Center, "Tank Destroyer History," One, I, p. 16.

22. Emory A. Dunham, "AGF Study No. 29: Tank Destroyer History" (Historical Section, AGF, 1946), p. 53.

23. "SOP TD Bn," Microfilm Reel 287, Item 4327, GCM Library. See also U.S. War Department, *Organization and Tactics of Tank Destroyer Units: Field Manual 18–5* (Washington, D.C.: Government Printing Office, 1942).

24. For an analysis of the tank destroyer program see Christopher R. Gabel, *Seek, Strike, and Destroy: U.S. Army Tank Destroyer Doctrine in World War II*, Leavenworth Paper 12 (Leavenworth, Kan.: U.S. Army Command and General Staff College, 1985).

25. Rpt, Col John B. Thompson [undated], Performance of AT, RG 337 57D, NA.

26. Brig Gen Orlando Ward to CofS, 2 Dec 41, Maneuvers Memoranda, General Corresp, RG 337 57, HQ AGF, GHQ, NA.

27. "Seek More Punch in Armored Units," *New York Times*, 26 Sep 41.

28. Memo, CofS for Gen Bryden, 4 Dec 41, Directives, DCofS 10–12/41, GCM Library.

29. Houston, *Hell on Wheels*, p. 105; "AGF Study No. 27: The Armored Force, Command, and Center" (Historical Section, AGF, 1946), p. 29.

30. "AGF Study No. 27," pp. 29–32.

31. Ibid.

32. Ibid., p. 89.

33. Ibid., pp. 29–32.

34. Richard M. Ogorkiewicz, *Armoured Forces* (New York: Arco, 1970), pp. 87–89.

35. Ogorkiewicz, *Armoured Forces*, p. 89.

36. HQ IV Corps, Critique on 2d Phase GHQ Carolinas Maneuvers, "Clark's Copy," RG 337 57D, NA; Memo, Maj Gen Arnold for CofS, 8 Oct 41, 354.2 Rpts, 1941, RG 337 57, NA; "War Games Over, Blues Near Goal," *New York Times*, 29 Sep 41.

37. Col William E. Kepner, 2d Phase Critique, 30 Nov 41, "Clark's Copy," RG 337 57D, NA.

38. Ibid.

39. Robert T. Finney, *History of the Air Corps Tactical School*, USAF Historical Study 100 (Maxwell AFB, Ala.: USAF Historical Division, Research Studies Institute, Air University, 1955), p. 36.

40. Greenfield, "AGF Study No. 35," pp. 3–4.

41. Ibid.

42. Memo, ACofS for TAG, 17 Jun 41, 353 (5/15/41) Sec 1, RG 407, NA; Laurence B. Epstein, "Army Organic Light Aviation: The Founding Fathers," *U.S. Army Aviation Digest*, Jun 77, pp. 2–17.

43. Richard K. Smith, "Marston Mat," *Air Force Magazine*, Apr 89, pp. 84–88; Dwight F. Johns, "Maneuver Notes of Aviation Engineers," *The Military Engineer*, Nov 41, pp. 10–12, and Mar 42, pp. 133–35; G.G. Greulich, "Steel Landing Mats for Airplane Runways," *Civil Engineering*, Sep 43, pp. 431–33.

Conclusion: The GHQ Maneuvers and the World War II Army

Even the men who saw the planes couldn't understand. One of them was Fireman Frank Stock of the repair ship *Vestal*, moored beside the *Arizona* along Battleship Row. . . . The men were mildly surprised—they had never seen U.S. planes come in from that direction. They were even more surprised when the rear-seat gunners sprayed them with machine-gun bullets. Then Stock recalled the stories he had read about "battle-condition" maneuvers in the Southern states. This must be the same idea—for extra realism they had even painted red circles on the planes. The truth finally dawned when one of his friends caught a slug in the stomach from the fifth plane that passed.[1]

When the Japanese Navy's First Air Fleet attacked Oahu on the morning of 7 December 1941, the U.S. Army's Protective Mobilization Plan instantly became obsolete. The basic goal of the 1941 training season, and of the GHQ maneuvers, had been to build up a combat-ready PMP Army of one million men, but with the attack on Pearl Harbor and the nation's entry into global war, the need for further expansion made that objective irrelevant. General McNair's post-maneuvers training program, predicated upon a period of stability and improvement rather than growth, gave way to urgent new mobilization schemes. On 14 December General Marshall received and immediately approved a mobilization and training plan calling for a permanent 2.2 million-man Army and the activation of 100 divisions over the next two years.[2] By 5 January 1942, the objective had risen to 3.6 million men and 69 divisions within one year.[3] In fact, 1942 would witness the activation of 9 new armored divisions, 27 infantry divisions, and 2 airborne divisions,[4] at the cost of cutting most mobilization training programs from thirteen to eight weeks, feeding selectees directly into tactical units, and, of course, abandoning McNair's leisurely post-maneuvers remedial training program.[5] Three years later the Army would number 8 million men and 89 combat divisions.

Expansion on such a scale entailed the cannibalization of the field-ready armies, corps, and divisions so laboriously built up in the course of the 1941 training and maneuvers program. Even General Headquarters ceased to exist; the scope of global war meant that there would be no single expeditionary force that could be trained at home and then dispatched wholesale to a theater of operations under the command of the chief of staff. Instead, forces were soon to be committed all around the world, and General Marshall's command post would of necessity be located in Washington, D.C., not on the battlefield. For this reason, and for the purpose of rationalizing the Army's command machinery, General Headquarters passed out of existence on 9 March 1942. A new organization called Army Ground Forces (AGF), commanded by General McNair, assumed training responsibilities. Operational authority over combat units passed to Operations Division (OPD), a new organization within the War Department General Staff.[6]

Since the overseas commitment of ground troops would initially be on a relatively small scale, the four existing field armies stayed on in the United States as training commands rather than opening as tactical headquarters in combat theaters. Eventually, the First and Third Armies became operational in Europe under new commanders and staffs, but the Second Army and Fourth Army (which had not participated in the GHQ army-versus-army maneuvers) served as training commands throughout the war. Similarly, by the time the various corps headquarters reached theaters of operations, most had been thoroughly reconstituted.

Even the divisions that had participated in the 1941 maneuvers were virtually unrecognizable by the end of 1942. The 30th Division, a veteran of the Carolinas maneuvers, gave up all but 3,000 of its men as cadres for new divisions and received raw recruits in return. The 31st and 33d, participants in the Louisiana maneuvers, lost all but 7,200 and 8,400 respectively.[7] The belated triangular configuring of these and all other National Guard divisions, which began in January 1942, cut each division's manpower requirements to approximately 15,000, but it also contributed to the extensive reconstitution of the maneuvers-experienced divisions. Ironically, the change occurred at a time when many officers, as a result of the GHQ maneuvers, recognized that the square division retained some desirable features lacking in the triangular division. The 45th Division in Louisiana and the 26th Division in the Carolinas, both square divisions, were among the best maneuvers units. General Griswold got such good service from his two square divisions, the 31st and 43d, that he acknowledged "a distinct need for both the triangular and the square division." [8] In the course of subsequent combat operation, the staying power of the massive square division would be missed in more than one bloody battle.

Thus, as an exercise in unit training the 1941 maneuvers ultimately did little to prepare the Army for war, inasmuch as the units and headquarters involved were largely reconfigured before seeing combat. A better case might be made for the assertion that the commanding officers involved in maneuvers benefited enormously from the experience of moving real troops through real terrain against a real opponent, and that this experience stood the Army in good stead during combat. However, most of the forty-two division, corps, and army commanders who took part in the GHQ maneuvers were either relieved or reassigned to new commands during 1942 (including twenty of the twenty-seven participating division commanders). Only eleven of the forty-two went on to significant combat commands during World War II. Among these, Krueger and Patton led field armies in combat; Griswold, Fredendall, Swift, and Millikin commanded corps; Hester, Walker, Persons, and Beightler held division commands; and Kepner led a fighter command. In addition to the maneuvers commanders who won combat commands, several others such as Richardson, Sultan, and Harmon filled important wartime administrative posts with distinction. (*Appendix B*)

The thirty-one caretakers, commanders of major units in the GHQ maneuvers who did not win combat commands, gave way to younger, more promising, officers. Terry Allen, Leonard Gerow, William Simpson, and Omar Bradley were among the officers who acquired major commands after the GHQ maneuvers and who rose to fame in combat. The most noteworthy of this group was, of course, Dwight D. Eisenhower, who won praise for his performance as Third Army chief of staff in Louisiana. Shortly thereafter, he embarked upon a meteoric ascent to the top ranks of the Army and to the most important line position of the war—supreme allied commander in Europe. [9] In all probability, General Marshall knew in 1941 who his wartime commanders would be, and he used the maneuvers period to groom the Eisenhowers and Bradleys in lower-level assignments. As a criterion for selection to higher command, one's showing in the maneuvers had relatively little significance.

Nor is it entirely clear that the maneuvers gave the officer corps an education in "operational art" (a term not then in use). A wide variety of operational styles emerged during the maneuvers, ranging from Patton's high-spirited armored raids to Drum's methodical general assaults. Patton's style seemed progressive at the time, but it actually owed more to J. E. B. Stuart than to Heinz Guderian. Drum's methods were enormously successful on maneuvers but held little appeal for Marshall and McNair, who wished to forge the Army into a rapier, not a battle-ax. Only one of the field armies involved in the maneuvers clearly anticipated the operational art that would characterize American operations in World War II— Krueger's Third Army, where Eisenhower served as chief of staff. Krueger fought on a broad front, yet retained a high degree of responsiveness owing to his skillful use of motor transport and to the latitude that he afforded his subordinates. His powerful operations were clear and straightforward, and they produced maximum results at minimum risk. Eisenhower did well to impart a similar operational style to his subsequent campaigns in Europe.

Although originally conceived as a training device, the GHQ maneuvers had their most lasting impact in the area of doctrine. Infantry and artillery doctrine, which the maneuvers validated (although execution left something to be desired), emerged relatively unchanged. Armor benefited enormously from its embarrassments in Louisiana and the Carolinas. The trend toward closer cooperation among tanks, infantry, and artillery that began with the 1942 division reorganization continued with yet another restructuring of the armored division in 1943. The 1943 division had three combat commands and three battalions each of tanks, infantry, and artillery. The sixteen armored divisions activated in World War II proved in combat to be sound, organizationally and doctrinally.[10]

Despite the success of its divisions in the field, the Armored Force as an institution within the Army declined significantly in status after the 1941 maneuvers. In Louisiana and the Carolinas, General McNair had provided I Armored Corps and its two divisions with the opportunity to strike decisive blows in battle, which they largely failed to do, for a variety of reasons. Thereafter, McNair relaxed his emphasis on armor and stressed instead the traditional infantry-artillery team as the centerpiece of ground combat.[11] This could be seen in his plans for post-maneuvers training, which did not encompass armor, but the decline of armor became even more obvious as 1942 progressed. The four armored corps headquarters that had been activated were disbanded, and the motorized division category, developed specifically for participation in large-scale armored operations, was also discontinued. General Devers, the Armored Force chief, had envisaged armored corps consisting of one motorized and two armored divisions each, but the actual wartime employment of armored divisions involved placing them into standard corps along with, typically, two infantry divisions. General McNair supported this procedure on the grounds that armored divisions were best suited to the exploitation of tactical advantages won by traditional units, and not to the creation of breakthroughs on their own.[12]

Although the maneuvers may have hastened the decline of large armored units, there was little in the Louisiana or Carolinas exercises to explain the dramatic upsurge in the numbers of independent tank battalions that followed. Only five such battalions existed in 1941, two of which participated in the GHQ maneuvers without much distinction.[13] As part of his shift in emphasis away from large armored forces, McNair asked for more of these independent tank battalions. By the end of the war there were more independent battalions than there were tank battalions within the sixteen armored divisions.[14] In the European theater the attachment of one tank battalion and one tank destroyer battalion (often equipped with tanklike weapons) to each infantry division on a semipermanent basis was the norm, thus fleshing out the lean triangular division and, incidentally, making a virtual armored division of it. Few German panzer divisions late in the war could boast an equal number of armored vehicles.

The loss of status sustained by the Armored Force after the GHQ maneuvers was nothing compared to that suffered by the Cavalry, which virtually ceased to exist as a distinct service. The maneuvers demonstrated that cavalry had lost its superiority in mobility. McNair concluded after the maneuvers that horse cavalry was no longer viable at all.[15] Troopers exchanged the last of their equestrian mounts for mechanized ones in 1942 and embarked upon a war in which cavalry would serve mainly in the unglamorous roles of reconnaissance, security, and defense of positions. Of the two cavalry divisions in 1941, only the 1st saw action, and that as infantry.[16] Diehard cavalrymen blamed their decline not on their own resistance to modernization in the years when cavalry could have dominated the Army's mechanization program, but on the special interests of "certain industries" that stood to profit from mechanization, and on the jealousy of "soft and inactive officers behind desks" who did away with the mounted service out of spite.[17]

The maneuvers did not lead to a sufficiently rigorous reappraisal of tactical air doctrine. Problems noted in 1941 resurfaced with a vengeance during the Tunisian campaign of 1942–43. In Tunisia, a dissipation of effort precluded the attainment of theater air supremacy, and yet the ground troops remained dissatisfied with the quality and quantity of direct support. The solution, which owed much to British experience, did not involve choosing between centralization and decentralization; rather, it involved centralization and decentralization simultaneously.

During the 1944–45 campaign in Europe, all American tactical aircraft came under one command, the Ninth Air Force, which assigned combat wings to tactical air commands (one per field army) on the basis of operational requirements. This centralization permitted the Ninth Air Force to maintain theaterwide control of the air and to channel combat power to decisive points.

Paradoxically, this system also facilitated decentralization. Tactical air command headquarters typically located with their respective field army headquarters and participated directly in the planning of ground operations, thus enhancing coordination and responsiveness. In a development of equal significance, Maj. Gen. Elwood Quesada, commander of the IX Tactical Air Command (assigned to the U.S. First Army), devised a means of providing continuous direct support for advancing armored divisions. Quesada assigned flights of four fighter-bombers to each combat command of the leading armored divisions and provided a tank-borne aircraft radio and air liaison officer to every combat command commander. Thus, the armored commander could communicate directly with the fighter-bombers, which were always immediately available, both to request attacks against specific targets in front of the combat command and to secure information about the route ahead.[18] In the GHQ maneuvers, air officers had rejected the idea of maintaining continuous support on the philosophical grounds that it would place aircraft under the control of ground commanders, and on the practical grounds that continuous support was "extremely costly, not . . . practical," and "not necessary."[19] General Quesada recognized both the need and the practicality, and in the words of the official Air Force history, his plan "was simple, and possibly on that very account it worked with a singular perfection."[20] Had the Army Air Forces possessed the same innovative spirit in 1941 that Quesada displayed three years later, a viable air-ground doctrine might have emerged from the GHQ maneuvers instead of from the hard school of war. Perhaps more to the point, by 1944 the Army Air Forces possessed such an abundance of aircraft and pilots that it could perform every conceivable air mission to satisfaction, ranging from strategic bombing to the direct support of frontline troops.

The GHQ maneuvers revealed problems in air-ground doctrine that were not heeded until they were confirmed by war, but in the related field of airborne warfare the apparent lessons of the GHQ maneuvers pointed in the wrong direction. To be fair, the maneuvers never provided a realistic tactical test of airborne warfare, in that none of the four maneuvers drops were of sufficient scale to have much impact on the greater scheme of the battle at hand. At best, airborne participation in the maneuvers provided good training, as General McNair claimed. Lt. Col. William C. Lee, commander of the Provisional Parachute Group and father of the American airborne force, dismissed even this marginal benefit on the grounds that the 502d Parachute Battalion, one of only three then active, spent so much time in preparation for the GHQ maneuvers that other essential training was neglected.[21]

In any event, such results as airborne troops obtained in the maneuvers seemed to indicate that parachute troops were most useful in small-scale sabotage activities and that drops against defended objectives should be made on a broad front at some distance from the intended targets in order to avoid the slaughter that befell the 502d when it dropped on Pope Field. Wartime practice cut directly across the maneuvers lessons. American airborne troops in Europe generally fought as divisions (a total of five were activated), performed key roles in the most crucial of ground operations, and preferred to drop as near their objectives as possible.

Whereas airborne lessons from the maneuvers held little interest for doctrine writers, the antitank concepts apparently validated in the maneuvers could not be set aside quite so easily. Put simply, tank destroyers never duplicated their maneuvers victories in combat. An impartial, critical analysis of antitank operations in the maneuvers might have warned of some of the difficulties ahead.

During the GHQ maneuvers, considerable confusion surrounded the antitank doctrine that General McNair had promoted: how could antitank defense be aggressive, and even offensive, in nature? Wartime tank destroyer doctrine incorporated all of the major characteristics of McNair's maneuvers doctrine, including the confusion. At one and the same time, tank destroyers were to "Seek, Strike, and Destroy"; were to take "offensive action" against armor; and yet were to avoid "slugging matches" with enemy tanks.[22] For two years General McNair and the Tank Destroyer Center struggled to clarify tank destroyer doctrine but could not even agree among themselves on exactly what that doctrine involved.[23]

Tactical commanders in the theaters of operations solved the problem by tacitly rejecting tank destroyer doctrine altogether. Instead of pooling tank destroyer battalions into corps and army reserves, commanders fragmented them into companies and platoons, which were then attached to infantry units for frontline antitank defense. When German armor went on the defensive, innovative tank destroyer officers developed valuable secondary missions for their units, particularly direct and indirect fire support. Tank destroyers served well in combat but never had the opportunity to re-fight the battles of Mount Carmel, Albemarle, or Pageland.[24]

As doctrine died in the field, so did the tank destroyer quasi-arm decline institutionally at home. In 1942, General McNair pro-posed that 222 tank destroyer battalions be activated, but the War Department approved only 144. At the peak of the program 106 battalions existed, but unfavorable reports from the field and a seri-ous shortage of infantry troops soon led to widespread deactiva-tions among tank destroyer battalions. By war's end only 68 battal-ions remained on the roster.[25] Shortly thereafter the Army disbanded the tank destroyer force altogether and adopted the dic-tum of General Devers, longtime opponent of the tank destroyer concept: "The separate tank destroyer arm is not a practical con-cept on the battlefield. Defensive AT weapons are essentially ar-tillery. Offensively the weapon to best the tank is a better tank."[26]

In the final analysis, were the GHQ maneuvers worthwhile? The advances made in unit training proved ephemeral, relatively few maneuvers-trained commanders ever saw combat, and as a doctri-nal laboratory the maneuvers ultimately proved to be a mixed suc-cess. In weighing the value of the GHQ maneuvers, however, it would be a mistake to overlook the most noteworthy result of the Protective Mobilization Plan period, of which the GHQ maneuvers were the climax: for the first time in the nation's history there ex-isted a field-tested, nearly combat-ready Army before the declara-tion of war. More than 1.6 million men wore the uniform and manned a force of 34 divisions organized into 9 traditional corps, 2 armored corps, 4 field armies, and an air arm of 32 active combat groups.[27] Of this force, over 740,000 men, 27 divisions, 3 armies, and 9 air force groups had taken part in one or both of the GHQ maneuvers. General McNair judged that 14 infantry, 2 armored, and 1 cavalry division had proven themselves marginally ready for combat by the time the United States entered World War II.[28]

Thanks to the Protective Mobilization Plan and the maneuvers, the Army responded well to the onset of hostilities. General Clark re-lates, "When Pearl Harbor happened . . . there was [a] great clamor to get troops to the west coast, and I thought to myself at the time . . . how lucky we [were] that we just had maneuvers. We'd moved a corps. Two or three months before that you would say, 'How do you move a corps?'"[29] And although the demands of wartime mobiliza-tion quickly dismembered that field-ready force and dispersed the veterans of Louisiana and the Carolinas, the training principles uti-lized in 1942 to create a new, larger Army were already in place, thanks to the Protective Mobilization Plan of 1939–41.[30]

Furthermore, in a psychological sense the 1941 maneuvers helped prepare the Army and the nation for war. Soldiers who had endured Louisiana or the Carolinas knew what to expect from campaigning, and some remarked during combat that, except for the shooting, "this is no worse than maneuvers."[31] The spirit of the troops on 7 December was higher than it had been six months before, and much of the improvement seemed to have come during maneuvers. Meaningful activity, even in a make-believe war, reinvigorated citizen-soldiers who had muttered "OHIO" (over the hill in October) only weeks before.

Public perception of the Army changed for the better during the 1941 maneuvers season. Initially, General Marshall had worried that the GHQ maneuvers might touch off a repetition of the "bad press" that had attended the unfortunate 1940 National Guard exercises.[32] But press coverage of the GHQ maneuvers was uniformly positive. Correspondents freely pointed out the faults and deficiencies that they observed, but throughout their articles and columns there sounds a note of pride and even wonder at what the Army had become in one year's time. The 1940 maneuvers had been playacting; 1941 was serious business. Some writers even went so far as to compare the 1941 Army with the apparently invincible German *Wehrmacht*—and the comparison was not altogether unfavorable.[33]

The public accepted the cost of the maneuvers without complaint. Sixty-one soldiers lost their lives in the Louisiana and Carolinas exercises, and yet there was no public outcry. In monetary terms the entire 1941 maneuvers season cost the nation approximately $20.6 million in expenses incurred directly by the field armies and armored and air forces.[34] Additional thousands went to cover damage claims filed by residents of the maneuvers areas. Compensation went out for stolen melons, rutted yards, wrecked barrooms, buildings damaged by errant tanks, drowned sheep (stampeded into water by artillery fire), and fatal accidents involving Army and civilian vehicles. The Army paid claims of up to $1,000 out of its own budget; the more serious claims, such as for the drowned sheep and the accident fatalities, meant compensation in the form of special appropriations from Congress.[35] But thousands of potential claims were never filed, and many of those filed were never paid because of their withdrawal by patriotic plaintiffs.[36]

All told, the cost of the GHQ maneuvers was low. Had the Army been forced to weed out unfit officers, experiment with new doctrine, and uncover training flaws in real combat, the price would have been measured in lives, not dollars. The Army learned lessons in transporting, maneuvering, administering, and supplying its forces in the field that nations such as France and the Soviet Union had just recently acquired in the midst of bloody and desperate fighting. The GHQ maneuvers enabled the United States to enter World War II with a degree of confidence that would have been lacking had the Army not already showed itself to be a functioning, potentially powerful, force.

The GHQ maneuvers of 1941 were unprecedented in U.S. Army history and have never been duplicated in size or scope since. Free, two-sided maneuvers remained a part of unit training throughout World War II, but these later exercises never exceeded the division-versus-division level. Indeed, from the perspective of the 1990s, the hope is that the circumstances that made the GHQ maneuvers necessary will be consigned forever to the past. Starting in 1939, with the world already enveloped in conflict, the Army was forced to make good two decades of virtual disarmament in two years' time. Conducted in an atmosphere of near desperation, the GHQ maneuvers of 1941 revealed both the penalties of military unpreparedness and the power of American resolve. The war that followed transformed both the Army and the nation forever.

Notes

1. Walter Lord, *Day of Infamy*, Bantam edition (New York: Holt, Rinehart, Winston, 1957), p. 67.
2. Mobilization and Training Plan, 14 Dec 41, Microfilm Reel 14, Item 450, GCM Library.
3. Memo for Sec GS, 15 Jan 42, G–3/6457–433, Microfilm Reel 14, Item 450, GCM Library.
4. Palmer, Wiley, and Keast, *Procurement*, p. 433.
5. Mobilization and Training Plan, 14 Dec 41, Microfilm Reel 14, Item 450, GCM Library.
6. Greenfield, Palmer, and Wiley, *Organization*, p. 155.
7. Palmer, Wiley, and Keast, *Procurement*, p. 457.
8. Critique on 1st Phase, GHQ Carolina Maneuvers, Gen Griswold, "General Clark's Personal Copy, First Army vs. IV Corps Maneuvers, November 15–30, 1941," RG 337 57D, HQ AGF, GHQ GS G–3, Subject File 1940–Mar 9, 1942, NA.
9. Pogue, *Marshall*, p. 162. See Appendix B, below, for a roster of maneuvers commanders and their wartime careers.
10. "AGF Study No. 27," p. 33; Ogorkiewicz, *Armoured Forces*, p. 93.
11. Greenfield, Palmer, and Wiley, *Organization*, p. 390.
12. Ogorkiewicz, *Armoured Forces*, p. 91.
13. "AGF Study No. 27," pp. 44–47.
14. Ogorkiewicz, *Armoured Forces*, p. 91.
15. Memo for Sec War, Notes on Conf, 4 Dec 41, Microfilm Reel 116, Item 2714, GCM Library.
16. Stubbs and Connor, *Armor-Cavalry I*, p. 71.
17. Herr and Wallace, *Cavalry*, p. 254.
18. Wesley F. Craven and James L. Cate, *Europe: Argument to V–E Day*, The Army Air Forces in World War II, vol. 3 (Chicago: University of Chicago Press, 1951), pp. 239–42.
19. "Report on 2d Air Task Force Participation in Louisiana Maneuvers," Sec II, p. 29, 353/2 Air Forces, RG 337 57, HQ AGF, GHQ, NA.
20. Craven and Cate, *Europe: Argument to V–E Day*, p. 240.
21. John T. Ellis, "AGF Study No. 25: The Airborne Command and Center" (Historical Section, AGF, 1951), p. 10; Memo, Lt Col Lloyd D. Brown for G–3 Dir, 28 Nov 41, Training Div File 1st Phase Critique, RG 337 57D, NA.
22. U.S. War Department, *Organization and Tactics of Tank Destroyer Units: Field Manual 18–5* (Washington, D.C.: Government Printing Office, 1942), p. 38.
23. See various ltrs between Ward and McNair, Jun–Aug 43, Orlando Ward Papers, MHI.
24. See Gabel, *Seek, Strike, and Destroy*.
25. Greenfield, Palmer, and Wiley, *Organization*, p. 161.
26. Extract of Gen Devers' Rpt, Andrew Bruce Papers, MHI.
27. Including Hawaiian Division. Watson, *Chief of Staff*, p. 202; H. H. Arnold, *Global Mission* (New York: Harper and Brothers, 1949), p. 267.
28. Greenfield, Palmer, and Wiley, *Organization*, p. 51.
29. Mark W. Clark, Oral History, Sec 1, p. 128, MHI Research Collection.
30. Palmer, Wiley, and Keast, *Procurement*, p. 454.
31. Ibid., p. 55; Edmund G. Love, *The 27th Infantry Division in World War II* (Washington, D.C.: Infantry Journal Press, 1949), p. 13.

32. Marshall to CGs, First, Second, Third, and Fourth Armies, 26 Jun 41, Directives (Chronological), GCM Library.

33. "Brickbats Outnumber Bouquets," *Newsweek*, 13 Oct 41, pp. 50–53.

34. TAG to CGs, First, Second, Third, and Fourth Armies, all 27 Jun 41, Sec 1; Acting ACofS for AG to Chief of Armd Force, 22 Sep 41, Sec 1; Memo, ACofS for AG, 31 Jul 41, Sec 1; TAG to CG, First Army, 2 Jul 41, Sec 2. All in 353 (5–15–41), RG 407, Army AG Decimal File 1940–45, NA.

35. For damage claims, see Sec 1a, 1b, AG 353 (5–15–41), RG 407, NA.

36. "Few Claims Are Made on Army in Louisiana," *New York Times*, 23 Sep 41.

Appendix A
Order of Battle, GHQ Maneuvers*

Louisiana Phase 1

Second Army (Red): Lt. Gen. Ben Lear, Regular Army
    5th Division (–): Brig. Gen. Cortlant Parker, Regular Army
    35th Division: Maj. Gen. Ralph E. Truman, Missouri National Guard

    VII Corps: Maj. Gen. Robert C. Richardson, Regular Army
        107th Cavalry Regiment (horse-mechanized)
        6th Division: Maj. Gen. Clarence S. Ridley, Regular Army
        27th Division: Maj. Gen. William N. Haskell, New York National Guard
        33d Division: Maj. Gen. Samuel T. Lawton, Illinois National Guard

    I Armored Corps: Maj. Gen. Charles L. Scott, Regular Army
        4th Cavalry Regiment (mounted)
        2d Cavalry Division: Maj. Gen. John Millikin, Regular Army
        1st Armored Division: Maj. Gen. Bruce Magruder, Regular Army
        2d Armored Division: Maj. Gen. George S. Patton, Regular Army

    2d Air Task Force: Maj. Gen. Millard Harmon, Regular Army
        17th Bomber Wing
        6th Pursuit Wing

Third Army (Blue): Lt. Gen. Walter Krueger, Regular Army
    1st Cavalry Division: Maj. Gen. Innis P. Swift, Regular Army
    56th Cavalry Brigade (mounted)
    1st Antitank Group
    2d Antitank Group
    3d Antitank Group
    1st Tank Group
    Company A, 502d Parachute Battalion

*The cavalry and armored divisions, as well as the single-numeral infantry divisions, were Regular Army formations. Infantry divisions numbered 26 and higher were National Guard organizations.

IV Corps: Maj. Gen. Jay L. Benedict, Regular Army
    6th Cavalry Regiment (horse-mechanized)
    31st Division: Maj. Gen. John C. Persons, Alabama National Guard
    38th Division: Maj. Gen. Daniel I. Sultan, Regular Army
    43d Division: Maj. Gen. Morris B. Payne, Connecticut National Guard

V Corps: Maj. Gen. Edmund L. Daley, Regular Army
    106th Cavalry Regiment (horse-mechanized)
    32d Division: Maj. Gen. Irving A. Fish, Wisconsin National Guard
    34th Division: Brig. Gen. Russell P. Hartle, Regular Army
    37th Division: Maj. Gen. Robert S. Beightler, Ohio National Guard

VIII Corps: Maj. Gen. George V. Strong, Regular Army
    113th Cavalry Regiment (horse-mechanized)
    2d Division: Maj. Gen. John N. Greely, Regular Army
    36th Division: Brig. Gen. Fred L. Walker, Regular Army
    45th Division: Maj. Gen. William S. Key, Oklahoma National Guard

3d Air Task Force: Maj. Gen. Herbert A. Dargue, Regular Army
    2d Bomber Wing
    10th Pursuit Wing

Louisiana Phase 2

Second Army (Red): Lt. Gen. Ben Lear, Regular Army
    2d Cavalry Division: Maj. Gen. John Milliken, Regular Army
    4th Cavalry Regiment (mounted)
    1st Antitank Group
    2d Antitank Group
    5th Division (-): Brig. Gen. Cortlant Parker, Regular Army
    6th Division: Maj. Gen. Clarence S. Ridley, Regular Army
    1st Armored Division: Maj. Gen. Bruce Magruder, Regular Army
    Company A, 502d Parachute Battalion

VII Corps: Maj. Gen. Robert C. Richardson, Regular Army
    107th Cavalry Regiment (horse-mechanized)
    27th Division: Maj. Gen. William N. Haskell, New York National
      Guard
    33d Division: Maj. Gen. Samuel T. Lawton, Illinois National Guard
    35th Division: Maj. Gen. Ralph E. Truman, Missouri National Guard

2d Air Task Force: Maj. Gen. Millard Harmon, Regular Army
    17th Bomber Wing
    6th Pursuit Wing

Third Army (Blue): Lt. Gen. Walter Krueger, Regular Army
    1st Cavalry Division: Maj. Gen. Innis P. Swift, Regular Army
    56th Cavalry Brigade (mounted)
    3d Antitank Group
    1st Tank Group

  IV Corps: Maj. Gen. Jay L. Benedict, Regular Army
    6th Cavalry Regiment (horse-mechanized)
    31st Division: Maj. Gen. John C. Persons, Alabama National Guard
    38th Division: Maj. Gen. Daniel I. Sultan, Regular Army
    43d Division: Maj. Gen. Morris B. Payne, Connecticut National Guard

  V Corps: Maj. Gen. Edmund L. Daley, Regular Army
    106th Cavalry Regiment (horse-mechanized)
    32d Division: Maj. Gen. Irving A. Fish, Wisconsin National Guard
    34th Division: Brig. Gen. Russell P. Hartle, Regular Army
    37th Division: Maj. Gen. Robert S. Beightler, Ohio National Guard

  VIII Corps: Maj. Gen. George V. Strong, Regular Army
    113th Cavalry Regiment (horse-mechanized)
    36th Division: Brig. Gen. Fred L. Walker, Regular Army
    45th Division: Maj. Gen. William S. Key, Oklahoma National Guard

  I Armored Corps: Maj. Gen. Charles L. Scott, Regular Army
    2d Division: Maj. Gen. John N. Greely, Regular Army
    2d Armored Division: Maj. Gen. George S. Patton, Regular Army

  3d Air Task Force: Maj. Gen. Herbert A. Dargue, Regular Army
    2d Bomber Wing
    10th Pursuit Wing

Carolinas Phase 1

IV Corps (reinforced) (Red): Maj. Gen. Oscar W. Griswold, Regular Army
    3d Cavalry Regiment (mounted)
    6th Cavalry Regiment (mechanized)
    107th Cavalry Regiment (mounted)
    4th Motorized Division: Brig. Gen. Fred C. Wallace, Regular Army
    31st Division: Brig. Gen. Louis F. Guerre, Louisiana National Guard
    43d Division: Brig. Gen. John H. Hester, Regular Army
    502d Parachute Battalion

  I Armored Corps: Maj. Gen. Charles L. Scott, Regular Army
    1st Armored Division: Maj. Gen. Bruce Magruder, Regular Army
    2d Armored Division: Maj. Gen. George S. Patton, Regular Army

3d Air Support Command: Col. Asa N. Duncan, Regular Army
    2d Bomber Wing
    10th Pursuit Wing

First Army (Blue): Lt. Gen. Hugh A. Drum, Regular Army
    GHQ–X (released to II Corps)
    GHQ–Y (released to VI Corps)
    GHQ–Z (released to I Corps)
    TA–1
    TA–2
    TA–3
    191st Tank Battalion
    AB–1
    1st Division: Maj. Gen. Donald C. Cubbison, Regular Army (released to VI Corps)
    9th Division: Brig. Gen. Rene E. DeRussey Hoyle, Regular Army

I Corps: Maj. Gen. Charles F. Thompson, Regular Army
    102d Cavalry Regiment (horse-mechanized)
    8th Division: Maj. Gen. James P. Marley, Regular Army
    30th Division: Maj. Gen. Henry D. Russell, Georgia National Guard

II Corps: Maj. Gen. Lloyd R. Fredendall, Regular Army
    104th Cavalry Regiment (horse-mechanized)
    28th Division: Maj. Gen. Edward Martin, Pennsylvania National Guard
    29th Division: Maj. Gen. Milton A. Reckord, Maryland National Guard (released to VI Corps)
    44th Division: Brig. Gen. James I. Muir, Regular Army

VI Corps: Maj. Gen. Karl Truesdell, Regular Army
    101st Cavalry Regiment (horse-mechanized)
    26th Division: Maj. Gen. Roger R. Eckfeldt, Massachusetts National Guard

1st Air Support Command: Col. William E. Kepner, Regular Army
    3d Bomber Group
    6th Pursuit Wing

Carolinas Phase 2

IV Corps (reinforced) (Red): Maj. Gen. Oscar W. Griswold, Regular Army
    3d Cavalry Regiment (mounted)
    6th Cavalry Regiment (mechanized)

107th Cavalry Regiment (mounted)
4th Motorized Division: Brig. Gen. Fred C. Wallace, Regular Army
31st Division: Brig. Gen. Louis F. Guerre, Louisiana National
   Guard
43d Division: Brig. Gen. John H. Hester, Regular Army

I Armored Corps: Maj. Gen. Charles L. Scott, Regular Army
   1st Armored Division: Maj. Gen. Bruce Magruder, Regular Army
   2d Armored Division: Maj. Gen. George S. Patton, Regular Army

3d Air Support Command: Col. Asa N. Duncan, Regular Army
   2d Bomber Wing (-17th Bomber Group)
   10th Pursuit Wing

First Army (Blue): Lt. Gen. Hugh A. Drum, Regular Army
   GHQ–X (released to II Corps)
   GHQ–Y (released to VI Corps)
   GHQ–Z (released to VI Corps)
   TA–1 (released to VI Corps)
   TA–2 (released to I Corps)
   TA–3
   191st Tank Battalion
   AB–1
   1st Division: Maj. Gen. Donald C. Cubbison, Regular Army (re-
      leased to VI Corps)
   8th Division: Maj. Gen. James P. Marley, Regular Army (released to
      I Corps)
   502d Parachute Battalion

I Corps: Maj. Gen. Charles F. Thompson, Regular Army
   102d Cavalry Regiment (horse-mechanized)
   30th Division: Maj. Gen. Henry D. Russell, Georgia National Guard

II Corps: Maj. Gen. Lloyd R. Fredendall, Regular Army
   104th Cavalry Regiment (horse-mechanized)
   9th Division: Maj. Gen. Rene E. DeRussey Hoyle, Regular Army
   28th Division: Maj. Gen. Edward Martin, Pennsylvania National
      Guard
   44th Division: Brig. Gen. James I. Muir, Regular Army

VI Corps: Maj. Gen. Karl Truesdell, Regular Army
   101st Cavalry Regiment (horse-mechanized)
   26th Division: Maj. Gen. Roger R. Eckfeldt, Massachusetts National
      Guard
   29th Division: Maj. Gen. Milton A. Reckord, Maryland National
      Guard

1st Air Support Command: Col. William E. Kepner, Regular Army
    3d Bomber Group
    17th Bomber Group
    6th Pursuit Wing

Appendix B

Principal Officers in the GHQ Maneuvers and Their Wartime Careers

Beightler, Maj. Gen. Robert S., Ohio National Guard. Commanding General, 37th Division. Assumed command October 1940, replacing Maj. Gen. G. D. Light, National Guard. Louisiana maneuvers. Commanding General, 37th Division, South West Pacific area, Solomons, Philippines, 1942–45.

Benedict, Maj. Gen. Jay L., Regular Army. Commanding General, VI Corps. Assumed command November 1940. Louisiana maneuvers. Replaced October 1941 by Maj. Gen. Oscar W. Griswold, Regular Army. Commanding General, IX Corps area, 1941–42. War Department, 1942.

Clark, Brig. Gen. Mark W., Regular Army. Deputy Director, GHQ maneuvers. G–3, GHQ, June 1941. Commanding General, II Corps, 1942. Deputy to Commanding General, ETO, 1942. Commanding General, Fifth Army, Italy, 1943. Commanding General, Fifteenth Army Group, Italy, 1944. Maj. Gen., April 1942; Lt. Gen., November 1942; General, March 1945.

Collins, Col. J. Lawton, Regular Army. Chief of Staff, VII Corps. Louisiana maneuvers. Commanding General, 25th Division, Pacific, Guadalcanal, New Georgia, 1942–43. Commanding General, VII Corps, ETO, 1944–45. Brig. Gen., February 1942; Maj. Gen., May 1942; Lt. Gen., April 1945.

Crittenberger, Brig. Gen. Willis D., Regular Army. Commanding General, 2d Armored Brigade. Louisiana and Carolinas maneuvers. Commanding General, 2d Armored Division, January 1942. Commanding General, III Armored Corps, 1942. Commanding General, IV Corps, Italy, 1945. Maj. Gen., February 1942; Lt. Gen., June 1945.

Cubbison, Maj. Gen. Donald C., Regular Army. Commanding General, 1st Division. Assumed command February 1941. Carolinas maneuvers. Replaced by Maj. Gen. Terry de la M. Allen, June 1942. Commanding Officer, Field Artillery Replacement Center, 1942.

Daley, Maj. Gen. Edmund L., Regular Army. Commanding General, V Corps. Assumed command April 1941, replacing Maj. Gen. C. B. Hodges. Louisiana maneuvers. Terminated, May 1942; retired, September 1942, at age 58.

Dargue, Maj. Gen. Herbert A., Regular Army. Commanding General, 3d Air Task Force. Louisiana maneuvers. Appointed Commander, Hawaiian Department, December 1941, and killed in air crash en route, 12 December.

Drum, Lt. Gen. Hugh A., Regular Army. Commanding General, First Army. Assumed command 1940 with full-time activation of First Army. Carolinas maneuvers. Offered post of Chief of Staff to Generalissimo Chiang Kai-shek, 31 December 1941. Retired, September 1943.

Duncan, Col. Asa N., Regular Army. Commanding Officer, 3d Air Support Command. Carolinas maneuvers. Temporary Commanding General, VIII Air Force, 1942. Died in ETO, November 1943. Brig. Gen., February 1942.

Eckfeldt, Maj. Gen. Roger W., Massachusetts National Guard. Commanding General, 26th Division. Carolinas maneuvers. Replaced May 1942 by Brig. Gen. Willard S. Paul, Regular Army. War Department Dependency Board, 1943.

Eddy, Col. Manton S., Regular Army. Commanding Officer, Anti-Airborne Detachment 1. Carolinas maneuvers. Commanding General, 9th Division, Tunisia, ETO, 1942–44. Commanding General, XII Corps, 1944–45. Brig. Gen., March 1942; Maj. Gen., August 1942.

Eisenhower, Col. Dwight D., Regular Army. Chief of Staff, Third Army. Louisiana maneuvers. Chief, Operations Division, War Department General Staff, 1942. Commanding General, U.S. Forces in Europe, 1942. Commander in Chief, Operation TORCH, North Africa, 1942. Commander in Chief, Operation HUSKY, Sicily, 1943. Commander in Chief, invasion of Italy, 1943. Supreme Allied Commander, ETO, 1944–45. Brig. Gen., October 1941; Maj. Gen., March 1942; Lt. Gen., July 1942; General, February 1943; General of the Army, December 1944.

Fish, Maj. Gen. Irving A., Wisconsin National Guard. Commanding General, 32d Division. Louisiana maneuvers. Replaced February 1942 by Maj. Gen. Edwin F. Harding, Regular Army.

Fredendall, Maj. Gen. Lloyd R., Regular Army. Commanding General, II Corps. Assumed command August 1941, replacing Maj. Gen. H. C. Pratt, Regular Army. Carolinas maneuvers. Commanding General, XI

Corps, 1942. Commanding General, Center Task Force, Operation
TORCH, Algeria, 1942. Commanding General, II Corps, Tunisia, 1943.
Commanding General, Second Army, Zone of the Interior, 1943. Lt.
Gen. (permanent list), June 1943.

Greely, Maj. Gen. John N., Regular Army. Commanding General, 2d Division. Assumed command April 1941. Louisiana maneuvers. Replaced
October 1941 by Maj. Gen. Walter M. Robertson, Regular Army. Military analyst and observer to Iran, Brazil, 1942. Terminated, February
1943; retired, March 1943, at age 57.

Griswold, Maj. Gen. Oscar W., Regular Army. Commanding General, IV
Corps. Assumed command October 1941, replacing Maj. Gen. Jay L.
Benedict, Regular Army. Commanding General, Red army, Carolinas
maneuvers. Commanding General, XIV Corps, South West Pacific
area, 1943–45. Lt. Gen., April 1945.

Guerre, Brig. Gen. Louis F., Louisiana National Guard. Commanding
General, 31st Division. Assumed temporary command, October 1941,
replacing Maj. Gen. John C. Persons, National Guard, for the maneuver. Carolinas maneuvers. Provost Marshal, VIII Corps area, 1942.

Harmon, Maj. Gen. Millard F., Regular Army. Commanding General, 2d
Air Task Force. Louisiana maneuvers. Commanding General, Army
Forces, South Pacific area, February 1943. Commanding General,
Army Air Forces, Pacific Ocean areas, and Deputy Commanding Gen-
eral, Twentieth Air Force, June 1944–February 1945. Died February
1945. Lt. Gen., February 1943.

Hartle, Brig. Gen. Russell P., Regular Army. Commanding General, 34th
Division. Assumed command August 1941, replacing Maj. Gen. E. A.
Walsh, National Guard. Louisiana maneuvers. Deputy Theater Com-
mander, ETO, 1942. Maj. Gen., November 1941.

Haskell, Maj. Gen. William N., New York National Guard. Commanding
General, 27th Division. Assumed command 1926. Louisiana maneuvers. Announced retirement 29 September 1941, effective 1 November 1941, at age 63. Replaced November 1941 by Brig. Gen. Ralph
McT. Pennell, Regular Army.

Hester, Brig. Gen. John H., Regular Army. Commanding General, 43d Division. Assumed command October 1941, replacing Maj. Gen. Morris
B. Payne, National Guard. Carolinas maneuvers. Commanding General, 43d Division, South West Pacific area, 1943. Commanding Officer, Tank Destroyer Center, 1943–44. Maj. Gen., February 1942.

Howell, Maj. George P., Regular Army. Commanding Officer, 502d Parachute Battalion. Carolinas maneuvers. Disabled, February 1942. Commanding Officer, Parachute Section, Airborne Command, May 1942. Retired, December 1945, at age 44.

Hoyle, Brig. Gen. Rene E. DeRussey, Regular Army. Commanding General, 9th Division. Assumed command August 1941, replacing Maj. Gen. Jacob L. Devers. Carolinas maneuvers. Replaced July 1942 by Brig. Gen. Manton S. Eddy. Retired August 1945, at age 61. Maj. Gen., February 1942.

Kepner, Col. William E., Regular Army. Commanding Officer, 1st Air Support Command. Carolinas maneuvers. Commanding General, VIII Fighter Command, ETO, 1943. Brig. Gen., February 1942; Maj. Gen., April 1943.

Key, Maj. Gen. William S., Oklahoma National Guard. Commanding General, 45th Division. Louisiana maneuvers. Provost Marshal General, ETO, 1942. Troop commander, Iceland, 1943–44. Control Commission, Hungary, 1945.

Krueger, Lt. Gen. Walter, Regular Army. Commanding General, Third Army. Assumed command May 1941, replacing Lt. Gen. Herbert J. Brees. Louisiana maneuvers. Replaced February 1943 by Lt. Gen. Courtney H. Hodges. Commanding General, Sixth Army, South West Pacific area, Philippines, 1943–45. General, March 1945.

Lawton, Maj. Gen. Samuel T., Illinois National Guard. Commanding General, 33d Division. Louisiana maneuvers. Replaced April 1942 by Maj. Gen. Frank C. Mahin, Regular Army. Commanding General, Great Lakes sector, Central Defense Command, April 1942.

Lear, Lt. Gen. Ben, Regular Army. Commanding General, Second Army. Assumed command October 1940, replacing Lt. Gen. Stanley H. Ford, Regular Army. Louisiana maneuvers. Temporary Commander, Army Ground Forces, 1944. Deputy Theater Commander (Manpower), ETO, 1945.

McNair, Lt. Gen. Lesley J., Regular Army. Director, GHQ maneuvers. Assumed post of Chief of Staff, General Headquarters, August 1940. Commanding General, Army Ground Forces, 1942–44. Killed in action July 1944, ETO.

Magruder, Maj. Gen. Bruce, Regular Army. Commanding General, 1st Armored Division. Assumed command July 1940 with activation of 1st Armored Division. Louisiana and Carolinas maneuvers. Replaced

March 1942 by Maj. Gen. Orlando Ward, Regular Army. Commanding Officer, Infantry Replacement Training Center, 1942.

Marley, Maj. Gen. James P., Regular Army. Commanding General, 8th Division. Carolinas maneuvers. Replaced August 1942 by Brig. Gen. Paul E. Peabody. Commanding Officer, U.S. Disciplinary Barracks, 1942. Terminated July 1942; retired November 1942, at age 60.

Martin, Maj. Gen. Edward, Pennsylvania National Guard. Commanding General, 28th Division. Assumed command February 1941. Carolinas maneuvers. Relieved January 1942 (over age). Replaced by Brig. Gen. J. Garesche Ord, Regular Army. Inactivated, April 1942. Elected Governor of Pennsylvania, 1942.

Millikin, Maj. Gen. John, Regular Army. Commanding General, 2d Cavalry Division. Assumed command June 1941. Louisiana maneuvers. Commanding General, 33d Division, August 1942–October 1943. Commanding General, III Corps, ETO, 1944–45. Commanding General, 13th Armored Division, ETO, 1945.

Muir, Brig. Gen. James I., Regular Army. Commanding General, 44th Division. Assumed command October 1941, replacing Maj. Gen. Clifford R. Powell, New Jersey National Guard. Carolinas maneuvers. Replaced August 1944 by Maj. Gen. Robert L. Spragins, Regular Army. Terminated November 1943; retired November 1945, at age 57. Maj. Gen., February 1942.

Parker, Brig. Gen. Cortlant, Regular Army. Commanding General, 5th Division. Louisiana maneuvers. Commanding General, 5th Division, Iceland, 1943. Replaced July 1943 by Maj. Gen. S. L. Irwin, Regular Army. Commanding Officer, Southern California sector, Western Defense Command, 1943–45. Maj. Gen., August 1942.

Patton, Maj. Gen. George S., Jr., Regular Army. Commanding General, 2d Armored Division. Assumed command December 1940. Louisiana and Carolinas maneuvers. Replaced January 1942 by Brig. Gen. Willis D. Crittenberger, Regular Army. Commanding General, I Armored Corps, January 1942. Commanding General, Western Task Force, Operation TORCH, Morocco, 1942. Commanding General, II Corps, Tunisia, 1943. Commanding General, Seventh Army, Sicily, 1943. Commanding General, Third Army, ETO, 1944–45. Lt. Gen., March 1943; General, April 1945.

Payne, Maj. Gen. Morris B., Connecticut National Guard. Commanding General, 43d Division. Louisiana maneuvers. Replaced October 1941 by Brig. Gen. John H. Hester, Regular Army.

Persons, Maj. Gen. John C., Alabama National Guard. Commanding General, 31st Division. Louisiana and Carolinas maneuvers. Replaced temporarily October 1941 by Brig. Gen. Louis F. Guerre, National Guard. Served on IV Corps staff during Carolinas maneuvers. Commanding General, 31st Division, South West Pacific area, Morotai, 1944. Replaced September 1944 by Maj. Gen. Clarence A. Martin. Inactivated January 1945.

Reckord, Maj. Gen. Milton A., Maryland National Guard. Commanding General, 29th Division. Carolinas maneuvers. Replaced February 1942 by Maj. Gen. Leonard T. Gerow, Regular Army. Commanding General, III Corps area, 1942. Provost Marshal, ETO, 1943.

Richardson, Maj. Gen. Robert C., Regular Army. Commanding General, VII Corps. Assumed command August 1941, replacing Maj. Gen. F. H. Smith. Louisiana maneuvers. Commanding Officer, Hawaiian Department, and Military Governor, June 1943. Commanding General, U.S. Army Forces in Pacific Ocean Areas, August 1944.

Ridley, Maj. Gen. Clarence S., Regular Army. Commanding General, 6th Division. Assumed command January 1941. Louisiana maneuvers. Replaced October 1942 by Maj. Gen. Franklin C. Sibert, Regular Army.

Russell, Maj. Gen. Henry D., Georgia National Guard. Commanding General, 30th Division. Carolinas maneuvers. Replaced May 1942 by Maj. Gen. William H. Simpson, Regular Army.

Scott, Maj. Gen. Charles L., Regular Army. Commanding General, I Armored Corps. Assumed command May 1941, replacing Maj. Gen. Adna R. Chaffee. Louisiana and Carolinas maneuvers. Replaced December 1941 by Maj. Gen. George S. Patton. Commanding Officer, Armored Force Replacement Training Center, 1942. Senior Military Observer to Mid-East, 1943.

Strong, Maj. Gen. George V., Regular Army. Commanding General, VIII Corps. Assumed command May 1941. Louisiana maneuvers. Assistant Chief of Staff, G–2, War Department General Staff, May 1942. Disabled; retired February 1944, at age 63.

Sultan, Maj. Gen. Daniel I., Regular Army. Commanding General, 38th Division. Assumed command April 1941, replacing Maj. Gen. Robert H. Tyndall, National Guard. Louisiana maneuvers. Replaced April 1942 by Maj. Gen. Henry L. C. Jones. Commanding General, VIII Corps, 1942–43. Deputy Commander in Chief, China-Burma-India Theater, 1943–44. Commanding General, U.S. Forces, Burma-India, 1944. Inspector General, 1945. Lt. Gen., September 1944.

Swift, Maj. Gen. Innis P., Regular Army. Commanding General, 1st Cavalry Division. Louisiana maneuvers. Commanding General, 1st Cavalry Division, South West Pacific area, Admiralty Islands, 1943–44. Commanding General, I Corps, Pacific, Luzon, 1945.

Thompson, Maj. Gen. Charles F., Regular Army. Commanding General, I Corps. Assumed command August 1941, replacing Maj. Gen. William E. Shedd. Carolinas maneuvers. Replaced June 1942 by Maj. Gen. Robert L. Eichelberger, Regular Army. Retired November 1945, at age 62.

Truesdell, Maj. Gen. Karl, Regular Army. Commanding General, VI Corps. Carolinas maneuvers. Deputy Commanding Officer, Panama Department, 1942. Commandant, Command and General Staff School, 1943.

Truman, Maj. Gen. Ralph E., Missouri National Guard. Commanding General, 35th Division. Louisiana maneuvers. Replaced October 1941 by Maj. Gen. William H. Simpson, Regular Army. Federal commission terminated January 1942.

Walker, Brig. Gen. Fred L., Regular Army. Commanding General, 36th Division. Assumed command September 1941, replacing Maj. Gen. Claude V. Birkhead, Texas National Guard. Louisiana maneuvers. Commanding General, 36th Division, Italy, 1943–44. Replaced July 1944 by Maj. Gen. John E. Dahlquist, Regular Army. Commandant, Army Ground Forces School, 1945. Maj. Gen., January 1942.

Wallace, Brig. Gen. Fred C., Regular Army. Commanding General, 4th Motorized Division. Assumed command October 1941, replacing Maj. Gen. Oscar W. Griswold. Carolinas maneuvers. Replaced June 1942 by Brig. Gen. Raymond O. Barton, Regular Army. Commanding Officer, 5th Service Command, 1942–43. Commanding Officer, garrison troops, Espiritu Santo Island, 1943–44. Commanding Officer, garrison troops, Okinawa, 1945.

Ward, Brig. Gen. Orlando, Regular Army. Commanding General, 1st Armored Brigade. Assumed command August 1941. Louisiana and Carolinas maneuvers. Commanding General, 1st Armored Division, March 1942, replacing Maj. Gen. Bruce Magruder. North Africa, 1942–43. Commanding Officer, Tank Destroyer Center, May–October 1943. Commanding General, 20th Armored Division, ETO, 1945. Maj. Gen., March 1942.

Wyche, Brig. Gen. Ira T., Regular Army. Commanding General, 1st Antitank Group. Louisiana maneuvers. Commanding General, 79th Division, U.S. and ETO, 1942–45. Maj. Gen., March 1942.

Bibliography

Primary Sources

Archival Sources

George C. Marshall Research Library. George C. Marshall Papers.
National Archives, Washington, D.C. Record Group 94. Office of
    the Adjutant General Central Files, 1926–39.
———. Record Group 337. Records of Army Ground Forces.
———. Record Group 337. Entry 57. Headquarters, Army Ground
    Forces, General Headquarters.
———. Record Group 337. Entry 57B. General Headquarters G–1
    Section Subject File 1940–March 1942.
———. Record Group 337. Entry 57D. Headquarters, Army Ground
    Forces, General Headquarters General Staff G–3, Subject File
    1940–March 9, 1942.
———. Record Group 407. Army Adjutant General Decimal File
    1940–45.
U.S. Army Command and General Staff College Library. General
    Headquarters Director Headquarters, Comments on First Phase
    Second Army vs. Third Army maneuvers, 22 September 1941.
———. Report on Second and Third Army Maneuvers, 1941.
U.S. Army Military History Institute. Archives. World War II U.S.
    Army War Game Maneuvers.
———. Reference Collection. Second and Third Army Maneuvers 1941.
———. Research Collection. Oral Histories: Mark W. Clark, Paul
    D. Harkins, Henry A. Miley, and Bruce Palmer, Jr.
———. Papers of Andrew D. Bruce.
———. Papers of Orlando Ward.

Printed Government Sources

General Headquarters, U.S. Army. *Umpire Manual.* Reproduced by
    the Command and General Staff School, 17 February 1941.

U.S. Army Command and General Staff School. *Antimechanized Defense (Tentative)*. Fort Leavenworth, Kan.: Command and General Saff School Press, 1939.

U.S. Army. Field Artillery School. *Field Artillery Gunnery*. Fort Sill, Okla.: Field Artillery School, 1941.

U.S. Congress. House. Committee on Appropriations. *HR Report No. 741 to Accompany HR 4965, Military Establishment Appropriation Bill, Fiscal Year 1942*. 77th Cong., 1st sess., 1941.

————. Subcommittee of the Committee on Appropriations. *Hearings on the Military Establishment Appropriations Bill for 1942*. 77th Cong., 1st sess., 1941.

————. *War Department Military Establishment Bill FY 1942, Hearings*. 77th Cong., 1st sess., 1941.

U.S. National Guard Bureau. *Official National Guard Register*. Washington, D.C.: Government Printing Office, 1943.

U.S. *Statutes at Large*. LV, Part 1, 367.

U.S. War Department. *Air Corps Field Manual. Employment of Aviation of the Army: Field Manual 1–5*. Washington, D.C.: Government Printing Office, 1940.

————. *Basic Field Manual. Infantry Drill Regulations: Field Manual 22–5*. Washington, D.C.: Government Printing Office, 1941.

————. *Organization and Tactics of Tank Destroyer Units: Field Manual 18–5*. Washington, D.C.: Government Printing Office, 1942.

————. *Tactical Employment, Tank Destroyer Units: Field Manual 18–5*. Washington, D.C.: Government Printing Office, 1944.

————. Adjutant General's Office. *Official Army Register*. Washington, D.C.: Government Printing Office, 1942–46.

Division Histories

Ewing, Joseph H. *29 Let's Go: A History of the 29th Infantry Division*. Washington, D.C.: Infantry Journal Press, 1948.

Hewitt, Robert L. *Work Horse of the Western Front: The Story of the 30th Infantry Division*. Washington, D.C.: Infantry Journal Press, 1946.

Houston, Donald E. *Hell on Wheels: The 2d Armored Division*. San Rafael, Calif.: Presidio Press, 1977.

Howe, George F. *Battle History of the 1st Armored Division*. Washington, D.C.: Combat Forces Press, 1954.

Kahn, Eli J., and McLemore, Henry. *Fighting Divisions: Histories of Each U.S. Army Combat Division in World War II*. Washington, D.C.: Infantry Journal, 1945.

Katcher, Philip. *U.S. 1st Infantry Division, 1939–45*. Warren, Mich.: Squadron/Signal Publications, 1978.

Love, Edmund G. *The 27th Infantry Divison in World War II.* Washington, D.C.: Infantry Journal Press, 1949.

Mittelman, Joseph B. "Eight Stars to Victory: A History of the Veteran 9th U.S. Infantry Division," 1948.

Robinson, Don, with Mauldin, Bill. *News of the 45th.* Norman: University of Oklahoma Press, 1944.

The [6th] Division Public Relations Section. *The 6th Infantry Division in World War II.* Washington, D.C.: Infantry Journal Press, 1947.

33d Infantry Division Historical Committee. *The Golden Cross: A History of the 33d Infantry Division in World War II.* Washington, D.C.: Infantry Journal Press, 1948.

U.S. Army 36th Division. *A Pictoral History of the 36th "Texas" Infantry Division.* Austin, Tex.: 36th Division Association.

Wright, Bertram C. *The 1st Cavalry Division in World War II.* Tokyo: Toppan Printing Co., 1947.

Secondary Sources

Government Studies

Abrahamson, James L. *The American Home Front.* Washington, D.C.: National Defense University Press, 1983.

Futrell, Robert F. *Ideas, Concepts, Doctrine: A History of Basic Thinking in the United States Air Force.* Maxwell Air Force Base, Ala.: Air University, 1971.

Gabel, Christopher R. *Seek, Strike, and Destroy: U.S. Army Tank Destroyer Doctrine in World War II.* Leavenworth Paper 12. Combat Studies Institute, U.S. Army Command and General Staff College, Fort Leavenworth, Kan., 1985.

Historical Section, Army Ground Forces. AFG Studies. Available in the U.S. Army Center of Military History, Washington, D.C.

———. Study No. 1. "Origins of the Army Ground Forces: General Headquarters, U.S. Army, 1940–42," by Kent Roberts Greenfield and Robert R. Palmer, 1946.

———. Study No. 16. "History of the Second Army," by Bell I. Wiley and William P. Govan, 1946.

———. Study No. 17. "History of the Third Army," by Francis G. Smith, 1946.

———. Study No. 25. "The Airborne Command and Center," by John T. Ellis, Jr., 1951.

———. Study No. 27. "The Armored Force, Command, and Center," 1946.

————. Study No. 29. "Tank Destroyer History," by Emory A. Dunham, 1946.

————. Study No. 35. "Army Ground Forces and the Air-Ground Battle Team," by Kent Roberts Greenfield, 1948.

Kennedy, Robert M. *The German Campaign in Poland (1939)*. Washington, D.C.: Department of the Army, 1956.

Kreidberg, Marvin A., and Henry, Merton G. *History of Military Mobilization in the United States Army, 1775–1945*. Washington, D.C.: Department of the Army, 1955.

Moenk, Jean R. *A History of Large-Scale Army Maneuvers in the United States, 1935–1964*. Fort Monroe, Va.: Headquarters, USCAC, 1969.

U.S. Air Force Historical Division. Research Studies Institute. Historical Studies.

————. Study No. 10. *Organization of the Army Air Arm 1935–45*, by Chase Curran Mooney. Maxwell AFB, Ala.: USAF Historical Division, 1956.

————. Study No. 89. *The Development of Air Doctrine in the Army Air Corps*, by Thomas H. Greer. Maxwell AFB, Ala.: USAF Historical Division, 1955.

————. Study No. 100. *History of the Air Corps Tactical School 1920–1940*, by Robert T. Finney. Maxwell AFB, Ala.: USAF Historical Division, 1955.

————. Study No. 160. *The Development of the German Air Force 1919–1939*, by Richard Suchenwirth. Maxwell AFB, Ala.: USAF Historical Division, 1968.

U.S. Air Force. Office of Air Force History. *Condensed Analysis of the Ninth Air Force in the European Theater of Operations*. USAF Warrior Studies. Washington, D.C.: Office of Air Force History, 1984. Reprint of 1946 study.

U.S. Army. Tank Destroyer Center. "Tank Destroyer History, Inception through 8 May, 1945," by Historical Officer, Tank Destroyer Center, 1945.

U.S. Congress. Senate. *The Army of the United States*. Senate Document No. 91, 76th Cong., 1st sess. Washington, D.C.: Government Printing Office, 1940.

Theses

Baily, C. M. "The Development of American Tank Destroyers in World War II." Master's thesis, U.S. Army Command and General Staff College, 1976.

Cluxton, Donald E., Jr. "Concepts of Airborne Warfare in World War II." Master's thesis, Duke University, 1967.

McKenna, Charles Douglas. "The Forgotten Reform: Field Maneuvers in the Development of the United States Army, 1902–1920." Ph.D. dissertation, Duke University, 1981.

Murray, George E. P. "The Louisiana Maneuvers, September, 1941: Practice for War." Master's thesis, Kansas State University, 1972.

Owens, John Patrick. "The Evolution of *FM 100–20, Command and Employment of Air Power, (21 July 1943)*: The Foundation of Modern Airpower Doctrine." Master's thesis, U.S. Army Command and General Staff College, 1989.

Nenninger, Timothy K. "The Development of American Armor, 1917–1940." Master's thesis, University of Wisconsin, 1968.

Shuffer, George Macon, Jr. "Development of the U.S. Armored Force: Its Doctrine and Its Tactics, 1916–1940." Master's thesis, University of Maryland, 1959.

Books

Arnold, H. H. *Global Mission.* New York: Harper and Brothers, 1949.

Blumenson, Martin, ed. *The Patton Papers.* Boston: Houghton Mifflin, 1972–74.

Brereton, Lewis H. *The Brereton Diaries.* New York: William Morrow and Co., 1946.

Chamberlain, Peter, and Ellis, Chris. *British and American Tanks of World War II.* 2d ed. New York: Arco, 1975.

Clark, Mark Wayne. *Calculated Risk.* New York: Harper and Brothers, 1950.

Clifford, J. Garry, and Spencer, Samuel R., Jr. *The First Peacetime Draft.* Lawrence: University Press of Kansas, 1986.

Cline, Ray S. *Washington Command Post: The Operations Division.* U.S. Army in World War II. Washington, D.C.: U.S. Army Center of Military History, Government Printing Office, 1951.

Coll, Blanche D., Keith, Jean E., and Rosenthal, Herbert H. *The Corps of Engineers: Troops and Equipment.* U.S. Army in World War II. Washington, D.C.: U.S. Army Center of Military History, Government Printing Office, 1958.

Collins, J. Lawton. *Lightning Joe: An Autobiography.* Baton Rouge: Louisiana State University Press, 1979.

Conn, Stetson, and Fairchild, Byron. *The Framework of Hemisphere Defense.* U.S. Army in World War II. Washington, D.C.: U.S. Army Center of Military History, Government Printing Office, 1960.

Cooper, Matthew. *The German Army, 1939–1945.* London: Macdonald and Jane's, 1978.

Craven, Wesley Frank, and Cate, James L., eds., *Europe: Argument to V–E Day*. The Army Air Forces in World War II, vol. 3. Chicago: University of Chicago Press, 1951.

―――. *Plans and Early Operations*. The Army Air Forces in World War II, vol. 1. Chicago: University of Chicago Press, 1948.

Doughty, Robert Allan. *The Seeds of Disaster: The Development of French Army Doctrine 1919–1939*. Hamden, Conn.: Archon Books, 1985.

Dupuy, R. Ernest and Trevor N. *The Encyclopedia of Military History*. New York: Harper and Row, 1977.

Earle, Edward Mead, ed. *Makers of Modern Strategy*. Princeton: Princeton University Press, 1943, 1971.

Eisenhower, Dwight D. *At Ease, Stories I Tell to Friends*. Garden City, N.Y.: Doubleday, 1967.

―――. *Crusade in Europe*. Garden City, N.Y.: Doubleday, 1948.

English, John A. *On Infantry*. New York: Praeger, 1981, 1984.

Farago, Ladislas. *Patton: Ordeal and Triumph*. New York: Obolensky, 1964.

Forty, George. *U.S. Army Handbook 1939–1945*. U.S. ed. New York: Scribner's, 1980.

Foss, Christopher F. *Jane's World Armoured Fighting Vehicles*. New York: St. Martin's, 1976.

Gillie, Mildred Hanson. *Forging the Thunderbolt*. Harrisburg, Pa.: Military Service Publishing Co., 1947.

Green, Constance M., Thomson, Harry C., and Roots, Peter C. *The Ordnance Department: Planning Munitions for War*. U.S. Army in World War II. Washington, D.C.: U.S. Army Center of Military History, Government Printing Office, 1955.

Greenfield, Kent Roberts, Palmer, Robert R., and Wiley, Bell I. *The Organization of Ground Combat Troops*. U.S. Army in World War II. Washington, D.C.: U.S. Army Center of Military History, Government Printing Office, 1947.

Griffith, Robert K. *Men Wanted for the U.S. Army*. Westport, Conn.: Greenwood Press, 1982.

Herr, John K., and Wallace, Edward S. *The Story of the U.S. Cavalry*. Boston: Little, Brown and Co., 1953.

Hill, Jim Dan. *The Minute Man in Peace and War*. Harrisburg, Pa.: Stackpole, 1964.

Horne, Alistair. *To Lose a Battle: France 1940*. New York: Little, Brown and Co., 1969.

Howe, George F. *Northwest Africa: Seizing the Initiative in the West*. U.S. Army in World War II. Washington, D.C.: U.S. Army Center of Military History, Government Printing Office, 1957.

Hunnicutt, R. P. *Sherman: A History of the American Medium Tank*. Belmont, Calif.: Taurus Enterprises, 1978.

James, D. Clayton. *The Years of MacArthur.* Vol. 1, *1880–1941.* Boston: Houghton Mifflin, 1970.

Kahn, Eli J. *McNair, Educator of an Army.* Washington, D.C.: Infantry Journal, 1945.

Krueger, Walter. *From Down Under to Nippon.* Washington, D.C.: Combat Forces Press, 1953.

Lewis, S. J. *Forgotten Legions: German Army Infantry Policy 1918–1941.* New York: Praeger, 1985.

Lord, Walter. *Day of Infamy.* New York: Holt, Rinehart, and Winston, 1957.

Marshall, George C. *George C. Marshall Interviews and Reminiscences for Forrest C. Pogue: Transcripts and Notes, 1956–57.* Lexington, Va.: George C. Marshall Research Foundation, 1986.

————. *The Papers of George Catlett Marshall.* Vol. 1, *"The Soldierly Spirit," December 1880–June 1939.* Edited by Larry I. Bland and Sharon R. Ritenour. Baltimore: Johns Hopkins University Press, 1981.

————. *The Papers of George Catlett Marshall.* Vol. 2, *"We Cannot Delay," July 1, 1939–December 6, 1941.* Edited by Larry I. Bland, Sharon R. Ritenour, and Clarence E. Wunderlin, Jr. Baltimore: Johns Hopkins University Press, 1986.

Ogorkiewicz, Richard M. *Armoured Forces, a History of Armoured Forces and their Vehicles.* New York: Arco, 1970.

Palmer, Robert R., and Wiley, Bell I. *Procurement and Training of Ground Combat Troops.* U.S. Army in World War II. Washington, D.C.: U.S. Army Center of Military History, Government Printing Office, 1948.

Pogue, Forrest C. *George C. Marshall: Ordeal and Hope 1939–1942.* New York: Viking, 1966.

Roosevelt, Franklin D. *The Public Papers and Addresses of Franklin D. Roosevelt.* Vol. 10, *The Call to Battle Stations, 1941.* New York: Russell and Russell, 1950.

Sherry, Michael S. *The Rise of American Air Power: The Creation of Armageddon.* New Haven: Yale University Press, 1987.

Smith, R. Elberton. *The Army and Economic Mobilization.* U.S. Army in World War II. Washington, D.C.: U.S. Army Center of Military History, Government Printing Office, 1959.

Stanton, Shelby L. *Order of Battle: U.S. Army, World War II.* Novato, Calif.: Presidio Press, 1984.

Stout, Wesley W. *Tanks Are Mighty Fine Things.* Detroit: Chrysler Corp., 1946.

Stubbs, Mary Lee, and Connor, Stanley Russell. *Armor-Cavalry Part I: Regular Army and Army Reserve.* Army Lineage Series. Washington, D.C.: U.S. Army Center of Military History, Government Printing Office, 1969.

Terret, Dulaney. *The Signal Corps: The Emergency, to December, 1941.*
     U.S. Army in World War II. Washington, D.C.: U.S. Army Cen-
     ter of Military History, Government Printing Office, 1956.
Tuchman, Barbara. *Stilwell and the American Experience in China.*
     New York: Macmillan, 1970.
*War Reports of General George C. Marshall, General H. H. Arnold, and
     Admiral Ernest J. King.* New York: Lippincott, 1947.
Wardlow, Chester. *The Transportation Corps: Responsibilities, Organi-
     zation, and Operations.* U.S. Army in World War II. Washington,
     D.C.: U.S. Army Center of Military History, Government Print-
     ing Office, 1951.
Watson, Mark Skinner. *Chief of Staff: Prewar Plans and Preparations.*
     U.S. Army in World War II. Washington, D.C.: U.S. Army Cen-
     ter of Military History, Government Printing Office, 1950.
Wedemeyer, Albert C. *Wedemeyer on War and Peace.* Edited by Keith
     E. Eiler. Stanford, Calif.: Hoover Institution Press, 1987.
Weigley, Russell F. *Eisenhower's Lieutenants.* Bloomington: Indiana
     University Press, 1981.
————. *History of the United States Army.* New York: Macmillan, 1967.
Who's Who. 1946–1947. Chicago: A. N. Marquis, 1946.

Periodicals

Army and Navy Journal September 1939 to December 1941.
Epstein, Laurence B. "Army Organic Light Aviation: The Found-
     ing Fathers." *U.S. Army Aviation Digest* June 1977: 2–17.
Field Artillery Journal September 1941 to May 1942.
Greulich, G.G. "Steel Landing Mats for Airplane Runways." *Civil
     Engineering* September 1943: 431–33.
Infantry Journal January–February 1938 to December 1941.
Johns, Dwight F. "Maneuver Notes of Aviation Engineers." *The Military
     Engineer* November 1941: 10–12, and March 1942: 133–35.
Life December 1940 to December 1941.
New York Times August to December 1941.
Newsweek August 1939 to October 1942.
Nichols, Herbert B. "Prepare for Action." *Christian Science Monitor
     Magazine* September 28, 1940: 8–14.
Smith, Richard K. "Marston Mat." *Air Force Magazine* April 1989:
     84–88.
Time May 1939 to December 1942.
Trudeau, Arthur G. "Mobility and Motors." *Military Review* April
     1942: 22–27.

Glossary

AA	Antiaircraft
AAF	Army Air Forces
AB–1	Antiairborne unit, Carolinas
ACofS	Assistant Chief of Staff
AG	Adjutant General
AGF	Army Ground Forces
AGO	Adjutant General's Office
ASC	Air Support Command
AT	Antitank
ATF	Air Task Force
CG	Commanding General
CGSC Library	U.S. Army Command and General Staff College Combined Arms Research Library, Fort Leavenworth, Kansas
CinC	Commander in Chief
CMH	U.S. Army Center of Military History, Washington, D.C.
CO	Commanding Officer
CofS	Chief of Staff
CPX	Command Post Exercise
DP	Delay Position
ETO	European Theater of Operations, World War II
FM	Field Manual
G–1	Personnel Section
G–2	Intelligence Section
G–3	Operations and Training Section
G–4	Supply Section
GCM Library	George C. Marshall Research Library, Lexington, Virginia

GHQ	General Headquarters
GHQ–X, –Y, –Z	Antitank Groups, Carolinas
MHI	Military History Institute, Carlisle Barracks, Pennsylvania
MTP	Mobilization Training Program
NA	National Archives Building, Washington, D.C.
NG	National Guard
PMP	Protective Mobilization Plan
RA	Regular Army
RCT	Regimental Combat Team
RG	Record Group
RTC	Replacement Training Center
TA–1, –2, –3	Antitank groups, First Army, Carolinas
TAC	Tactical Air Command
TAG	The Adjutant General
TD	Tank Destroyer
WDGS	War Department General Staff

Military Map Symbols

Infantry

Cavalry

Cavalry, Mechanized

Artillery

Armored

Armored Infantry

Antitank

XXXX	Army
XXX	Corps
XX	Division
X	Brigade
III	Regiment
II	Battalion
I	Company

Index